ADOBE®
ACROBAT® 7
QuickSteps

MARTY MATTHEWS

JOHN CRONAN

McGraw-Hill/Osborne

New York Chicago San Francisco
Lisbon London Madrid Mexico City
Milan New Delhi San Juan
Seoul Singapore Sydney Toronto

W

McGraw-Hill/Osborne
2100 Powell Street, 10th Floor
Emeryville, California 94608
U.S.A.

To arrange bulk purchase discounts for sales promotions, premiums, or fund-raisers, please contact McGraw-Hill/Osborne at the above address. For information on translations or book distributors outside the U.S.A., please see the International Contact Information page on the last page of this book.

Adobe®, Adobe® Reader®, Acrobat®, Distiller®, Illustrator®, InDesign®, PostScript®, and Photoshop® are registered trademarks of Adobe Systems, Incorporated in the United States and/or other countries.

Microsoft®, Windows®, FrontPage®, Outlook®, PowerPoint®, and Visio® are registered trademarks of Microsoft Corporation in the United States and/or other countries.

This book was composed with Adobe® InDesign®

Information has been obtained by McGraw-Hill/Osborne from sources believed to be reliable. However, because of the possibility of human or mechanical error by our sources, McGraw-Hill/Osborne, or others, McGraw-Hill/Osborne does not guarantee the accuracy, adequacy, or completeness of any information and is not responsible for any errors or omissions or the results obtained from use of such information.

ADOBE® ACROBAT® 7 QUICKSTEPS

1234567890 WCK WCK 0198765

ISBN 0-07-226032-7

VICE PRESIDENT, GROUP PUBLISHER / Philip Ruppel

VICE PRESIDENT, PUBLISHER / Jeffrey Krames

ACQUISITIONS EDITOR / Roger Stewart

ACQUISITIONS COORDINATOR / Agatha Kim

SERIES CREATORS & EDITORS / Marty and Carole Matthews

TECHNICAL EDITORS / Marty Matthews, John Cronan

COPY EDITORS / Lisa McCoy, Karyle Kramer

PROOFREADERS / Harriet O'Neal, Lisa McCoy

INDEXER / Valerie Perry

LAYOUT ARTIST / Bailey Cunningham

ILLUSTRATORS / Kathleen Edwards, Pattie Lee, Bruce Hopkins

SERIES DESIGN / Bailey Cunningham

COVER DESIGN / Pattie Lee

Contents at a Glance

1 2 3 4 5 6 7 8 9 10

Contents

4

5

Chapter 6   Searching and Indexing PDF Files 111

Chapter 7   Collaborating with Acrobat............................ 131

Chapter 8   Creating and Using Forms 155

9

10

Introduction

QuickSteps books are recipe books for computer users. They answer the question "How do I...?" by providing quick sets of steps to accomplish the most common tasks in a particular operating system or application.

The sets of steps are the central focus of the book. QuickSteps sidebars show how to quickly perform many small functions or tasks that support primary functions. Notes, Tips, and Cautions augment the steps, presented in a separate column so as not to interrupt the flow of the steps. Introductions are minimal rather than narrative, and numerous illustrations and figures, many with callouts, support the steps.

QuickSteps books are organized by function and the tasks needed to perform that function. Each function is a chapter. Each task, or "How To," contains the steps needed for accomplishing the function with the relevant Notes, Tips, Cautions, and screenshots. You can easily find the tasks you need through:

- The Table of Contents, which lists the functional areas (chapters) and tasks in the order they are presented

- A How To list of tasks on the opening page of each chapter

- The index, which provides an alphabetical list of the terms that are used to describe the functions and tasks

- Color-coded tabs for each chapter or functional area with an index to the tabs in the Contents at a Glance (just before the Table of Contents)

Conventions Used in this Book

Adobe Acrobat 7 QuickSteps uses several conventions designed to make the book easier for you to follow:

- A ⬤ in the table of contents and in the How To list in each chapter references a QuickSteps sidebar in a chapter, and a ⬤ references a QuickFacts sidebar.

- **Bold type** is used for words or objects on the screen that you are to do something with—for example, "click the **Start** menu and then click **My Computer**."

- *Italic type* is used for a word or phrase that is being defined or otherwise deserves special emphasis.

- Underlined type is used for text that you are to type from the keyboard.

- SMALL CAPITAL LETTERS are used for keys on the keyboard such as ENTER and SHIFT.

- When you are expected to enter a command, you are told to press the key(s). If you are to enter text or numbers, you are told to type them.

How to...

- Starting Acrobat in Different Ways
- Use All Programs to Start Acrobat
- Leave Acrobat
- Explore the Acrobat Window
- Using Acrobat Toolbars
- Use the Mouse
- Using Menus
- Understanding the PDF Concept
- Use Acrobat Navigation
- Using the How To Window
- Use Offline Help
- Connect to Online Support
- Change Document History Settings
- Update Acrobat

Chapter 1
Stepping into Acrobat

Acrobat allows computer users to open and view files created from a myriad of programs. Acrobat lets you convert content from many disparate sources into a common file format: a portable document format, or *PDF*. For example, once your Word document, Excel spreadsheet, or InDesign layout is converted to a PDF document, Acrobat provides a plethora of tools and features that provide editing, organizing, searching, linking, and collaborative functions. To provide universal access to PDF documents, Adobe offers a free program, *Adobe Reader*, so that anyone can view a PDF file. Extending Acrobat's reach, you can create electronic forms that are tied to data collection engines; use *Distiller*, a companion program that is normally used in the background to create PDF files but can be used separately to handle complex conversions; and perform *preflighting*– a check of the document's font, graphics, and other characteristics to assure high-end printing requirements.

QUICKSTEPS

STARTING ACROBAT IN DIFFERENT WAYS

In addition to using All Programs on the Start menu, Acrobat can be started in several other ways.

USE THE START MENU

The icons of the programs you use most often are displayed on the left side of the Start menu. If you frequently use Acrobat, its icon will appear there, as shown in Figure 1-1. To use this icon to start Acrobat:

1. Click **Start**. The Start menu opens.
2. Click the **Acrobat** icon on the left of the Start menu.

PIN ACROBAT TO THE TOP OF THE START MENU

If you think you may use other programs more frequently, you can keep Acrobat at the top of the Start menu by "pinning" it there.

1. Click **Start** to open the Start menu.
2. Right-click (click the right mouse button) the **Acrobat** icon, and click **Pin To Start Menu**.

USE A DESKTOP SHORTCUT

During installation, Acrobat automatically creates an icon on the desktop that you can double-click to open the program.

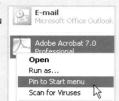

Adobe Acrobat 7.0 Professional

Continued...

In this chapter you will familiarize yourself with Acrobat and see how to start and leave it; use Acrobat's windows, panes, toolbars, and menus; learn how to navigate in a PDF; see how to get help; and find out how to customize Acrobat.

How You Start Acrobat

How you start Acrobat depends on how Acrobat was installed and what has happened to it since its installation. In this section you'll see a surefire way to start Acrobat and some alternatives. You'll also see how to leave Acrobat.

Use All Programs to Start Acrobat

If no other icons for or shortcuts to Acrobat are available on your desktop, you can always start Acrobat using the All Programs option on the Start menu.

1. Start your computer if it is not already running, and log on to Windows if necessary.
2. Click **Start**. The Start menu opens.
3. Click **All Programs** and click **Adobe Acrobat 7.0 Standard** or **Adobe Acrobat 7.0 Professional**, whichever you have, as shown in Figure 1-1.

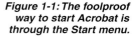

Figure 1-1: The foolproof way to start Acrobat is through the Start menu.

TIP

If you drag the Acrobat icon from the Start menu to the Quick Launch toolbar and nothing happens, the toolbar is probably locked. To unlock the toolbar, right-click a blank area of taskbar, and click **Lock The Taskbar** on the context menu to remove the check mark.

Leave Acrobat

To leave Acrobat when you are done using it:

- Click the **File** menu and click **Exit**.

  –Or–

- Click **Close** on the right of the title bar.

  –Or–

- Press **CTRL+Q**.

Explore Acrobat

Acrobat uses a wide assortment of windows, toolbars, menus, and special features to accomplish its functions. Much of this book explores how to find and use all of these items. In this section you'll learn how to use the most common features of the Acrobat window, including panes and windows that can occupy the main window, the buttons on the principal toolbars, and the menus.

Explore the Acrobat Window

The Acrobat window has many features to aid you in creating PDF files and working with documents. The view presented to you when you open a document is shown in Figure 1-2. The principal features of the Acrobat window are introduced in Table 1-1 and will be described further in this and other chapters of this book.

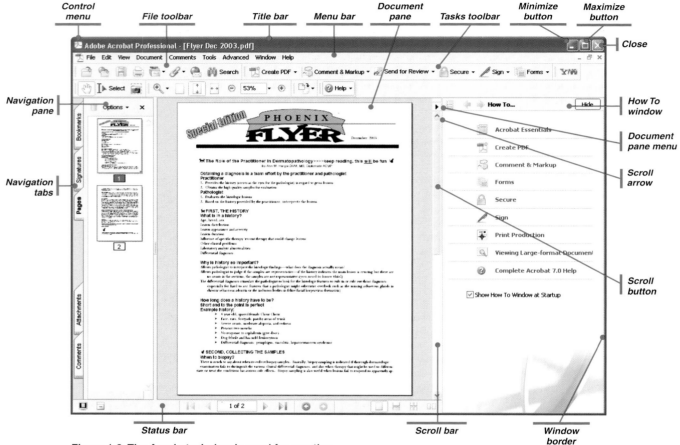

Figure 1-2: The Acrobat window is used for creating PDF files and working with documents.

USING ACROBAT TOOLBARS

Toolbars hold buttons, or tools, that allow you to perform a direct function, such as saving a file or rotating a document. Some special tools contain menus of additional options.

SEE WHAT A TOOL DOES

Hold the mouse pointer over the tool. A *Tooltip* will appear telling you what the tool does.

Zoom In

USE A TOOL

Click the button or icon that represents the tool.

–Or–

Click the down arrow next to a tool, and then click one of the options in the menu that appears.

DISPLAY A TOOLBAR

Right-click a toolbar and then click the toolbar you want displayed.

–Or–

Click the **View** menu, click **Toolbars**, and click the toolbar you want displayed.

MOVE A TOOLBAR

- When the toolbar is docked (placed in the toolbar area below the menu bar), place your pointer on the handle on the left of the toolbar (the column of dashes), and drag it to the new location.

- When the toolbar is floating (see Figure 1-3), place your pointer on the title bar of the toolbar, and drag it to the new location.

Advanced Editing	
✔ Basic	
Commenting	
Drawing Markups	
Edit	
✔ File	
Find	
✔ Help	
Measuring	
Navigation	
Object Data	
Print Production	
✔ Rotate View	
✔ Search the Internet	
✔ Tasks *	
✔ Zoom	
Properties Bar	Ctrl+E
Reset Toolbars	Alt+F8
Hide Toolbars	F8
Lock Toolbars	
Show Button Labels	▶

Continued...

TABLE 1-1: PRINCIPAL FEATURES OF THE ACROBAT WINDOW

ACROBAT FEATURES	DESCRIPTION
Title bar	Contains the name of the open document and the controls for the window
Menu bar	Contains the primary controls for Acrobat, divided into categories
File toolbar	Allows direct access to many of the document file functions for Acrobat
Tasks toolbar	Provides drop-down menus containing options for many of the common tasks performed in Acrobat
Minimize button	Minimizes the window to an icon on the taskbar
Maximize button	Maximizes the window to fill the screen
Close	Exits Acrobat and closes the window
Navigation tabs	Provides quick access to several aspects of the open document
Navigation pane	Displays contents of the selected Navigation tab
Document pane	Displays one or more pages of the open document
Document pane menu	Opens a menu of options related to the open document
Scroll arrow	Moves the contents of the pane in the direction of the arrow
Scroll button	Moves the contents of the pane in the direction it is dragged
Scroll bar	Moves the contents of the pane in the direction it is clicked
Status bar	Contains buttons and controls that enable you to change the view of the open document
How To window	Displays categories of actions you can perform and links to specific tasks
Window border	Sizes the window by being dragged
Control menu	Contains the controls for resizing, moving, and closing the window itself

USING ACROBAT TOOLBARS

(Continued)

HIDE A TOOLBAR

1. Right-click any displayed toolbar or the menu bar.
2. In the context menu, click the toolbar to remove the check mark.

HIDE ALL TOOLBARS

You can hide all open toolbars to quickly gain space within the Acrobat window.

Click **Hide Toolbars** on the status bar. To display the hidden toolbars, click the same button again (now displayed as Show Toolbars).

TIP

To decrease the width of a toolbar, you can hide the text labels that accompany many buttons. Right-click a toolbar, click **Show Button Labels** at the bottom of the context menu, and click **No Labels**.

Use the Mouse

A *mouse* is any pointing device—including trackballs, pointing sticks, and graphic tablets—with two or more buttons. This book assumes you are using a two-button mouse. Moving the mouse moves the pointer on the screen. You *click* an object on the screen by moving the pointer so that it is on top of the object and then pressing the left button on the mouse.

You may control the mouse with either your left or right hand; therefore, the buttons may be switched. (See *Windows XP QuickSteps*, published by McGraw-Hill/Osborne, for information on how to switch the buttons.) This book assumes the right hand controls the mouse and the left mouse button is "*the* mouse button." The right button is always called the "right mouse button." If you switch the buttons, you must change your interpretation of these phrases.

Figure 1-3: A toolbar can be docked in the toolbar area of the Acrobat window, or it can be floating in or out of the window.

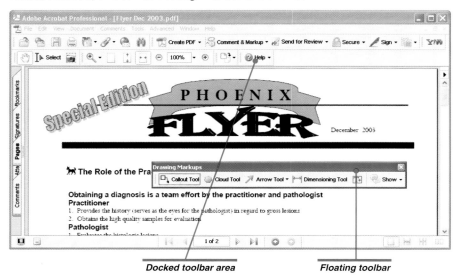

Docked toolbar area   Floating toolbar

QUICKSTEPS

USING MENUS

OPEN A MENU WITH THE MOUSE

Click the menu name.

OPEN A MENU WITH THE KEYBOARD

Press **ALT+** the underlined letter in the menu name (the underlines appear after you press **ALT**). For example, press **ALT+F** to open the File menu.

OPEN A SUBMENU

A number of menu options have a right-pointing arrow on their right to indicate that a submenu is associated with that option. To open the submenu:

Move the mouse pointer to the menu option with a submenu, and the submenu will open.

SELECT A MENU OPTION

To select a menu option:

Click the menu to open it, and then click the option.

HIDE THE MENU BAR

Click the **View** menu and click **Menu Bar**.

–Or–

Press **F9**. (Press **F9** again to redisplay the menu

NOTE

The mouse pointer in Acrobat changes appearance depending on the tool selected and the object it's placed over. Outside the document pane, the pointer is typically the Select arrow used to select commands and buttons. Inside the document pane, the pointer appears as an I-beam when working with text and a crosshair when using tools to draw or select objects. The Hand tool pointer allows you to browse a document using your mouse (see "Use Acrobat Navigation" later in this chapter).

Five actions can be accomplished with the mouse:

- **Point** at an *object* on the screen (a button, an icon, a menu or one of its options, or a border) to highlight it. To *point* means to move the mouse so that the tip of the pointer is on top of the object.

- **Click** an object on the screen to *select* it, making that object the item that your next actions will affect. Clicking will also open a menu, select a menu option, or activate a button or "tool" on a toolbar. *Click* means to point at an object you want to select and quickly press and release the left mouse button.

- **Double-click** an object to open or activate it. *Double-click* means to point at an object you want to select, then press and release the left mouse button twice in rapid succession.

- **Right-click** an object to open a context menu containing commands used to manipulate that object. *Right-click* means to point at an object you want to select and then quickly press and release the right mouse button. For example, right-clicking selected text opens the context menu on the right.

- **Drag** an object to move it on the screen to where you want it moved within the document. *Drag* means to point at an object you want to move and then press and hold the left mouse button while moving the mouse. The object is dragged as you move the mouse. When the object is where you want it, release the mouse button.

Copy To Clipboard	Ctrl+C
Copy As Table	
Save As Table...	
Open Table in Spreadsheet	
Select All	Ctrl+A
Deselect All	Shift+Ctrl+A
Replace Text (Comment)	
Highlight Text (Comment)	
Add Note to Text (Comment)	
Underline Text (Comment)	
Cross Out Text (Comment)	
Add Bookmark	Ctrl+B
Create Link	
Lookup "effort"	

QUICK**FACTS**

UNDERSTANDING THE PDF CONCEPT

One of the great frustrations of computing is receiving a document or picture and not being able to view or print it because you have neither the program that created it nor a program to adequately convert it. Windows promised us this valuable, integrated environment, but in practice, how we exchange information is still very program-parochial. Acrobat, in blood-type terminology, acts as a universal recipient, accepting many file and graphics formats for conversion to its PDF file format— and what a conversion it is! Converted documents and web pages appear exactly as they did in their source formats. Once a document is converted to a PDF file in Acrobat, a myriad of features and benefits can be universally applied. For example, using Acrobat you can:

- Combine several documents into a single PDF
- Reduce the file size associated with documents by selecting one of several PDF file compression levels
- Distribute a PDF among several reviewers and use commenting and marking tools
- Navigate within larger PDF documents using several techniques (see "Use Acrobat Navigation" in this chapter)
- Create tables of contents and indexes
- Provide document security using encryption and digital signatures
- Create electronic forms (Adobe Reader can be used to fill out the forms)

NOTE

If you need to make any significant changes to the content of the PDF, you are better off doing the work in the original program, saving the file, and reconverting the file to a PDF.

Use Acrobat Navigation

One of the key elements of working with documents, especially lengthy ones, is being able to quickly move to where you want to perform a task. Acrobat provides several tools and techniques to allow you to get to where you want, and provide assistance to others viewing your documents.

USE THE NAVIGATION PANE

The navigation pane (see Figure 1-2) provides tabs that categorize many of the elements found in a PDF, allowing you to quickly focus in on the information you want. To display tabs that don't appear on the left edge of the navigation pane, click **View**, click **Navigation Tabs**, and click the tab you want from the submenu.

Some of the tabs appear in their own window and are not docked along the left edge of the navigation pane. To dock an open tab, click **View**, click **Navigation Tabs**, and click **Dock All Tabs**.

The tabs that provide additional navigation properties include:

- **Bookmarks** allow you to quickly jump to specific areas or objects in a document or perform an action, such as opening a page view. Bookmarks can be created from a table of contents, but they can also be created by selecting text, graphics, or portions of graphics. Chapter 9 describes how to create and use bookmarks. To view bookmarks in a document, click the **Bookmarks** tab in the navigation pane.

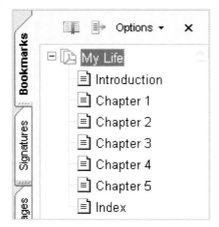

TIP

The vertical and horizontal scroll bars that appear when all content doesn't fit in a pane have enhanced properties. Right-click a scroll bar to display its context menu (the Scroll Here option lets you move to content that's proportionally located along the scroll bar near where you right-clicked it).

Scroll Here
Top
Bottom
Page Up
Page Down
Scroll Up
Scroll Down

NOTE

The Hand tool works in conjunction with the Views buttons on the right end of the status bar. For example, when in Single Page view, you will be limited to moving within the displayed page. If you want to be able to move through the entire document, ensure you are in Continuous view (see Chapter 2 for more information on viewing PDFs).

TIP

To temporarily switch to the Hand tool when using another tool, press **SPACEBAR**.

- **Thumbnails** of each page in a document are displayed in the Pages tab of the navigation pane. You can quickly display a page in the document pane by clicking its thumbnail, though that is just the beginning as to what you can do with page thumbnails. Right-clicking a thumbnail displays a context menu of several actions, as shown in Figure 1-4, that you can perform on the document's pages.

- **Articles** allow you to string together contiguous content that is spread over multiple columns and pages so readers can more easily navigate through the content. See Chapter 4 for more information on creating articles.

USE NAVIGATION BUTTONS

The Navigation buttons at the bottom of the document pane provide page-by-page movement through a document, direct first page and last page access, and page numbering information.

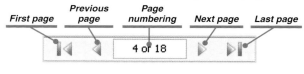

BROWSE WITH THE HAND TOOL

The Hand tool provides a "grabber hand" you can use to move within a document.

1. Click **Hand Tool** on the Basic toolbar.

2. Click the document and drag the page opposite to the direction where you want to go. For example, to see the document above your current view, drag the grabber hand down.

Insert Pages...
Extract Pages...
Replace Pages...
Delete Pages...
Crop Pages...
Rotate Pages...
Set Page Transitions...
Number Pages...
Print Pages...
Embed All Page Thumbnails
Remove Embedded Page Thumbnails
Reduce Page Thumbnails
Enlarge Page Thumbnails
Page Properties...

Figure 1-4: The Pages tab provides fast page retrieval and access to a plethora of actions you can perform on the pages in a document.

USE ORGANIZER

The Organizer window, shown in Figure 1-5, allows you to find and view any PDF files on your computer or network by location, history, or collections of files you create. Chapter 2 describes the Organizer in more detail.

Figure 1-5: The Organizer provides a PDF locating and viewing service.

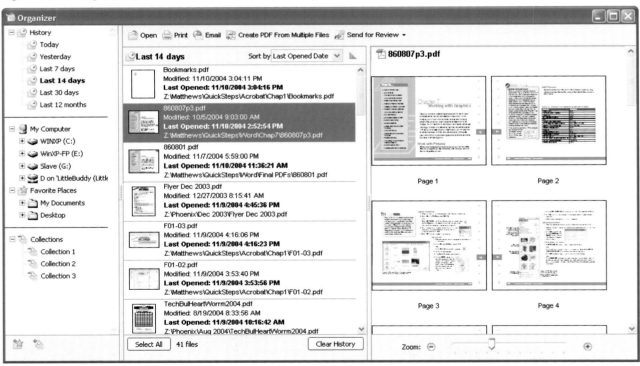

USING THE HOW TO WINDOW

The How To window on the right of the Acrobat window (see Figure 1-2) displays options for common tasks. When you first start Acrobat, the How To window is not displayed, though you can easily choose to display it. Eight categories of tasks are available, with several links to related tasks in each category. Clicking a task link opens a page with brief instructions, as shown in Figure 1-6.

DISPLAY THE HOW TO WINDOW

If the How To window is not currently open:

Click **Help** on the menu bar, click **How To**, and click the category of tasks from the submenu.

Acrobat Essentials
Create PDF
Comment & Markup
Forms
Secure
Sign
Print Production
Viewing Large-format Documents

–Or–

Click the **Help** button on the Help toolbar, and click the category of tasks from the submenu.

Help ▾

OPEN A HOW TO CATEGORY

Click the **Home Page** button on the How To window toolbar, and click the category of assistance you want.

CLOSE THE HOW TO WINDOW

To close the task pane, click **Hide** on the How To window toolbar.

SCROLL THROUGH PAGES BEING USED

To move back and forth through the How To pages you have been working with, click the **Back** and **Forward** arrows on the How To window toolbar.

Continued…

Get Help

Acrobat provides substantial assistance, tailored to whether you are working online or offline. If you are offline, you will get quick, but more limited, help. If you are or can be online, help will be slower, but potentially more comprehensive (and possibly more expensive). Access Help using one of the techniques in the following sections:

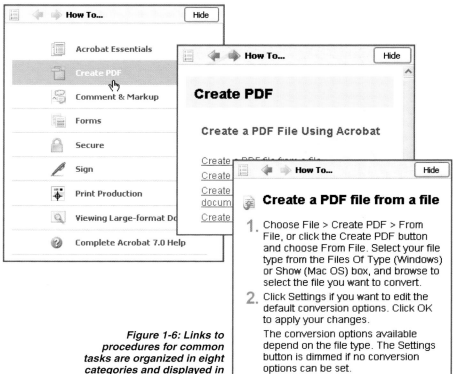

Figure 1-6: Links to procedures for common tasks are organized in eight categories and displayed in the How To window.

USING THE HOW TO WINDOW

(Continued)

MOVE THE HOW TO WINDOW

The How To window is initially docked on the right side of the Acrobat window. You can move it to the left side of the window. To move the pane:

Right-click the **Home Page** button, and click **Docked Left** on the context menu.

RESIZE THE HOW TO WINDOW

You can enlarge the How To window from its default width to more easily view task procedures.

1. Place the mouse pointer over the left border (right-docked) or right border (left-docked) How To window.

2. Drag the double-headed arrow toward the center of the Acrobat window. Drag toward the Acrobat window sides to reduce the width. (You cannot reduce the width less than its default size.)

TIP

To display the How To window when you start Acrobat, click the **Show How To Window At Startup** check box on the home page of the How To window (see Figure 1-2).

Use Offline Help

Acrobat's integrated Help facility is available from several avenues. Use any of these techniques to open the Help window shown in Figure 1-7:

Click the **Help** menu and click **Complete Acrobat 7.0 Help**.

–Or–

Open the How To window home page (see the QuickSteps "Using the How To Window"), and click **Complete Acrobat 7.0 Help**.

–Or–

Click the **Help** button and click **Complete Acrobat 7.0 Help**.

–Or–

Press **F1**.

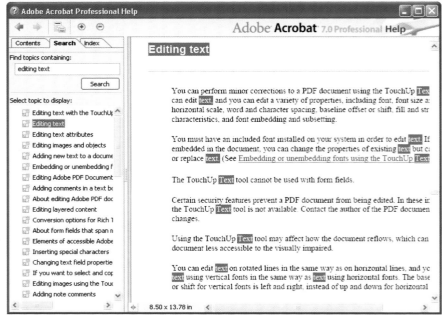

Figure 1-7: Acrobat Help is available by browsing topics, searching by keywords, or using an alphabetical index.

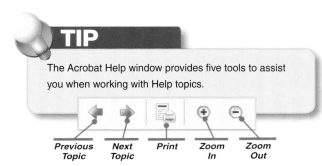

The Acrobat Help window provides five tools to assist you when working with Help topics.

Previous Topic   Next Topic   Print   Zoom In   Zoom Out

BROWSE FOR TOPICS

You can find the information you need by browsing through the topics in the Contents tab.

1. Click the **Contents** tab in the Help navigation pane.

2. Use the plus and minus controls to the left of each topic to expand or contract the topic's hierarchy.

3. Point at a topic of interest, and click its title when the mouse pointer turns into a pointing hand. The information displays in the Topic pane on the right side of the window.

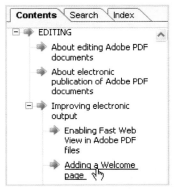

SEARCH FOR INFORMATION USING KEYWORDS

1. Click the **Search** tab in the Help navigation pane.

2. Type one or more keywords in the Find Topics Containing text box that identifies the information you seek, and click **Search**.

3. Click a topic in the list of topics that Help generates. The information displays in the topic pane with your keywords highlighted (see Figure 1-7).

LOCATE INFORMATION ALPHABETICALLY

1. Click the **Index** tab in the Help navigation pane to locate information alphabetically.

2. Type the beginning of the topic in the Select Index Entry text box to automatically scroll down the index to entries that begin with those letters. The more letters of the topic name you type, the more focused the search.

–Or–

Use the scroll bar to locate the topic you want, and click the plus control to the left of entries to see subtopics.

3. Point at an entry of interest, and click its title when the mouse pointer turns into a pointing hand. The information displays in the topic pane on the right side of the window.

Connect to Online Support

If you cannot find the answers to your questions using the Help provided by Acrobat, do not despair—you have online options at Adobe's web site (assuming you're connected to the Internet).

SEARCH FOR ANSWERS

Click **Help** and click **Online Support**. Your browser opens to the Acrobat support page, as shown in Figure 1-8. You can find information by:

- Clicking one of the Top Issues links
- Typing keywords and searching for Acrobat-unique or Adobe-wide topics
- Clicking **Tutorials** under Acrobat Resources to see how to work with new features and incorporate Acrobat with other Adobe products

Figure 1-8: In-depth information on Acrobat is available from Adobe's web site.

CONTACT OTHERS

If you cannot find the information you want, offline or online, you can ask others for their expertise.

1. On the Adobe support page (see "Search for Answers"), under Acrobat Resources, click **Forums**.

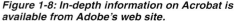
Share your Acrobat questions, suggestions, and information with other Adobe product users and expert guest hosts through the Adobe User to User Forums.

2. On the User To User Forums page, click the **Win** link next to the Acrobat product name.

TIP

If money is no object in seeking the Acrobat truth, click **Help** and click **Adobe Expert Support**. Review the plan offerings on the Adobe web page (see Figure 1-9), and sign up for the one that meets your needs (and credit card limit).

3. Enter name and password details, and click **Log In** to participate in topic threads. (If you aren't already registered on the forums, you will need to do so—Adobe Online particulars won't work!)

–Or–

Click **Log In As A Guest** to only view topics.

Figure 1-9: You can talk to Adobe product experts by subscribing to pay-for-use plans.

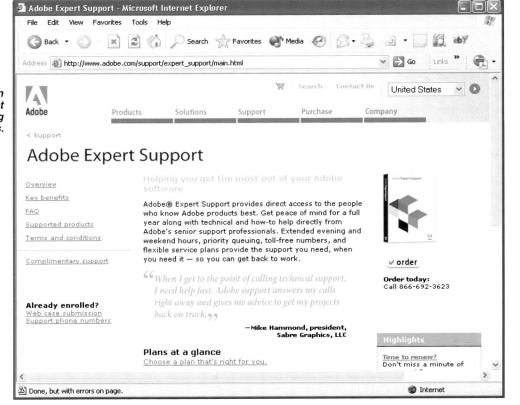

Customize Acrobat

Acrobat offers a preponderance of customization options. Fortunately, for most users, the default settings work just fine 99 percent of the time. If you need more control over Acrobat, the Preferences dialog box, shown in Figure 1-10, provides a long list of areas where you can change settings (many settings are covered in the remaining chapters in this book). Additionally, as they become available, online updates can be installed to update Acrobat.

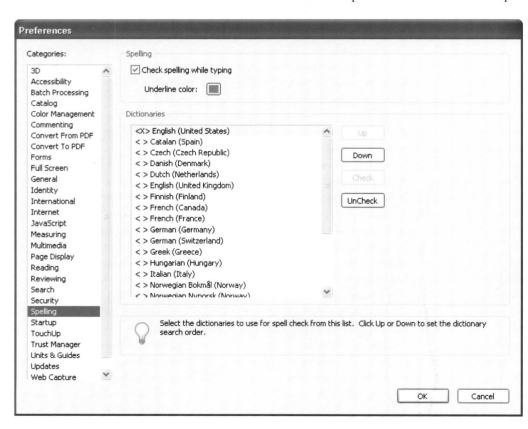

Figure 1-10: The Preferences dialog box lets you change settings to fully customize your Acrobat environment.

Change Document History Settings

You can modify how many recently opened documents appear in the File menu for easy opening and how long you want to maintain a history of documents in the Organizer.

1. Click **Edit** and click **Preferences**. The Preferences dialog box opens (see Figure 1-10).

2. In the Categories list box, click **StartUp**. The right side of the dialog box changes to reflect startup-related options, as shown in Figure 1-11.

3. In the Opening Documents area:

   ● Click the **Maximum Documents In Most-Recently Used List** spinner to increase or decrease the number of document file names that appear at the bottom of the File menu. Clicking a file name opens the document (see Chapter 2 for other methods to open PDF files).

   ● Click the **Remember Files In Organizer History For** down arrow, and click the duration you want Organizer to track opened PDFs.

4. Click **OK** when finished.

Opening Documents

Maximum documents in most-recently used list: 5

Remember files in Organizer History for: Last 12 months

(Takes effect at next launch)

Reopen Documents to Last Viewed Page: Digital Editions Only

☐ Use page cache

☑ Allow layer state to be set by user information

☑ Display the Document Status dialog when these status items appear:

   ☐ Documents that enable extended features in Adobe Reader

   ☑ Documents with object data

   ☐ Documents with file attachments

   ☐ Documents with layers

   ☐ Secured documents

Application Startup

☐ Display splash screen

☐ Use only certified plug-ins   Currently in Certified Mode: Yes

Figure 1-11: You can change several attributes that govern how the program is started as well as how documents are opened.

Update Acrobat

Adobe periodically releases updates for Acrobat and Reader (these are both problem fixes and enhancements). You can check on available updates, download them, and install them from the respective programs.

1. Click **Help** and click **Check For Updates Now**. This will open your Internet browser and connect to the Adobe web site. Your system will be checked for any necessary updates. If none are needed, you will be told so; if updates are available, you will be given the opportunity to download and install them if you choose, as you can see in Figure 1-12.

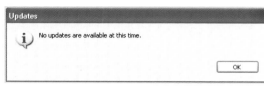

2. When you have installed the updates you want, close your web browser.

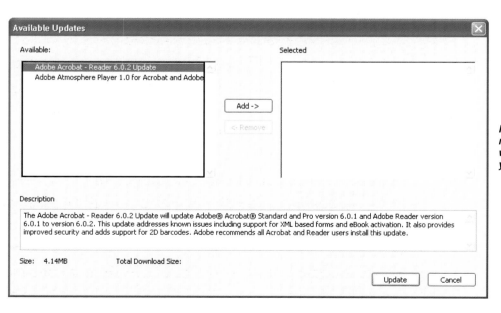

Figure 1-12: You can review and choose which Acrobat updates you want to install.

How to...

Chapter 2

Viewing and Printing PDF Files

No matter which member of the Acrobat family of products you use (Standard or Professional), or if you use the free program, Adobe Reader, you have powerful tools to locate, view, and navigate in PDF files. (In fact, if all you wanted to do was view files, you would do just fine with only Reader.) Through several easy-to-use organizational, navigational, and viewing options, you can see PDFs as you want. You can view a single PDF in several configurations as well as view multiple files on your screen. When you want to locate PDF files, Acrobat provides the Organizer, which supplies an enhanced, Explorer-like display that lets you find PDFs you've viewed on your local system, network, or even on the Internet. If you need a paper-based record of a PDF, Acrobat provides a full assortment of printing options to allow you to set up a document and preview it before you send it to a printer.

Most of the tasks described in this chapter work the same for Acrobat or Reader. Those features that are available only to Acrobat users are noted.

Locate and Display PDF Documents

You can find and open PDFs using tools common to Windows programs or use special features that make locating PDFs a snap. Once a document is open, you can choose to view it in different magnifications, by the number of pages displayed at one time, and by utilizing the entire screen without menus, toolbars, and other display "hogs."

Install Adobe Reader

You can obtain the free PDF viewing program, Adobe Reader, from the Acrobat (Standard or Professional) CD, or you can download it from Adobe's web site.

1. To install Reader from the Acrobat CD, insert the CD in your CD or DVD drive. When the opening Acrobat splash screen appears, click the **Explore** button and then click **Install Adobe Reader 7.0** to start the installation program.

Explore

–Or–

Figure 2-1: Acrobat or Reader can be your default program for opening PDF files.

To install Reader from the Adobe web site, type www.adobe.com in your browser's address text box, and press **ENTER**. On the Adobe home page, click **Get Adobe Reader**. Choose your language, platform, connection speed, and whether you want the full version and any free products. Click **Continue** and then click **Download**. Save the file on your local system, and double-click the file to start the installation program.

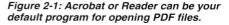

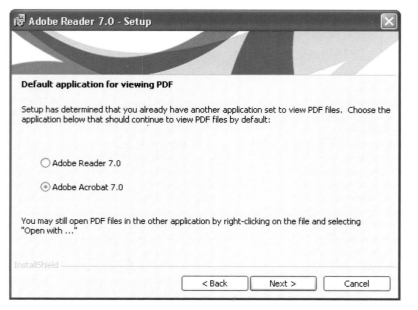

2. Move through the installation dialog boxes by clicking **Next** after reading the information provided in each box. The installation steps are fairly standard except for the dialog box, shown in Figure 2-1, that lets you choose whether you want Acrobat or Reader to be the default program to open PDFs. (If you typically view PDFs more often than edit them, you will find Reader opens a little faster.)

3. After making any changes to where you want the program files located, click **Next** twice, then click **Install**, and finally click **Finish**.

QUICKSTEPS

OPENING A PDF FILE

PDF documents can be opened using techniques common to Windows programs.

USE THE OPEN DIALOG BOX

1. Start Acrobat or Reader.
2. Click the **File** menu and click **Open**.

   –Or–

   Press **CTRL+O**.

   –Or–

   Click **Open** on the File toolbar.
3. Use the Look In drop-down list box or the button on the left sidebar to find the folder where the PDF you want to open is stored.
4. Select the file and click **Open**.

USE WINDOWS EXPLORER

1. Click **Start**, right-click **My Computer** on the right column of the Start menu, and click **Explore** in the context menu.
2. Click **Folders** on the toolbar to display Folders view in the left pane of the Explorer window.
3. Use the drive and folder hierarchy in the left pane to locate the folder that contains the PDF you want to open. Click the folder to display its contents in the right pane.
4. Double-click the PDF file you want to open in your default Adobe program.

   –Or–

   Right-click the PDF and click the Adobe program you want to use.

   Open with Acrobat 7.0
   Print
   Open with Adobe Reader 7.0

Browse and View Files with Organizer

Organizer (available in Acrobat, but not Reader) is a tri-pane window that provides listings of PDFs you have previously viewed. You can zoom in and out of page thumbnails to quickly locate just the information you want and then open the file in Acrobat. You also can group PDFs in *collections*, which are virtual containers that allow you to categorize PDFs by a common subject. To open Organizer, click the **File** menu, click **Organizer**, and click **Open Organizer**. The Organizer opens in its own window, as shown in Figure 2-2.

Folders and collections are listed in the left pane

PDF files in a folder or collection are listed in the middle pane

Page thumbnails of a selected PDF are displayed in the right pane

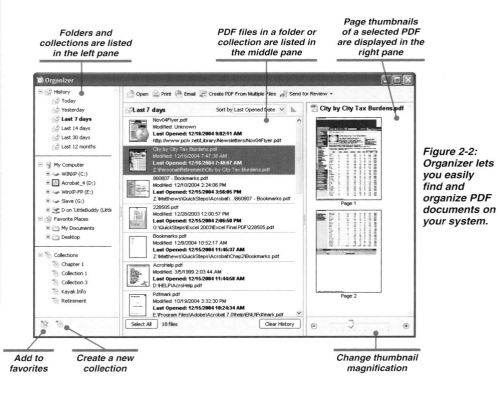

Figure 2-2: Organizer lets you easily find and organize PDF documents on your system.

Add to favorites

Create a new collection

Change thumbnail magnification

LOCATE A PDF IN ORGANIZER

You can find previously opened PDFs in Organizer folders or collections listed in the left pane. PDFs found in the selected folder or collection are listed in the center pane. The left pane can include:

- **History** folder, which provides six blocks of time from which you can choose to list PDFs you viewed. (Be careful when choosing Last 12 Months—you might be surprised by the number of PDFs you can view in a year!)

- **My Computer** folder, which allows you to explore the physical and mapped drives, and folders, on your local system and network for PDFs.

- **Favorite Places** folder, which provides a listing of folders you can open to quickly display the PDFs in them. To add your own favorite folders, click **Add A Favorite Place**. In the Browse For Folder dialog box, select an existing folder, or click **Make New Folder** to create and name a new one. Click **OK** when done.

- **Collections** are virtual folders that let you combine shortcuts to PDFs from anywhere on your system, network, or the Internet. Since collections contain only shortcuts and not the actual PDF files, you can add the same PDF to more than one collection (see the QuickSteps "Working with Collections" for information on using collections).

VIEW PDF PAGES IN ORGANIZER

From the list of PDFs found in a selected Organizer folder or collection (displayed in the center pane), you can select one or more files and view page thumbnails in the right pane.

- Use the left pane to locate the folder or collection that contains the PDFs you want.

- Select one or more documents in the center pane (to select multiple documents, press and hold **CTRL** while clicking noncontiguous files, or press and hold **SHIFT** and click the first and last file in a contiguous list).

- In the right pane, the pages of selected PDFs are displayed as thumbnails. Use the scroll bar to locate pages hidden from view, and use the Zoom slider and buttons to change magnification.

QUICKSTEPS

WORKING WITH COLLECTIONS

Organizer provides three empty collections to get you started. You can rename these, add PDFs to them, as well as create new ones.

> 🗎 Collection 1
> 🗎 Collection 2
> 🗎 Collection 3

CREATE A COLLECTION

In Acrobat, click the **File** menu, click **Organizer**, click **Collections**, and click **Create A New Collection**. Organizer opens with a new, untitled collection added to the Collections folder.

–Or–

In Organizer, right-click an existing collection, and click **Create a New Collection** in the context menu. A new, untitled collection is added to the Collections folder.

ADD DOCUMENTS TO A COLLECTION

In Acrobat, display the PDF you want to add to a collection. Click the **File** menu, click **Organizer**, and click **Add To A Collection**. In the Add To Collection dialog box, click the collection you want, and click **OK**.

–Or–

In Organizer, right-click the collection into which you want to add documents, and click **Add Files** in the context menu. Locate the folder that contains the files, select the files you want, and click **Add**.

DISPLAY A PDF LOCATED IN A COLLECTION

In Acrobat, click the **File** menu, click **Organizer**, click **Collections**, click the collection that contains the PDF, and click the PDF that you want to open. The PDF opens in Acrobat.

RENAME A COLLECTION

1. In Organizer, right-click the collection you want to rename, and click **Rename Collection**.

2. Type the new name and press ENTER.

DELETE A COLLECTION

1. In Organizer, right-click the collection you want to delete, and click **Delete Collection**.

2. Click **Yes** to confirm the collection will be deleted and that no files will be removed from your disk.

SORT PDFS LISTED IN ORGANIZER

In folders and collections that contain several PDFs, you can arrange the list according to sorting criteria.

1. In the left pane, click the folder or collection that contains the PDF you want to open.

2. In the center pane, click the **Sort By** down arrow, and click the criteria that you want used to sort the list of PDFs.

3. Click 📑 to toggle between an ascending and descending sort of the PDFs.

> Sort by Last Opened Date ∨
> Filename
> Modified Date
> Last Opened Date
> File Size
> Number of Pages
> Title
> Subject
> Author
> Keywords
> Creator
> Producer

OPEN A PDF IN ORGANIZER

You can open a PDF to a specific page:

1. In the left pane, click the folder or collection that contains the PDF you want to open.

2. Right-click the PDF in the center pane, and click **Open** on the context menu. The PDF opens in Acrobat at the beginning of the document.

–Or–

Select the PDF in the center pane, and then right-click a specific page thumbnail in the right pane. Click **Open _PDF file name_ to page _x_**. The PDF opens in Acrobat to the page you specified.

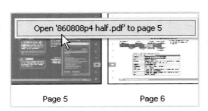

Open '860808p4 half.pdf' to page 5

Page 5   Page 6

NOTE

Individual page thumbnails shown in the right pane of Organizer are not displayed for PDFs you viewed on the Internet.

TIP

You can choose to have documents displayed in a specific layout when initially opened. In Acrobat or Reader, click the **Edit** menu, click **Preferences**, and click the **Page Display** category. Click the **Default Page Layout** down arrow at the top of the dialog box, and click the layout you want. Click **OK** when finished.

Page Display

Default Page Layout: | Automatic ▾

Automatic
Continuous
Continuous - Facing
Facing
Single Page

☐ Display art, trim, ble
☑ Display large images
☐ Display page to edge
☐ Display transparency

NOTE

The first page of a document in either of the two facing pages views is shown by itself in the right hand position. This mimics the convention that a book's page 1 typically starts on the right side of the spine.

View Single or Facing Pages

The Views buttons in the bottom-right corner of the Acrobat window let you control whether you see a single page or facing pages in the document pane, as shown in Figure 2-3. Further, you can determine how you want to scroll between single pages or sets of facing pages—either in a continuous scroll or jumping between successive views when you scroll to the bottom of a document. Table 2-1 describes the page layout options.

Click the **Views** button for the layout you want.

–Or–

Click the **View** menu, click **Page Layout**, and click the layout you want.

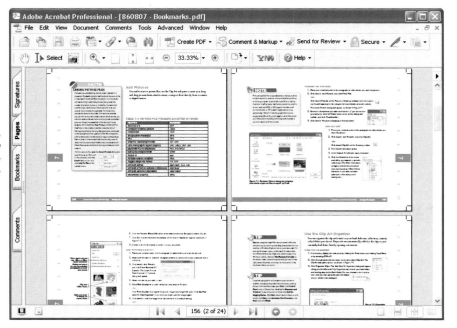

Figure 2-3: Facing pages are helpful when reviewing documents that are part of a book.

TABLE 2-1: THE VIEWS BUTTONS CHANGE DISPLAY AND SCROLLING BEHAVIOR

VIEW	CONTINUOUS SCROLLING BETWEEN LAYOUTS	"JUMP" BEHAVIOR BETWEEN LAYOUTS
Single page		
Facing pages		

TIP

You can return to a layout, magnification level, or area of a document you recently viewed by using the Previous View and Next View buttons on the status bar at the bottom of the Acrobat or Reader window.

NOTE

Adobe thinks so highly of its zooming capabilities that it has not one, but two, Zoom-related toolbars. The standard Zoom toolbar displays by default in the toolbar area at the top of the Acrobat window and can be displayed or hidden from the Toolbars option on the View menu. The Zoom Tools toolbar can be displayed by clicking the **Zoom Tool** down arrow on the Zoom toolbar and clicking **Show Zoom** (*Tools*) **Toolbar**. See the "Using Zoom Tools" QuickSteps later in this chapter.

- Zoom In
- Zoom Out
- Dynamic Zoom
- Loupe
- Pan & Zoom Window

Show Zoom Toolbar

Enlarge or Reduce a Document

Acrobat and Reader provide an extensive array of zoom tools and options so you can adjust your view in the document pane just as you want.

CHANGE MAGNIFICATION VALUE

You can choose a predefined magnification value, toggle through the values, or enter any value between 1 percent and 6400 percent.

- To select a predefined magnification:

  On the Zoom toolbar (click the **View** menu, click **Toolbars**, and click **Zoom** if it's not displayed), click the **Zoom** down arrow and click the magnification value you want.

  –Or–

  Click the **View** menu, click **Zoom To**, click the **Magnification** down arrow in the Zoom To dialog box, and select the magnification value you want. Click **OK**.

- To toggle through the predefined magnification values:

  Click the **Zoom In** or **Zoom Out** buttons on the Zoom toolbar. The layout increases or decreases magnification by one increment with each click.

- To enter a magnification value:

  On the Zoom toolbar, select the current magnification value in the Zoom text box, and type the new value you want. Press **ENTER**.

  –Or–

  Click the **View** menu, click **Zoom To**, select the current value in the **Magnification** text box, and type the new value you want. Click **OK**.

TIP

You can choose to have documents displayed at a specific magnification when initially opened. In Acrobat or Reader, click the **Edit** menu, click **Preferences**, and click the **Page Display** category. Click the **Default Zoom** down arrow at the bottom of the dialog box, and click the magnification you want. Click **OK** when finished.

FIT A VIEW

You can force a document to fit into one of several display criteria. Figure 2-4 shows how the view changes as you change the fit.

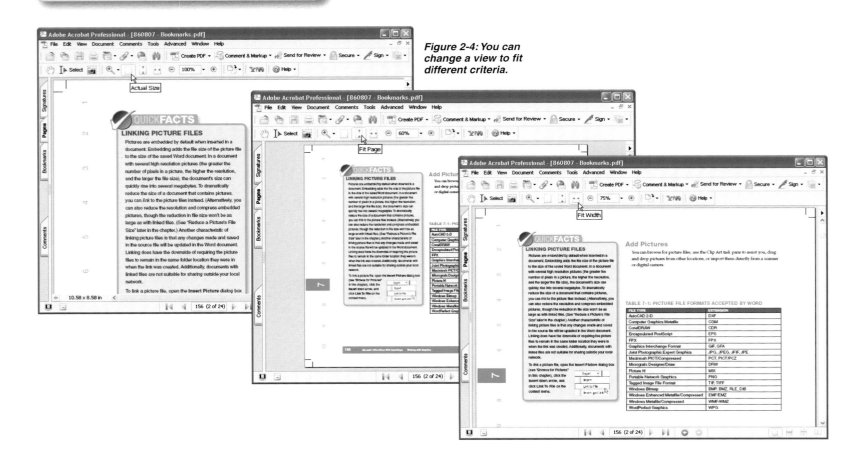

Figure 2-4: You can change a view to fit different criteria.

Click the **View** menu and click one of the fit options (the first three options are also available on the Zoom toolbar):

- **Actual Size** displays a document at 100 percent magnification.

- **Fit Page** changes the view so the entire layout (single or facing pages) is visible at the maximum magnification that will fit within the Acrobat or Reader window.

- **Fit Width** changes the view so the width of the entire layout is visible at the maximum magnification that will fit within the width of the Acrobat or Reader window (content at the bottom of the layout might be hidden).

- **Fit Visible** changes the view so the width of the content only is visible (trims margins on left and right sides) at maximum magnification (content at the bottom of the layout might be hidden).

- **Full Screen View** lets you display a single page at a time without menus, toolbars, and other window elements obstructing your view, as shown in Figure 2-5. Click the **Full Screen View** button in the bottom-left corner of the Acrobat window, or click the **Window** menu and click **Full Screen View**. Press **UP ARROW** and **DOWN ARROW** on your keyboard to move between pages; press **ESC** to return to the standard view.

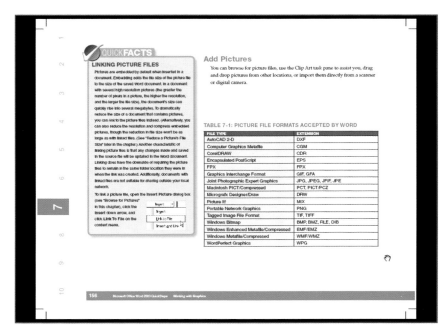

Figure 2-5: Full Screen View provides the most focused view of a layout.

QUICKSTEPS

USING ZOOM TOOLS

You can adjust the magnification for a specific area of the layout (the Loupe tool and the Pan & Zoom window are not available in Reader).

DRAG TO CHANGE MAGNIFICATION

1. On the Zoom toolbar, click the **Zoom Tool** down arrow, and click **Dynamic Zoom**.

2. Drag (meaning to press and hold the mouse button while moving the mouse) the magnification icon over the area you want to change:

   - Drag upwards to increase magnification.
   - Drag downwards to decrease magnification.

DEFINE AN AREA TO MAGNIFY

The Loupe tool lets you focus the area under magnification and adjust the zoom.

1. On the Zoom toolbar, click the **Zoom Tool** down arrow, and click **Loupe**.

2. Click the loupe pointer on the object you want to see magnified. The Loupe Tool dialog box opens, as shown in Figure 2-6.

3. Use the slider, Zoom In and Zoom Out buttons, or the magnification value text box to change the magnification level.

4. Drag and size the loupe focus rectangle to change the size and location of the loupe's focus. You can also change the color of the rectangle by clicking its down arrow and selecting a new color from the palette.

MOVE THE AREA TO MAGNIFY

The Pan & Zoom window lets you use the grabber hand to move, or *pan*, the area that's under magnification.

1. On the Zoom toolbar, click the Zoom Tool down arrow, and click **Pan & Zoom Window**.

Continued...

Split a Document into Multiple Views

You can display a document in two panes (Split view) or four panes (Spreadsheet Split view) to let you see more than one area of the PDF in the document pane.

Figure 2-6: The Loupe tool lets you focus on an area you want magnified.

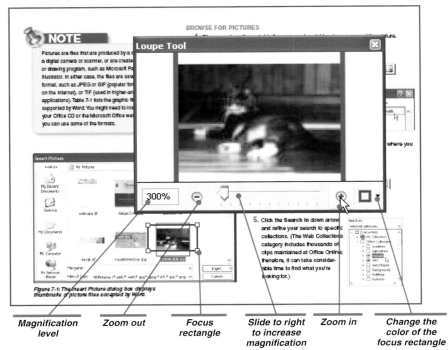

| Magnification level | Zoom out | Focus rectangle | Slide to right to increase magnification | Zoom in | Change the color of the focus rectangle |

USING ZOOM TOOLS *(Continued)*

2. With the Pan & Zoom window displayed, use the grabber hand icon to slide the focus rectangle to where you want it. Resize the rectangle by dragging the sizing handles on the corners.

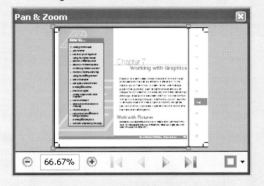

3. Use the Zoom text box to enter a magnification percentage or the Zoom In and Zoom Out buttons to adjust the magnification value.

4. Use the page navigation buttons to change pages to the first page, the previous page, the next page, or the last page. You can also change the color of the focus rectangle by clicking its down arrow and selecting a new color from the palette.

TIP

To rotate a layout 90 degrees, click the **Rotate** down arrow on the Rotate View toolbar, and click the direction you want; or click the **View** menu, click **Rotate View**, and click the rotation direction.

USE SPLIT VIEW

In Split view, the two panes act independently of each other so you scroll each to different areas of the document, use different layouts, and change the magnification of each view, as shown in Figure 2-7. For example, you can leave the first page of a document that shows the table of contents of a chapter in the upper pane in Single Page layout and use the lower pane in Continuous-Facing layout to scroll to content you want to see.

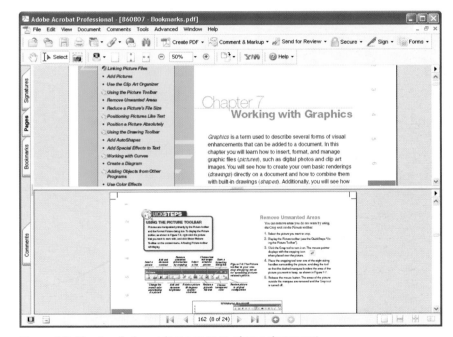

Figure 2-7: Use two independent panes to view a document.

1. Click the **Window** menu and click **Split**. The currently displayed layout is divided into two horizontal panes, each with its own vertical and horizontal scroll bars.

2. Size the panes by dragging the split border.

3. Click one of the panes to make it active. A thin black border will appear on the perimeter of the  active pane. Change the layout and magnification, and navigate to where you want to go (see "Move Around in a File" later in the chapter for information about navigating in a PDF).

4. Click the second pane, change the view, and navigate to another area of the document.

5. To return to a single pane, click the **Window** menu and click **Remove Split**. The document displays at the location and magnifica- tion of the active pane.

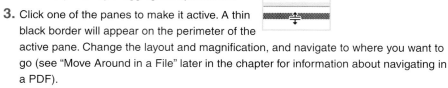

Figure 2-8: Spreadsheet view is handy for viewing Excel worksheets and tables.

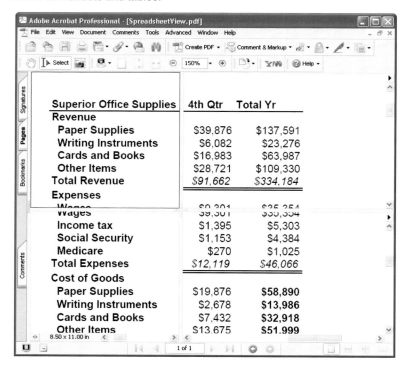

USE SPREADSHEET SPLIT VIEW

In Spreadsheet Split view (not available in Reader), the panes act in concert to allow you to, for example, freeze column or row headings in a larger spreadsheet or table.

1. Click the **Window** menu and click **Spreadsheet View.** The cur- rently displayed layout is divided into four panes with two sets of vertical scroll bars and two sets of horizontal scroll bars, as shown in Figure 2-8.

2. Size the panes by dragging the horizontal and vertical borders.

3. Click one of the panes to make it active. A thin black border will ap- pear on the perimeter of the active pane. Change the magnification and navigate to where you want to go. All panes receive the same magnification value, the layout defaults to Single Page view, and the two adjacent panes move in unison.

4. Click another pane and move to another part of the page (the views in all four panes move through successive pages together).

5. To return to a single pane, click the **Window** menu and click **Remove Split**. The document displays in its original layout with the magnification last used in the split panes.

VIEWING MULTIPLE DOCUMENTS

You can display all open PDFs in their own Document window within the program window.

DISPLAY MULTIPLE DOCUMENTS

Open those documents you want to display and close any you don't want shown. Figure 2-9 shows the three configurations.

Click the **Window** menu and click **Cascade** to display each open document in overlapping windows.

–Or–

Click the **Window** menu, click **Tile**, and click **Horizontally** to display each open document in a stacked windows array.

–Or–

Click the **Window** menu, click **Tile**, and click **Vertically** to display each open document in a side-by-side windows array.

WORK WITH MULTIPLE DOCUMENTS

Each document window has the properties of a standard window. You can resize them by dragging a border or corner; expand or reduce them by using the Maximize, Minimize, and Restore buttons on the title bar; move them by dragging their title bars; and close them by clicking their respective Close buttons.

To close all open document windows, click the **Window** menu and click **Close All**.

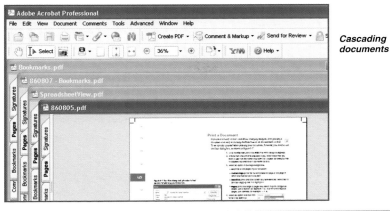

Cascading documents

Documents tiled horizontally

Documents tiled vertically

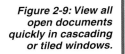

Figure 2-9: View all open documents quickly in cascading or tiled windows.

Move around in a File

Chapter 1 briefly introduced features you can use to navigate through a PDF—this section provides the details on how to do it. You can find the information you want by using Bookmarks and Pages, two of the several Navigation tabs that categorize a document; by manual or automatic scrolling; by interactively moving content with the Hand tool; and by viewing pages. (Searching techniques are described in Chapter 6.)

Use Bookmarks

When you are looking to move around in a file according to the elements contained in the document, the Acrobat or Reader windows provide several categories, organized by tabs (Acrobat has thirteen; Reader has six), that you can use. The Bookmarks tab, displayed in the navigation pane on the left side of the Acrobat window (not in Reader by default), shows one or more levels of links to locations in the currently displayed PDF, as shown in Figure 2-10. Typically, the author of the document adds bookmarks to help readers find major sections or to highlight specific information; however, depending on how the PDF is created, bookmarks may be created from headings in the source document. (Chapter 3 describes how to create PDFs, and Chapter 9 covers adding bookmarks.)

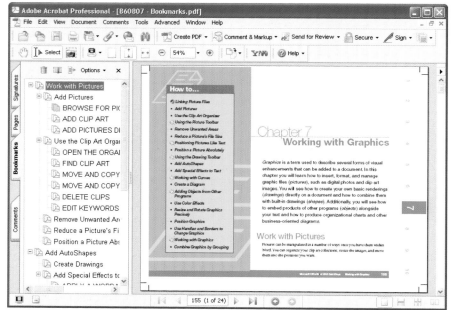

Figure 2-10:
Bookmarks can provide
a table of contents set
of links to navigate
longer documents.

To display bookmarks in a PDF, first expand the Bookmarks tab in the navigation pane:

1. Open the document in Acrobat or Reader.

2. Click the **Bookmarks** tab on the navigation pane, if shown.

    –Or–

    Click the **View** menu, click **Navigation** tabs, and click **Bookmarks**.

MOVE TO A BOOKMARK

In the Bookmarks tab:

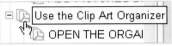

Point at the bookmark whose location you want to see, and click when the pointer changes to a pointing hand.

–Or–

Right-click the bookmark and click **Go To Bookmark** on the context menu.

In either case, the page that contains the bookmark displays in the document pane.

MODIFY THE BOOKMARKS TAB

You can make changes to how you view the Bookmarks tab and the bookmarks that are listed.

- **Float the tab** by dragging the tab handle from the navigation pane to another area of the screen. Resize the window by dragging borders and corners. To return the window to the navigation pane, click the **View** menu, click **Navigation Tabs**, and click **Dock All Tabs** (this procedure works for any tab).

- **Expand the navigation pane** by dragging the right border to the right.

- **Expand or collapse the bookmark's hierarchy** by clicking the plus and minus icons to the left of a bookmark level, or click **Options** on the Bookmarks toolbar and click **Collapse** (or *Expand*) **Top-Level Bookmarks**.

- **Expand an individual bookmark** by selecting the bookmark. On the Bookmarks toolbar, click **Expand Current Bookmark**, or click **Options** and click **Expand Current Bookmark**.

- **Display the full bookmark** by clicking **Options** on the Bookmarks toolbar and clicking **Wrap Long Bookmarks**.

- **Adjust text size** by clicking **Options**, clicking **Text Size**, and clicking a different size.

Navigate by Page

You can quickly move through a PDF by viewing thumbnails of the pages in the document, or by using navigation buttons to cycle through the document.

USE PAGE THUMBNAILS

1. Open the document in Acrobat or Reader.

2. Click the **Pages** tab on the navigation pane.

   –Or–

   Click the **View** menu, click **Navigation** tabs, and click **Pages**.

   In either case, a single column of page thumbnails is displayed.

3. To view more thumbnails:

   Use the vertical scroll bar (see "Scroll through a File Automatically" in the following section).

   –Or–

   Drag the right border of the navigation pane to the right to increase the number of columns displaying thumbnails.

   –Or–

   Click **Options** on the Pages tab toolbar, and click **Reduce Page Thumbnails**. Repeat the procedure to continue to reduce the size/increase the number of thumbnails displayed.

4. Click the thumbnail that you want displayed in the document pane.

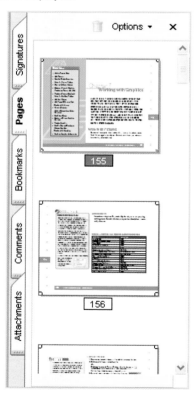

TIP

Each time the Pages tab is opened on the navigation pane, all thumbnails are drawn from their respective pages. To avoid waiting for the thumbnails to redraw each time you open the Pages tab for a document, you can embed the thumbnails. Click the **Options** down arrow on the Pages tab, and click Embed All Page Thumbnails. Click **Remove Embedded Page Thumbnails** to return to the default behavior.

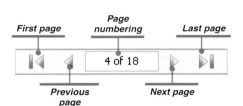

First page — Page numbering — Last page

4 of 18

Previous page — Next page

TIP

If you find the location of the status bar navigation buttons awkward to use, you can activate the Navigation toolbar (click the **View** menu, click **Toolbars**, and click **Navigation**), which has the same navigation controls. Float that toolbar anywhere on the screen, or dock it in the toolbar area (see Chapter 1 for information on using toolbars).

Navigation

TIP

If you purchased a mouse (other than a bargain-basement model) in the last few years, you should have a scroll wheel incorporated into the design. By rotating the wheel, you can vertically scroll through the open document (to get full functionality of a newer mouse, you typically need to install additional software provided by the manufacturer).

PAGE THROUGH A DOCUMENT

Navigation buttons, menu options, and the keyboard let you move sequentially through a document or zip you to the first and last page.

1. Open the document in Acrobat or Reader.

2. On the status bar, click the button to perform the movement you want. To go directly to a page, select the current page number in the page numbering text box, type the page number of the page you want to see, and press **ENTER**.

   –Or–

   Click the **View** menu, click **Go To**, and click the action you want. To go directly to a page, click the **Page** option, type the number of the page you want to see, and click **OK**.

   –Or–

   Use the keyboard:

   • Press **HOME** to move to the first page.

   • Press **LEFT ARROW** to move to the previous page.

   • Press **RIGHT ARROW** to move to the next page.

   • Press **END** to move to the last page.

Scroll through a File Automatically

Acrobat and Reader allow you to page through a document without the constant mouse or keyboard input required by traditional means.

1. Open the document in Acrobat or Reader. Move to the point in the document where you want to start continuous scrolling.

2. Click the **View** menu and click **Automatically Scroll**. The document starts scrolling at a leisurely viewing rate.

3. To stop automatically scrolling, press **ESC**.

If you find yourself in a position where looking at a computer screen is inconvenient, for instance, when you're trying to read a report in traffic while balancing a cup of coffee and fielding a few cell phone calls, you can have Acrobat or Reader recite the text for you. (You will need speakers integrated with, or attached to, your computer. *Windows XP QuickSteps*, from McGraw-Hill/Osborne, provides details on how to use sound with your PC.)

1. Open the document in Acrobat or Reader.

2. Display the page in the document where you want the reading to start. Start and stop the reading by clicking the **View** menu, clicking **Read Out Loud**, and then clicking one of the following menu options or use keyboard shortcuts:

   • Click **Read To End Of Document** (or press **CTRL+SHIFT+B**) to read continuously to the end of the document.

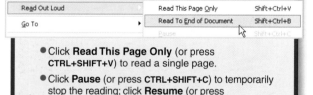

Read Out Loud	▶	Read This Page Only	Shift+Ctrl+V
Go To	▶	Read To End of Document	Shift+Ctrl+B
		Pause	Shift+Ctrl+C

   • Click **Read This Page Only** (or press **CTRL+SHIFT+V**) to read a single page.

   • Click **Pause** (or press **CTRL+SHIFT+C**) to temporarily stop the reading; click **Resume** (or press **CTRL+SHIFT+C** a second time) to continue the reading.

   • Click **Stop** (or press **CTRL+SHIFT+E**) to end the reading.

TIP

You can adjust the pitch, volume, tempo, and even gender, of the voice that reads text to you. Click the **Edit** menu, click **Preferences**, and click the **Reading** category in the Preferences dialog box, as shown in Figure 2-11. Click **OK** when finished.

Move around a Document by Hand

One of the "handiest" features found in most Adobe products (and conspicuously absent in Microsoft's) is the Hand tool, or *grabber* hand. Using this tool, you can interactively move the current layout up, down, sideways, and everything in between so you can see whatever portion of the PDF you want.

1. Click the **Hand** tool on the Basic toolbar.

   –Or–

   To temporarily use the Hand tool while working with another tool, press and hold **SPACEBAR**.

   In either case, your mouse pointer turns into an open-faced hand when moved over the document pane.

2. Click the document (the hand turns into a grabbing fist) and drag the page in the direction you want it to move.

3. If you reach the edge of the screen, release the mouse button, and "grab" and drag another fistful of page.

Figure 2-11: You can customize several attributes of the Read Out Loud feature.

UNDERSTANDING PRINTING

In Acrobat, you can print in a few clicks using default or custom settings, but you also can delve into options generally used by professionals. Adobe has long been associated with higher-end digital printing used by graphic artists and commercial printing shops. The key difference between Windows and Adobe printing is that Adobe products first came from the Apple world, where the printing medium is *PostScript*, a print language that provides much greater control over the printing process than the language used by Windows, especially for graphics.

Going hand-in-hand with choosing printing options are the options you choose when creating a PDF document. Again, you can use default settings to cover 90 percent of the documents you work with, but you also can use advanced techniques to give precise control over the creation process, including downloading fonts and working with images and colors. Chapter 3 describes how to set up options for creating PDF documents using the more automated techniques. Chapter 5 describes PostScript in more detail and how to use Adobe Distiller (a companion program installed with Acrobat) to exercise greater control when creating PDF documents.

TIP

For those road warriors who don't want to lug a portable printer around with them, Acrobat and Reader provide a link with an online service that allows you to print on a system of printers in airports, hotels, and other public facilities. Click the **File** menu and click **PrintMe Internet Printing** to be connected to the fee-based service, shown in Figure 2-12.

Print a PDF Document

While producing a paper-based copy of a PDF can be as simple as clicking a button, Acrobat and Reader provide extensive options from which to choose. Also, the particular printer you use might have additional features you can apply before you perform the print job.

Define Printer-Specific Options

You can select paper and orientation options for the printer and, depending on the printer, select several other features such as color settings, print quality, and dry times.

Figure 2-12: With only an Internet connection, you can print a PDF in many public facilities.

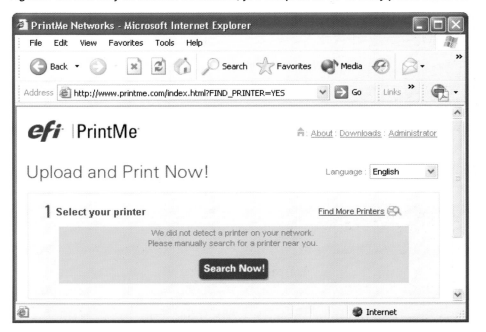

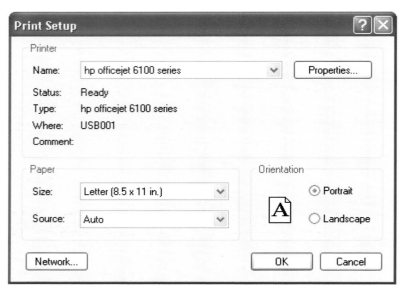

Figure 2-13: Set up paper specifications and other printer-
specific settings in the Print Setup dialog box.

SELECT PRINTER OPTIONS

1. Open the document you want to print in Acrobat or Reader.

2. Click the **File** menu and click **Print Setup**. The Print Setup dialog box, shown in Figure 2-13, displays basic options common to most printers.

3. Click the **Name** down arrow to display a drop-down listing of printers that are connected to your system. Click the  printer you want (if the printer you want isn't listed, see "Connect to a Networked Printer" in the next section). The options might change as you choose different printers.

4. If you need to change any of the default settings:

   - Click the **Size** down arrow, and select the correct size, dimensions, or format—for example, an envelope.

   - Click the **Source** down arrow, and select the paper tray or feeder that you want the printer to use.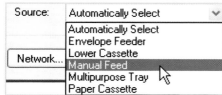

   - Click **Landscape** if you want your pages printed across the short and wide dimensions of the paper instead of the default tall and narrow Portrait option.

5. Click **Properties** and review the printer-specific options you have available to you, as shown in Figure 2-14. Make any changes you want, and click **OK**.

6. Click **OK** to close the Print Setup dialog box.

Figure 2-14: Printers enhance your printing options with printer-specific features.

CONNECT TO A NETWORKED PRINTER

1. Open the document you want to print in Acrobat or Reader.

2. Click the **File** menu, click **Print Setup**, and click **Network**. The Connect To Printer dialog box opens.

    [Network...]

3. If you know the printer's name, type it in the Printer text box.

    –Or–

    Under Shared Printers, double-click the network where the printer you want is connected, and if necessary, double-click the workgroup where the printer is located. Select the printer you want, as shown in Figure 2-15.

4. Click **OK** when finished. The printer is displayed in the Name drop-down list box in the Print Setup dialog (see "Select Printer Options" earlier in the chapter).

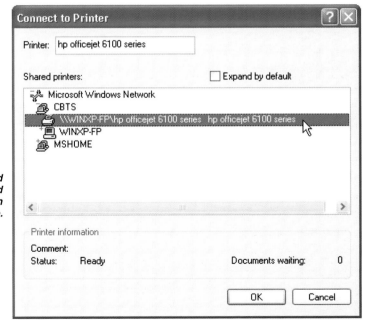

Figure 2-15: Find shared, networked computers you can connect to.

Print a Document

The business end of printing is done in the Print dialog box, which provides several options on how the PDF can be printed.

1. Open the document you want to print in Acrobat or Reader.

2. Click **Print** on the File toolbar.

   –Or–

   Click the **File** menu and click **Print**.

   –Or–

   Press **CTRL+P**.

   In any case, the Print dialog box opens, as shown in Figure 2-16.

3. In the Printer area, change the printer and set any printer-specific properties (see "Define Printer-Specific Options" earlier in the chapter). If your document contains comments or forms, select additional options from the Comments And Forms drop-down list. (Chapter 7 discusses comments, and Chapter 8 describes how to create forms.)

4. Click **OK** to print with default options.

   –Or–

   Choose options (described in the following sections) to refine your print job, and then click **OK**.

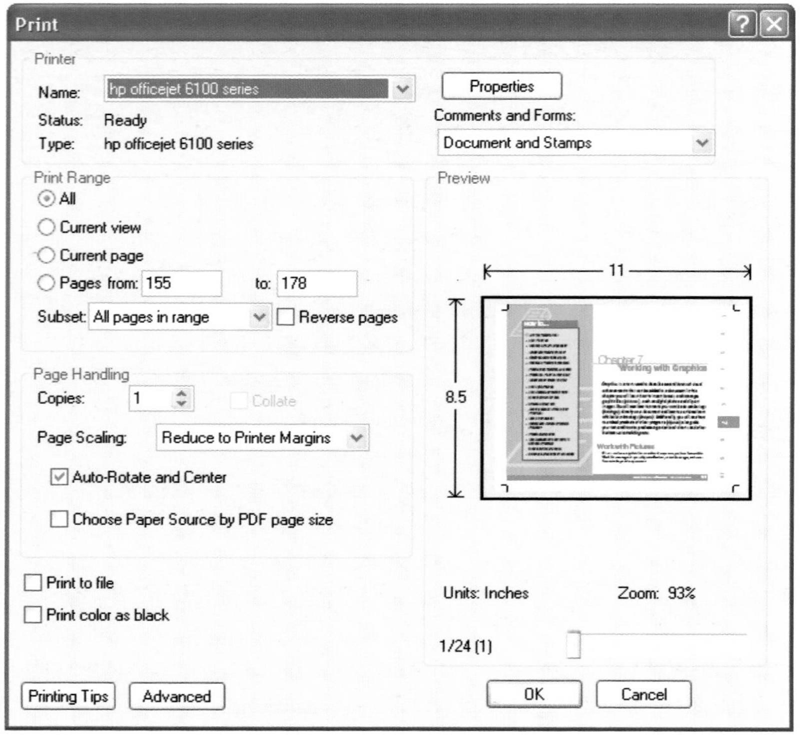

Print

Printer

Name: hp officejet 6100 series   Properties

Status: Ready
Type: hp officejet 6100 series   Comments and Forms:
                                   Document and Stamps

Print Range
- ○ All
- ○ Current view
- ○ Current page
- ○ Pages from: 155   to: 178
- Subset: All pages in range   ☐ Reverse pages

Page Handling
- Copies: 1   ☐ Collate
- Page Scaling: Reduce to Printer Margins
- ☑ Auto-Rotate and Center
- ☐ Choose Paper Source by PDF page size

☐ Print to file
☐ Print color as black

Preview

11

8.5

Chapter 7
Working with Graphics

Work with Pictures

Units: Inches   Zoom: 93%

1/24 (1)

Printing Tips   Advanced   OK   Cancel

Figure 2-16: The Print dialog box is your gateway to Acrobat and Reader printing options.

QUICKSTEPS

SELECTING AN AREA TO PRINT

You can select an area of a document to print by dragging a rectangular marquee around it.

1. Open the document in Acrobat or Reader, and navigate to the page that contains the content you want to print.

2. Click **Snapshot Tool** on the Basic toolbar. The mouse pointer changes to a crosshair.

3. Place the mouse pointer over the upper-left corner of the area you want to print, and drag down and to the right. Release the mouse button when the marquee has surrounded the content you want. A dialog box informs you the selected area is copied to the Clipboard. Click **OK**.

TABLE 7-1: PICTURE FILE FORMATS ACCEPTED BY WORD

FILE TYPE	EXTENSION
AutoCAD 2-D	DXF
Computer Graphics Metafile	CGM
CorelDRAW	CDR
Encapsulated PostScript	EPS
FPX	FPX
Graphics Interchange Format	GIF, GFA
Joint Photographic Expert Graphics	JPG, JPEG, JFIF, JPE
Macintosh PICT/Compressed	PCT, PICT/PCZ
Micrograph Designer/Draw	DRW
Picture It!	MIX
Portable Network Graphics	PNG
Tagged Image File Format	TIF, TIFF
Windows Bitmap	BMP, BMZ, RLE, DIB
Windows Enhanced Metafile/Compressed	EMF/EMZ
Windows Metafile/Compressed	WMF/WMZ
WordPerfect Graphics	WPG

4. In the Print dialog box (see "Print a Document"), under Print Range, click **Selected Graphic**. Choose other print options and click **OK** when finished.

NOTE

The Preview area in the Print dialog box (see Figure 2-16) displays a thumbnail of a page that represents what a printed page will look like based on the options you've selected. Use the slider at the bottom of the Preview area to see each page if you selected multiple pages to be printed.

SELECT WHICH PAGES TO PRINT

The Print Range area of the Print dialog box lets you determine which pages print and in what order.

- Click **All** to print the entire document. (Click the **Subset** down arrow to print only odd or even pages.)

- Click **Current View** to print just the portion of a single page layout that is currently displayed on your screen. Only a portion of a page may be printed.

- Click **Selected Graphic** if you selected an area to print with the Snapshot tool. See the QuickSteps, "Selecting an Area to Print."

- Click **Current Page** to print the entire page listed in the page numbering text box at the bottom of the document pane.

- Click **Pages From** and type the first and last page numbers to print a range of pages. (Click the **Subset** down arrow to print only odd or even pages.)

- Click the **Reverse Pages** check box to select it and change the print order from first-to-last to last-to-first.

DETERMINE PAGE SCALING AND ALIGNMENT

The Page Handling area of the Print dialog box provides options for fitting document pages to the paper by reducing, enlarging, or dividing pages; choosing the number of copies you want; and aligning the pages on the printed output.

1. Use the Copies text box to enter the number of copies you want, or click the spinner to increase or decrease the number. Click the **Collate** check box to print each copy from the first page to the last page; otherwise, the first page is printed the number of times you specified, followed by multiple printing of the second page, and so on.

2. Click the **Page Scaling** down arrow, and choose how you want pages to appear on the printed output. One or more of the features listed in Table 2-2 are available for each of the scaling options:

   - **None** does not scale the page. The page prints starting from the upper-left corner or center (if Auto-Rotate And Center is selected) of the page.

   - **Fit To Printer Margins** changes the scale of each page to match the printable margins determined by the paper size and printer.

- **Reduce To Printer Margins** reduces large pages to match the printable margins determined by the paper size and printer but does not enlarge smaller pages.

- **Tile Large Pages** (Acrobat only) divides a document page or selected area whose dimensions exceed the size of the printer paper into rectangular areas, or *tiles*, that match the paper size.

- **Tile All Pages** (Acrobat only) divides all pages or selected areas into tiles.

- **Multiple Pages Per Sheet** (also referred to as *N*-Up; for example, printing four pages per sheet is called 4-Up) lets you determine the number of pages you want printed on a single sheet of paper and the order in which they are printed (see Figure 2-17). This option is not available when you've selected an area using the Snapshot tool.

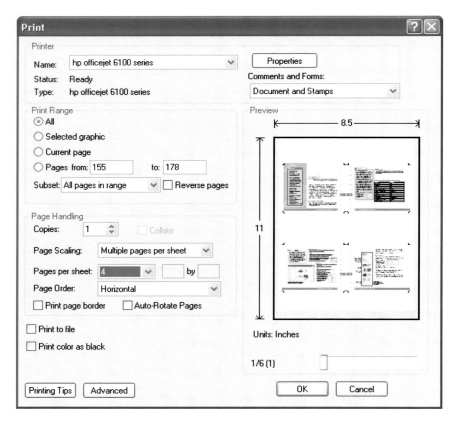

Figure 2-17: You can print multiple pages per sheet of paper, as shown in a 4-Up layout here.

NOTE

The printing features described in this chapter are only the tip of iceberg of the printing options Acrobat provides. To get a sense of the breadth of features available (which are beyond the scope of this book), click the **Advanced** button in the Print dialog box, and click each of the categories on the left side of the dialog box. One feature that might come in handy is the Print As Image option at the top of the dialog box. Try this option, at different resolutions, if your printed output using normal options doesn't come out as you expect.

☑ Print As Image   300 ⌄   dpi

TABLE 2-2: PAGE SCALING AND MISCELLANEOUS PRINTING OPTIONS

FEATURE	DESCRIPTION	PAGE SCALING OPTION USED WITH...
Auto-Rotate And Center	Matches the page orientation to the orientation selected in the printer properties and centers the page on the paper.	None, Fit To Printer Margins, Reduce To Printer Margins
Choose Paper Source By PDF Page Size	Selects the printer's paper tray that holds paper that best matches the page size.	None, Fit To Printer Margins, Reduce To Printer Margins
Tile Scale (Acrobat only)	Lets you change the page scale, thereby increasing or decreasing the number of tiles required to print a page.	Tile Large Pages, Tile All Pages
Overlap (Acrobat only)	Lets you determine how much duplicated content you want to appear in each tile. Aids in reassembling tiles.	Tile Large Pages, Tile All Pages
Cut Marks (Acrobat only)	Provides different styles for marks that aid in cutting tiles into individual pieces.	Tile Large Pages, Tile All Pages
Labels (Acrobat only)	Adds descriptive information to each tile so the tiles can be reassembled in the correct order.	Tile Large Pages, Tile All Pages
Pages Per Sheet	Prints a predefined number of pages per sheet of paper using the best orientation, or lets you enter any number of sheets per page up to 99.	Multiple Pages Per Sheet
Page Order	Lets you choose the order multiple pages are printed on a sheet.	Multiple Pages Per Sheet
Print Page Border	Prints a border around each page. Also called a crop box.	Multiple Pages Per Sheet
Auto-Rotate Pages	Matches the page orientation to the orientation selected in the printer properties.	Multiple Pages Per Sheet
Print To File	Prints to a PostScript file instead of a physical printer (you get better results by using the Save As dialog box and choosing the PostScript file type).	All
Print Color As Black (Acrobat only)	Prints all non-white objects in black.	All

TIP

If your document contains JPEG pictures (.jpg) that were created in Adobe programs such as Photoshop Elements 2.0, you will see a Pictures Tasks button on the Task toolbar. Click the button to display several picture-related options. Click **Print Pictures** to open a special Print dialog box which allows you to choose photo-related features, as shown in Figure 2-18.

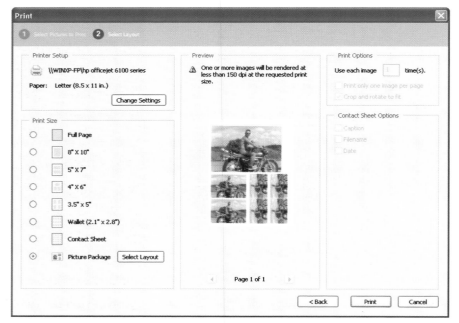

Figure 2-18: You can choose from several photo-printing options when printing .jpg files from the Picture Tasks' Print dialog box.

Chapter 3

Creating PDF Files

You can create a PDF file from just about any application that you can install on your system—and depending on the application, you might be able to create it with a single click from within the application. With such convenience, you don't sacrifice much flexibility in how the PDF is created, since there are several settings you can change for most file types (although the default settings work just fine in most cases). In this chapter you will learn how to create PDF files from Acrobat; from other applications, with and without convenient macros; and even from the Internet, e-mail, and scanned documents. Furthermore, you can use Acrobat to combine multiple files into one PDF document and add files to existing PDF documents.

UNDERSTANDING PDF CONVERSION TERMINOLOGY

Creating a PDF file is actually much easier than trying to grasp the concept of how a PDF is created. Two basic steps are involved in creating a PDF—how you decide to create one will determine the degree to which you are involved in the process:

1. The source document or image file is translated into an imaging model.

2. The imaging model is "printed" using a printer driver, a virtual, nonphysical software device, and converted to a PDF file.

- **Abode PDF** is a printer driver added to your list of available printers when you installed Acrobat. When you create a PDF by most methods, the source file is converted to PostScript behind the scenes and sent to the Adobe PDF printer driver. You can change a number of settings in the Properties dialog box for the printer or in the Abode PDF Settings dialog box (see "Modify Conversion Settings" later in the chapter). These changes can be saved for future use. Using this method to create a PDF, you cannot change the PostScript code prior to sending the file to the printer driver (and for most users, that's just fine).

- **Adobe Distiller** is a secondary print driver in the form of a companion application that is installed with Acrobat, providing tools that give you a wide range of options to optimize PDFs being created. Distiller converts PostScript files that have been created from the source document—you cannot directly convert a source document. Advanced users, however, can modify the PostScript file prior to converting (see Chapter 5 for more information on PostScript and Distiller).

- **PDFMaker** is a macro added to most Microsoft Office programs (as well as a few others) that allows bookmarks, links, and other elements to be transferred from the Office document to the PDF file. PDFMaker also provides a one-click start to the conversion process. See Table 3-1 for a list of supported programs.

Convert Files to PDFs

You can convert existing files to PDF documents in several ways. Whether you're working in Acrobat, using the application that created the content, or browsing files in Windows Explorer or on the desktop, you can start the process to create a PDF. Using these methods, PDFs are created with default settings (see "Modify Conversion Settings" later in this chapter for information on conversion options).

Create PDFs in Acrobat

Acrobat provides several ways for you to convert files to PDFs, including combining multiple files into a single PDF and processing more than one file at a time.

CREATE A SINGLE PDF

You can use menus or toolbar commands to locate a file and convert it to PDF.

1. Start Acrobat.

2. Click the **File** menu, click **Create PDF**, and click **From File**.

   –Or–

   Click **Create PDF** on the Tasks toolbar, and click **From File**.

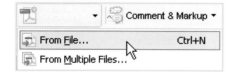

TABLE 3-1: PDFMAKER-SUPPORTED PROGRAMS

PROGRAM	VERSION
Microsoft	
Access	2000, 2002, 2003
Excel	2000, 2002, 2003
Internet Explorer	6
Outlook	2000, 2002, 2003
PowerPoint	2000, 2002, 2003
Project	2000, 2002, 2003
Publisher	2002, 2003
Visio	2000, 2002, 2003
AutoDesk AutoCAD (Professional version only)	2002, 2004, 2005

NOTE

PDFMaker is added to PDFMaker-supported programs on your system when you install Acrobat, and it is also added to many of the supported programs if they are installed after Acrobat is set up on your computer. If a supported program (see Table 3-1 for a list of supported programs) does not obtain the PDFMaker macro when installed, you might have to reinstall Acrobat in order to add PDFMaker to the program.

TIP

When converting Microsoft Office content to PDFs, it is best to start the Office program, open the file that contains the content you want to convert, and then use the Adobe PDF menu options that Acrobat added to Office. Each program provides conversion options tailored to the type of content it uses. If you use Acrobat directly to convert the content, you might wind up having to convert all content in a file instead of choosing specific objects to convert. See "Create PDFs in Office Programs" later in this chapter for information on the conversion options available in Office programs.

3. In the Open dialog box, shown in Figure 3-1, click the **Look In** down arrow, and click the drive and folder where your file is located; or use the shortcut buttons on the left side of the dialog box. Open any subfolders. Click the **Files Of Type** down arrow, and select the applicable file type to narrow the files displayed. Select the file you want to convert, and click **Open**.

Depending on the file type of the source file, you will see dialog boxes that show the conversion progress or provide hints on how you can work with the PDF document. When completed, the file displays as an unsaved PDF in the document pane.

4. Save the PDF, either before or after making any changes (the remaining chapters in this book describe those features you can use to modify a PDF). See "Save Converted Content" later in this chapter for saving options and procedures.

Figure 3-1: Use the Files Of Type drop-down list in the Open dialog box to display a focused list of files in a folder.

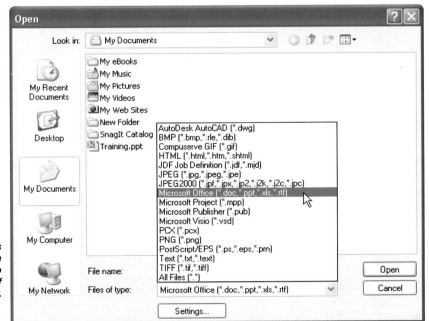

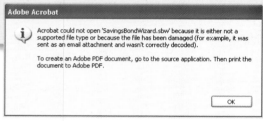

NOTE

You can view the file types that Acrobat can convert from the Open dialog box. Click the **Files Of Type** down arrow to view the list. If you try to convert a file type not on the list, you will be told to open the file in its parent program and print it to the Adobe PDF printer driver. See "Use the Adobe PDF Printer Driver to Create PDFs" later in this chapter for information on creating PDFs from most programs.

> **Adobe Acrobat**
>
> ⓘ Acrobat could not open 'SavingsBondWizard.sbw' because it is either not a supported file type or because the file has been damaged (for example, it was sent as an email attachment and wasn't correctly decoded).
>
> To create an Adobe PDF document, go to the source application. Then print the document to Adobe PDF.
>
> [OK]

TIP

You can create multiple PDFs by selecting more than one file in the Open dialog box. Browse to the folder that contains the files you want to convert. Press and hold **CTRL** and click the files you want to convert. Click **Open** to start the conversion process. When completed, all selected files will have separate PDF documents available in Acrobat.

CREATE A PDF FROM MULTIPLE FILES

You can combine the content from several source files into a PDF document (also known as creating a *binder*). For example, you can consolidate a narrative report written in Word, a supporting spreadsheet created in Excel, and research materials from the Internet.

1. Start Acrobat.

2. Click the **File** menu, click **Create PDF**, and click **From Multiple Files**.

–Or–

Click **Create PDF** on the Tasks toolbar, and click **From Multiple Files**.

3. In the Create PDF From Multiple Documents dialog box, shown in Figure 3-2 with added files, click **Browse**. Use the Open dialog box to locate the first folder that contains one or more files you want. Select a file (press and hold **CTRL** and click additional files to select them), and click **Add**. The file names are added to the Files To Combine list box.

Figure 3-2: You can add and arrange files, combining them into a single PDF.

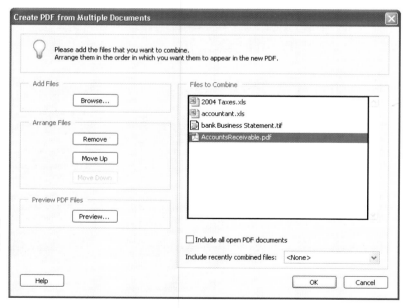

CREATING PDFS FROM PAGES

You can select pages in an existing PDF document and create one PDF or a separate PDF for each page you choose.

1. Create a PDF in Acrobat, and display it in the document pane.

   –Or–

   Open an existing PDF (see Chapter 2 for information on opening PDF files).

2. Click the **Document** menu and click **Extract Pages**. In the From and To text boxes, type the page numbers of the pages you want to create in separate PDFs.

3. Click the **Extract Pages As Separate Files** check box if you want each selected page converted to a separate PDF. Click the **Delete Pages After Extracting** check box if you want to delete the pages in the original file. Click **OK**.

4. If you chose to extract each page to a PDF, the Browse For Folder dialog box appears. Find the folder where you want the PDFs located, or create a new folder, and click **OK**. Otherwise, a new PDF, which you will need to save, opens with the extracted pages. (Pages extracted as separate files to PDFs are named using the original PDF's file name appended with the page number. If you chose to add the extracted pages to one PDF, the words "Pages From" are added as a prefix to the original file name.)

Adobe Acrobat Professional - [Pages from Organization Chart (US units).pdf]

4. Repeat step 3 to locate and add other files you want to be a part of the PDF.

5. If a file you want to add is a PDF, you might be able to add it without browsing:

   - Click the **Include All Open PDF Documents** check box, and currently opened PDFs will be added to the Files To Combine list box.

   - Click the **Include Recently Combined Files** down arrow, and select any binder PDFs you recently created and want to add to the new PDF.

6. To verify that a PDF is the correct file you want, select the file name in the Files To Combine list box, and click **Preview** to open the PDF in a window.

7. Reorganize the files in the Files To Combine list box in the order they will appear in the PDF by selecting a file name (press and hold **CTRL** and click additional files to select them), and using the buttons under **Arrange Files**.

8. When finished, click **OK**. In the Save As dialog box, locate the folder where you want the file located. Change the file name, if needed, and click **Save**.

Convert Files from Windows

If you are comfortable working with the folder and file hierarchy in Windows Explorer, or if you use the desktop to store files, you can easily convert files by dragging them to Acrobat or to an Acrobat shortcut, or by using context menus.

TIP

You can add files from outside of Acrobat when creating a binder PDF. Right-click a file icon (typically found in Windows Explorer or on the desktop) of a type that can be converted to a PDF, and click **Combine In Adobe Acrobat**. The file is added to the Files To Combine list box in the Create PDF From Multiple Documents dialog box.

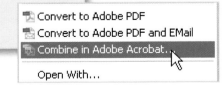

CREATE PDFS BY DRAGGING

1. Start Acrobat.

2. Click the **Start** button, right-click **My Computer**, and click **Explore**.

3. If necessary, click **Folders** on the toolbar to display the Folders pane on the left side of the Explorer window.

4. Use the drive and folder hierarchy in the Folders pane to find the folder in which the files you want to convert are located. Click the folder to display its files in the contents pane, located to the right of the Folders pane.

5. Drag files from the contents pane in the Explorer window to the document pane in the Acrobat window, as shown in Figure 3-3 (press and hold **CTRL** and click additional files to select them, and then drag the selected files to copy them all at once).

   –Or–

   Drag files from the Explorer contents pane to an Acrobat shortcut icon. In either case, the files are converted and opened in Acrobat.

Select files in the Explorer contents pane...

...and drag to the Acrobat document pane

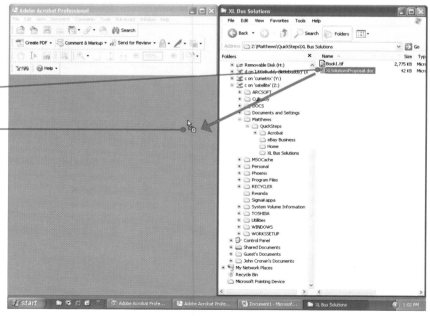

Figure 3-3: Drag a file to the document pane in Acrobat to convert it to a PDF.

CREATE PDFS FROM CONTEXT MENUS

Right-click a file icon (typically found in Windows Explorer or on the desktop), and click **Convert To Adobe PDF**. Acrobat is started, if needed, and the file is converted and opened.

Save Converted Content

Saving converted files ensures that the files are copied to a disk and can be retrieved for future use. You will also want to save a PDF document after making any changes. Furthermore, you can save (or convert) a PDF file to other file types, such as a PostScript document or one of several image formats.

SAVE SOURCE FILES AS PDFS

If you convert a file to a PDF in Acrobat (or if you are not prompted to save the file in a conversion dialog box when converting from another program), you will need to save the file in the Save As dialog box.

To save the new PDF:

1. In Acrobat, click the **File** menu and click **Save** or **Save As**.

   –Or–

   Click **Save** on the File toolbar.

   –Or–

   Click the **File** menu and click **Close**, or click the document's **Close** button. Confirm you want to save the file. In all cases, the Save As dialog box appears.

2. Navigate to the drive and folder where you want to store the PDF file. Change the file name, if needed (the Adobe PDF Files file type is selected and added to the original file name by default), and click **Save**.

NOTE

In some conversions (for example, when using PDFMaker in Word), the converted file does not display in Acrobat immediately after it's converted. If you are not prompted to save the file, it is automatically saved in the same folder as the source file, with the same file name, and a .pdf file extension is added. Some programs, such as Internet Explorer, prompt you to save converted files, as shown in Figure 3-4. As with similar Save and Save As dialog boxes, locate the drive and folder where you want the file stored, and click **Save** (there is only one file type available—PDF Files).

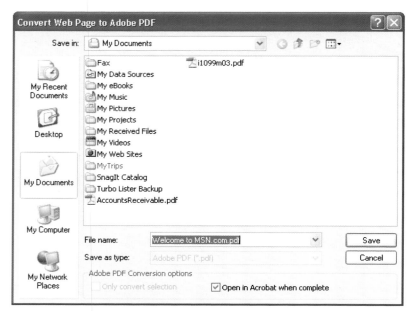

Figure 3-4: Some programs prompt you to save content before displaying it as a PDF in Acrobat.

SAVE MODIFIED PDFS

If you make changes to a PDF after initially saving it, subsequent saves simply codify the modifications in the current file. It's a good practice to perform a save after expending any significant effort working on a PDF document. Acrobat offers several ways to save a modified PDF.

Click the **File** menu and click **Save**.

–Or–

Click **Save** on the File toolbar.

–Or–

Close the file and confirm that you want to save your changes.

–Or–

Press **CTRL+S**.

CONVERT PDFS TO OTHER FILE TYPES

You can convert a PDF to one of several document and image file types. The "cleanest" conversions occur when converting a PDF back to the file type from which it was originally converted or if you convert an image in a PDF to an image file.

1. Open Acrobat and the PDF you want to convert.

2. Click the **File** menu and click **Save As**.

3. In the Save As dialog box, locate the drive and folder where you want the converted file stored, and change the file name, if needed.

4. Click the **Save As Type** down arrow, and choose the file type to which you want to convert the PDF.

5. Click the **Settings** button. In the Save As Settings dialog box pertaining to file types, shown in Figure 3-5, select the conversion options you want, and click **OK**.

6. Click **Save** in the Save As dialog box to convert the PDF.

TIP

If the Settings button is unavailable for a file type when trying to convert a PDF, close the Save As dialog box, click the **Edit** menu, click **Preferences**, and click the **Convert From PDF** category. In the Converting From PDF list box, select the file type whose settings you want to change, and click the **Edit Settings** button. Make any changes, click **OK** twice to close the Save As Settings and Preferences dialog boxes, and use the **Save As** option again (any settings changes you make are retained for future conversions to that particular file type).

Save As DOC Settings

Comments Settings
- ☑ Include Comments

Layout Settings
- ☑ Retain Columns
- ☑ Retain Page Size and Margin

Image Settings
- ☑ Include Images

Output Format: ◉ JPG   ○ PNG

Use Colorspace: [Determine Automatically ▾]

- ☐ Change Resolution

Downsample To: [150 dpi ▾]

Untagged Document Settings
- ☑ Generate tags for untagged files

[OK] [Restore Defaults] [Cancel]

Figure 3-5: Each file type has an associated Save As Settings dialog box.

Create PDFs in Office Programs

Adobe recognizes the prevalence of the Microsoft Office suite of programs and accommodates its users by adding menus and toolbars to automate the creation of PDFs using PDFMaker (see the QuickFacts "Understanding PDF Conversion Terminology" earlier in this chapter for information on PDFMaker). Each Office program has a similar set of conversion options, although many options are tuned to the specific nature of the program. For example, in Word or Publisher, you convert a complete document or publication file; in other programs, you convert objects such as tables or messages contained within a file. Table 3-2 lists the conversion options offered by the Office programs.

1. Start the relevant Office program.
2. Open the file whose content you want to convert to a PDF.
3. Click the **Adobe PDF** menu, and click the conversion option you want.

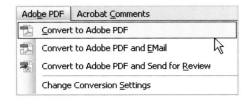

–Or–

Click a conversion option button on the PDFMaker 7.0 toolbar.

4. In either case, a Save Adobe PDF File As dialog box appears. If necessary, change the folder location where the PDF document will be stored, and change the file name. Click **Save** when finished. The PDF document opens in the Acrobat document pane.

TIP

Most Office programs provide options on the Abode PDF menu and PDFMaker toolbar that combine converting and sending the PDF file to others by e-mail or for review (Convert To Adobe PDF And Email and Convert To Adobe PDF And Send For Review). Using Acrobat to collaborate with others is covered in Chapter 7.

TABLE 3-2: OFFICE PROGRAMS CONVERSION OPTIONS

OFFICE PROGRAM	TAILORED CONVERSION OPTION	DESCRIPTION
Word	Convert To Adobe PDF	Converts each document page to a PDF document page. Bookmarks are created for headings, links, and other document elements.
	Acrobat Comments menu	Provides options for working with comments (see Chapter 7 for information on inserting comments and reviewing PDF documents).
Excel	Convert To Adobe PDF	Converts the active worksheet to a PDF.
	Convert Entire Workbook	If selected (a check mark displays next to the option), all worksheets in the workbook convert to a single PDF when Convert To Adobe PDF is clicked. Bookmarks are created for each worksheet.
Access	Convert To Adobe PDF	Converts the active object or the selected object in the Database window to a PDF.
	Convert Multiple Reports To Single PDF	Opens an Acrobat PDFMaker dialog box that allows you to select the reports you want to add to a single PDF and the order in which they appear. Bookmarks are created for each report.
Outlook	Convert To Adobe PDF Selected Messages	Converts selected messages into a single PDF. Bookmarks are created, sorting the messages by several categories.
	Convert To Adobe PDF Selected Folder	Converts the selected folder into a single PDF. Bookmarks are created, sorting the messages by several categories.
	Convert And Append To Existing Adobe PDF Selected Messages	Adds the selected messages to the end of the existing PDF you select. Bookmarks are created, sorting the messages by several categories.
	Convert And Append To Existing Adobe PDF Selected Folder	Adds the messages in the selected folder to the end of the existing PDF you select. Bookmarks are created, sorting the messages by several categories.
Outlook Message Window	Attach As Adobe PDF	Converts files to PDF that you want to attach to a new, reply, or forwarded message.
	Attach As Secured Adobe PDF	Converts files to PDF that you want to attach to a new, reply, or forwarded message, and allows you to restrict their use based on recipients or security policies (see Chapter 10 for more information on securing PDF documents).
PowerPoint	Convert To Adobe PDF	Converts each slide in a presentation to a separate page in a PDF. Bookmarks are created for each slide.
Publisher	Convert To Adobe PDF	Converts each publication page to a PDF document page. Bookmarks are created for headings, links, and other publication elements.
Visio	Convert To Adobe PDF	Converts the current page in the drawing to a PDF.
	Convert All Pages In Drawing	Converts all pages in a drawing to a single PDF when Convert To Adobe PDF is clicked. You are asked if you want to include or flatten layers in the PDF, and you are informed the PDF might contain object data (see the QuickFacts "Viewing Object Data").

VIEWING OBJECT DATA

Programs such as Microsoft Visio and AutoDesk
AutoCAD can provide supplemental information to many
of the layout objects they use to create architectural,
business, and engineering drawings. The information
available to the objects after the source file is converted
to a PDF file is referred to as *object data*. When
documents with object data are opened in Acrobat, the
Object Data button is displayed on the toolbar. You can
click the button to view the data, and a Document Status
dialog box informs you data is available. To view the
object data for an object:

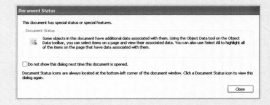

Click the **Object Data** button, and click the object
whose data you want to view. The object is
surrounded by a red border, and an Object Data
dialog box displays its
associated data, as
shown in Figure 3-6.

PDFs displayed in the document pane that contain object
data are identified by an icon at the
leftmost end of the Status bar.

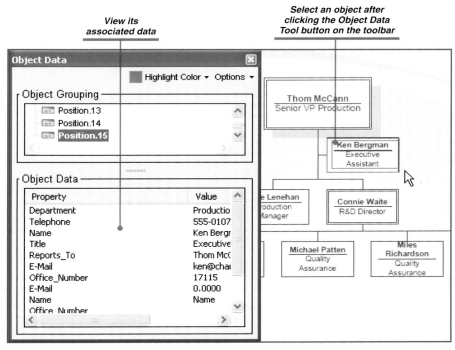

*View its
associated data*

*Select an object after
clicking the Object Data
Tool button on the toolbar*

*Figure 3-6: Object data in this PDF converted from Microsoft Visio provides
supplemental information on the selected object.*

Create PDFs from Adobe Programs

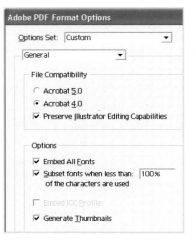

Some Adobe programs use the Save As or Export options as the means to create a PDF within the program. For example, to create a PDF in Adobe Illustrator (version 9.0), a popular drawing program:

1. Open or create a file in Illustrator.

2. Click the **File** menu and click **Save As** to open the Save dialog box. Browse to the folder where you want the PDF stored.

3. Click the **Save As Type** down arrow, click **Adobe PDF**, rename the file, if needed, and click **Save**.

4. Accept the default settings in the Adobe PDF Format Options dialog box, and click **OK**.

   –Or–

   Make any formatting changes and click **OK**. In either case, the file is converted and displayed in Illustrator as a PDF.

Use the Adobe PDF Printer Driver to Create PDFs

Programs that don't use the PDFMaker macro or that have other built-in methods to create PDFs can convert files when you manually print them to the Adobe PDF printer driver. Behind the scenes, the source file is converted to PostScript and processed by Distiller using current settings (see Chapter 5 for information on using Distiller to optimize settings when creating PDFs).

1. Start the parent program and, if needed, open the file or select the report you want to convert to a PDF (for example, in Quicken, you convert reports instead of a file).

2. Click the **File** menu and click **Print**. Although there are differences in programs' Print dialog boxes, they all should provide a means to select a printer from those installed on your system.

3. Select **Adobe PDF** as your printer, and click **OK** or **Print**.

4. In the Save PDF File As dialog box, browse to the folder where you want the PDF stored, change the file name, if needed, and click **Save**. A progress dialog box shows the status of the conversion, and the PDF is displayed in the Acrobat document pane.

Capture Content and Convert to PDF

For many applications, we don't think in terms of working with files. For example, when browsing the Web, we work with web sites and web pages and don't really care about the underlying files. Similarly, we use scanners to capture paper-based information and screen captures to grab content displayed on a screen. Acrobat has features that accommodate these "fileless" items when creating PDF files.

Capture Web Pages in IE

Converting web pages in Internet Explorer lets you quickly capture content using current conversion settings.

Figure 3-7: You can choose to convert selected content and display the PDF in Acrobat when converted.

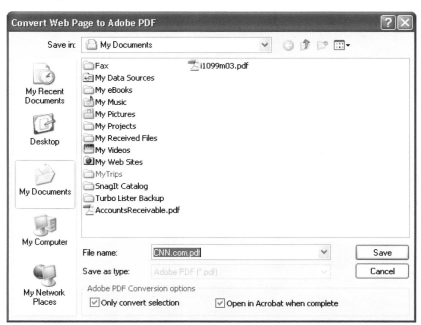

CAPTURE A WEB PAGE IN INTERNET EXPLORER

1. Open Internet Explorer and browse to the page you want to capture. (If you only want to convert a portion of the content on a page, select the content by dragging the mouse pointer over it.)

2. On the Internet Explorer toolbar, click the **Convert Current Web Page** button.

   –Or–

   Click **Convert** on the Adobe PDF Explorer bar (see "Use the Adobe PDF Explorer Bar" at the end of this section).

3. In the Convert Web Page To Adobe PDF dialog box, shown in Figure 3-7, browse to the folder where you want the PDF located, change the file name, if needed, and select or deselect the **Only Convert Selection** and **Open In Acrobat When Complete** check boxes, depending on what you want.

4. Click **Save**. The web page or selected content is converted, saved in the location you specified, and opened in Acrobat (if you chose to do that).

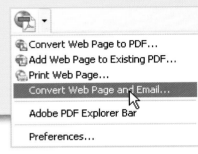
ADD WEB PAGES IN INTERNET EXPLORER

1. Open Internet Explorer and browse to the page you want to add to an existing PDF document. (If you only want to add a portion of the content on a page, select the content by dragging the mouse pointer over it.)

2. On the Internet Explorer toolbar, click the **Convert Current Web Page** down arrow, and click **Add Web Page To Existing PDF**. (Alternatively, use the Adobe PDF Explorer bar. See "Use the Abode PDF Explorer Bar" at the end of this section.)

3. In the Add Web Page To Existing Adobe PDF dialog box, browse to the folder that contains the PDF to which you want to add pages or selected content. (If you have selected content, the Only Convert Selection check box is selected.) Click the PDF file to select it, and click **Save**. The converted web page is added to the end of the PDF document.

USE THE ADOBE PDF EXPLORER BAR

Acrobat adds to Internet Explorer an Adobe PDF feature that lets you quickly find PDF files stored on your system and add web pages to them.

1. Open Internet Explorer and browse to the page you want to add to an existing PDF document or convert to a PDF document.

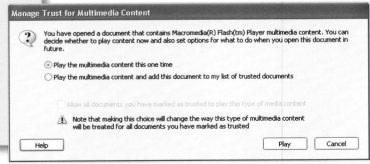

Using the Adobe PDF Explorer bar, you can perform folder maintenance similar to that performed in Windows Explorer. You can open, add, remove, and rename folders by right-clicking them and using the context menu, and you can create new folders from the bar's toolbar.

2. On the Internet Explorer toolbar, click the **Convert Current Web Page** down arrow, and click **Adobe PDF Explorer Bar**.

–Or–

Click the **View** menu, click **Explorer Bar**, and click **Adobe PDF**. In either case, the folders on your system appear in the pane to the left of the contents pane along with PDF files contained in each, as shown in Figure 3-8.

3. Browse to the folder that contains the PDF to which you want to add the displayed web page. Click the PDF to select it, and click **Add** on the Explorer toolbar.

4. Click **Yes** to confirm your decision (click the **Don't Ask Me Again** check box if in the future you want the web page added without further intervention on your part). The converted web page is added to the end of the PDF document.

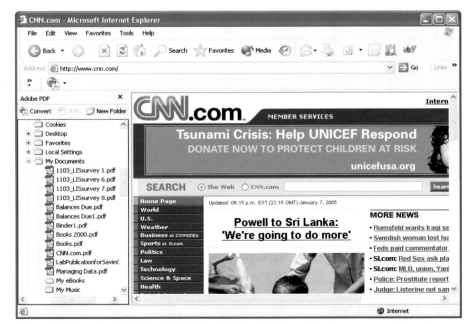

Figure 3-8: Only folders and PDF files are displayed in the Adobe PDF Explorer bar.

UNDERSTANDING WEB PAGE CONVERSIONS

If there's one area where it's ideal to use Acrobat to convert source information into PDFs, it's on the Web. Saving web pages as .htm files has never been one of the more satisfying computing tasks—links are broken, graphics do not display properly, ancillary folders need to be created to store linked objects, and some pages just can't be saved. Web pages converted to PDFs resolve these annoyances and provide several additional benefits.

CAPTURE TO PDF THE CONTENT YOU WANT

You can choose from several capture options using Acrobat (see "Capture Web Pages in IE" for a more limited choice of capture options):

- Capture only selected information by dragging the **Select** tool over it.
- Capture a single web page, from the Web or as an .htm file located on your system.
- Capture a web page and all the links displayed on it (each linked web page is added (appended) to the end of the web page PDF as a separate page).
- Capture web pages in a web site based on *levels*. Level 1 captures just the identified web page to a PDF document; Level 2 captures the identified web page and all links and converts them to PDF pages; Level 3 captures the identified web page, all links, and any links on the pages linked to the original web page and converts them to PDF pages; and so on through the remaining levels. Figure 3-9 shows an example of a web site with four layers.
- Capture all of the web pages on a web site.

RETAIN ACCUSTOMED FEATURES

- Links in the web page are converted to links in the PDF document. You can choose whether to have the target web page of a link open in Acrobat or in your browser.

Continued…

Convert Web Pages in Acrobat

When you capture web pages in Acrobat, you have more options—you can convert everything from a single web page to entire web sites.

CAPTURE WEB PAGES IN ACROBAT

1. Start Acrobat.

2. Click **Create PDF From Web Page** on the File toolbar.

   –Or–

   Click the **File** menu, click **Create PDF**, and click **From Web Page**.

   –Or–

   Click **Create PDF** on the Tasks toolbar, and click **From Web Page**. The Create PDF From Web Page dialog box appears.

3. Type the address of the web page in the URL text box. You can also click the **URL** down arrow, and select a previously used address; or click **Browse** and locate a web page on your system.

4. Determine the scope of your conversion by choosing options in the Settings area. Click **Get Only** and click the **Levels** spinner to change how "deep" you want to go to convert web pages (see the QuickFacts "Understanding Web Page Conversions").

   –Or–

   Click **Get Entire Site** to convert all web pages in the web site (see the Caution on this topic).

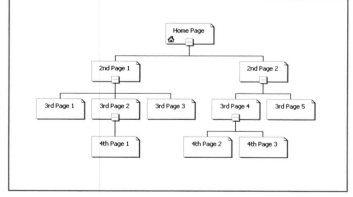

Figure 3-9: A simple but efficient web tree structure helps users navigate through several layers.

UNDERSTANDING WEB PAGE CONVERSIONS *(Continued)*

- Entry forms, such as Search boxes in the web page, are converted to interactive form fields in the PDF. You can type information in the fields, choose from drop-down lists, and initiate actions.

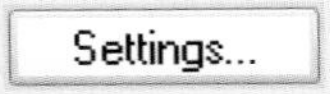

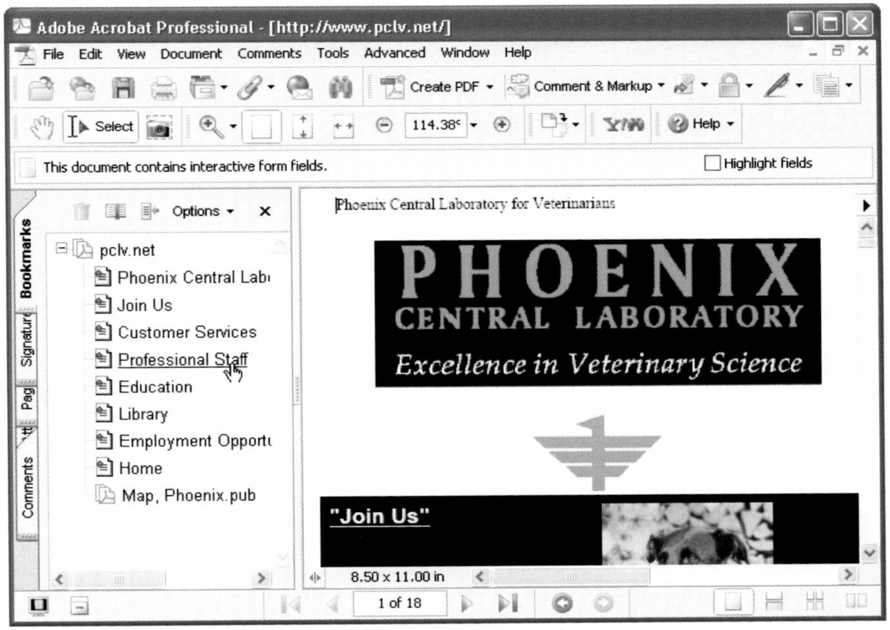

CAUTION

Acrobat provides an option, Get Entire Site, in the Create PDF From Web Page dialog box, that will convert all web pages in a web site to PDF documents. This is a handy feature when converting content on www.my_trip_to_yellowstone.com, but a really bad idea when converting all web pages on www.microsoft.com. Large web sites can contain gigabytes of content that might bog down your system, if not cause it to completely crash.

CAUTION

The settings in the Create PDF From Web Page dialog box determine how web pages are converted in *both* Acrobat and Internet Explorer. It's a good policy to change the settings back to their defaults after creating a PDF with any significant changes. Changes to settings are effective in Internet Explorer after they've been exercised once in Acrobat. Additional conversion settings are available by clicking the **Settings** button. See "Change Web Page Settings" later in this chapter.

5. Click the **Stay On Same Path** check box to capture and convert only those web pages in the web site that are *child* pages, or subordinate to, the identified web page.
6. Click the **Stay On Same Server** check box to capture and convert only those web pages that are stored on the same web server as the identified web page.
7. Click **Create**. The web pages you selected are added to a new PDF document displayed in the document pane. Each captured page appears as a bookmark under its parent web site, as shown in Figure 3-10 (unless you changed the default conversion settings).

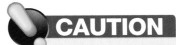

Figure 3-10: Links on a web page can be captured as PDF pages and are listed as bookmarks.

ADD WEB PAGES TO THE ACTIVE PDF

1. Open the PDF to which you want to add web pages.

2. Click the **Advanced** menu, click **Web Capture**, and click **Append Web Page**.

3. In the Add To PDF From Web Page dialog box, provide the address of the web page by typing it in the URL text box; by clicking the **URL** down arrow, and selecting a previously used address; or by clicking **Browse** and locating a web page on your system.

4. Determine the scope of your conversion by choosing options in the Settings area (see the previous section, "Capture Web Pages in Acrobat," for descriptions of the options).

5. Click **Create**. The web pages you selected are added to the end of the PDF document displayed in the document pane. Each captured page appears as a bookmark under its parent web site (unless you changed the default conversion settings).

CONVERT WEB LINKS IN EXISTING PDFS

You can capture web pages that appear as links in a PDF and add the pages to the end of a PDF.

1. Open the PDF in Acrobat, and navigate to the page that contains the links you want to capture.

2. Click the **Advanced** menu, click **Web Capture**, and click **View Web Links**. The Select Page Links To Download dialog box displays all web links on the page.

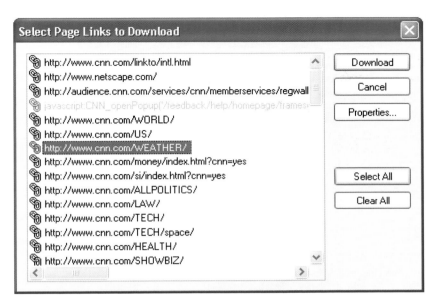

Figure 3-11: You can select the web links in a PDF and add the content to the end of the document.

3. Select one or more links that you want to download to Acrobat. Press and hold **CTRL** and click the files you want to convert, or click **Select All**, as shown in Figure 3-11.

4. Determine the scope of the download of a single link by selecting the link and clicking **Properties**. On the Download tab, set options in the Settings area (see the previous section, "Capture Web Pages in Acrobat," for descriptions of the options). Click **OK** when done.

5. Click **Download**. A Download Status dialog box displays the downloading and conversion progress. The pages are added to the end of the PDF, and bookmarks are created.

Create PDFs from Scans

You can capture paper-based documents directly from your scanner into a new PDF document or add them to the current document in your document pane. Scanned text can be converted to fully searchable and editable text using optical character recognition (OCR) technology (see Chapter 4 for information on working with text in PDF documents).

1. Place the documents you want captured in the scanner's document feeder or on its glass scanning window, and start Acrobat.

2. Click the **File** menu, click **Create PDF**, and click **From Scanner**.

   –Or–

   Click **Create PDF** on the Tasks toolbar, and click **From Scanner**. In either case, the Create PDF From Scanner dialog box appears, as shown in Figure 3-12.

3. Click the **Scanner** down arrow, and click the scanner you want to use.

4. Click the **Scan** down arrow, and choose between scanning one or two sides of the document pages.

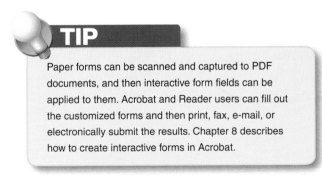

TIP

Paper forms can be scanned and captured to PDF documents, and then interactive form fields can be applied to them. Acrobat and Reader users can fill out the customized forms and then print, fax, e-mail, or electronically submit the results. Chapter 8 describes how to create interactive forms in Acrobat.

NOTE

Paper documents that contain text you want to make editable and searchable using OCR must be scanned at 144 dots per inch (dpi) resolution or greater (Acrobat supports scanning resolutions between 10 and 3,000 dpi). The optimum input scanning resolution for OCR is 300 dpi, which is the sweet spot between increased font-recognition errors at lower resolutions and slower performance and larger file sizes at higher resolutions (if your document contains text 9 points or smaller, you might have to increase the resolution to reduce errors, although resolutions higher than 600 dpi are downsampled to 600 dpi or lower). Also, you should scan text-based documents in black and white for better OCR results.

Figure 3-12: The Create PDF From Scanner dialog box lets you select a scanner connected to your system and choose options, such as OCR, to create editable and searchable text.

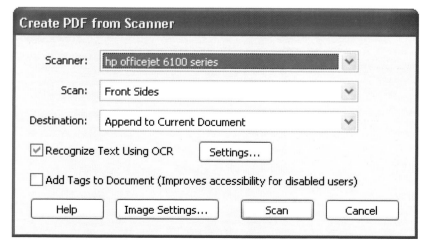

5. Click the **Destination** down arrow, and click **New Document** to send the captured pages to a new PDF.

–Or–

Click **Append To Current Document** to add the captured pages to the end of the PDF in the document pane.

6. To capture text as editable and searchable characters using OCR technology, click the **Recognize Text Using OCR** check box. For additional options related to OCR scanning, click the **Settings** button. In the Recognize Text – Settings dialog box that appears:

- Click the **Primary OCR Language** down arrow to select a different primary OCR language used to recognize text besides your system default language.

- Click the **PDF Output Style** down arrow to change how text and graphics appear in the PDF. Click **Searchable Image** to create the searchable text in a separate, invisible layer below the page image. Click **Formatted Text & Graphics** to reconstruct the page based on text, graphics, and other elements recognized by Acrobat. Either method provides searchable text, although Formatted Text & Graphics seems to provide a more accurate representation of the original document (at the cost of a slightly larger PDF document).

- Click the **Downsample Images** down arrow, and change the compression level used in images. As an image is compressed, pixels are removed and the quality of the image is decreased. A 72-dpi image is more highly compressed and of lesser quality than a 600-dpi image.

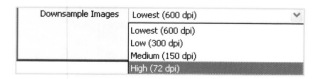

7. Click **OK** to close the Recognize Text – Settings dialog box and accept any changes. Click the **Add Tags To Document** check box if you want Acrobat to identify elements in a captured PDF so they can be more accurately reflowed when used on smaller screens, such as PDAs.

8. Click the **Image Settings** button to adjust image compression and filtering, as shown in Figure 3-13 (experiment with the options in the Image Settings dialog box; click **Defaults** if you need to return to a known set of acceptable values). Click **OK** when done. See Chapter 5 for more information on converting images.

9. Click **Scan** to start your scanning software. Accept the preview in your scanning software, or make changes to the capture settings.

10. After the first page is scanned, the Acrobat Scan dialog box appears and provides options to continue scanning additional pages, including front and back, if that's what you chose. Click **Next** to continue scanning; click **Done** when finished. After a few moments, the pages are displayed in the document pane.

Figure 3-13: The Image Settings dialog box provides several compression and filtering options for PDF content acquired from a scanner.

You can apply OCR to pages that were initially scanned without OCR having been applied. Drag the **Select** tool over a portion of the non-OCR text to create a selection box. Right-click the selection box and click **Recognize Text Using OCR**, as shown in Figure 3-14. In the Recognize Text dialog box, select the pages to which you want OCR applied. Click **Edit** to change capture settings in the Recognize Text – Settings dialog box. (See "Create PDFs from Scans" for an explanation of the settings. Using this method to open the Recognize Text – Settings dialog box, you can choose between an exact or compressed version of the Searchable Image option). Click **OK** to close any open dialog boxes and start the OCR procedure.

Convert Screen Captures to PDF

Screen captures are a snapshot of what is displayed on your screen. For example, if you wanted to help a friend configure a new computer, you could capture a Properties dialog box on your screen that shows all the correct settings, convert the capture to PDF, and then e-mail the PDF document to that person.

1. Set up your screen to display the content you want to convert to a PDF document.

2. Press and release **PRINT SCREEN** (might be also displayed as **PRINT SCRN** or **PRTSC**) on your keyboard to capture the entire screen.

   –Or–

   Press **ALT + PRINT SCREEN** to capture only the active window. In either case, the captured content is copied to the Windows Clipboard as an image.

3. Start Acrobat.

4. Click the **File** menu, click **Create PDF**, and click **From Clipboard Image**.

   –Or–

   Click **Create PDF** on the Tasks menu, and click **From Clipboard Image**.

   In either case, the image is displayed in the document pane as an untitled PDF document. (See Chapters 4 and 5 for options you have when working with images in Acrobat.)

Invoice the Buyer

An invoice is a document sent by you, the seller, stating the amount owed by the buyer who is receiving the goods or services. Invoicing used to be a personal e-mail from the seller directly to the buyer (and still can be) in which payment and shipping details were reiterated; however, the ease-of-use features in the eBay and PayPal system-generated invoices make the automated process hard to ... the invoice is mostly a personal ... you spend in PayPal. Some sell... clear for them.)

USE EBAY TO SEND AN INVOICE

1. Send an eBay invoice by:

   • Clicking the **Create And Send An Invoice** link in the end-of-auction e-mail a seller receives (see Figure 8-4).

Copy Image to Clipboard	Ctrl+C
Save Image As...	
Add Bookmark	Ctrl+B
Create Link	
Recognize Text Using OCR	

Figure 3-14: You can recognize text in a scanned document that didn't initially have OCR applied.

Modify Conversion Settings

Although default conversion settings work for 90 percent of users 95 percent of the time, situations might arise in which you want greater control over how a PDF is converted. *Settings* affect core conversion of the PDF file, while *options* are generally more program- or file type-specific.

Change File Type- or Program-Specific Conversion Options

Programs that provide the means to create PDFs from within their interfaces also provide general options—some tailored to the file types they support. For example, Word adds options related to converting footnotes and cross references to links, and Outlook adds options related to page layout. (There are also core PDF conversion settings that apply to most documents and images. See "Change Core PDF Conversion Settings" later in the chapter.)

CHANGE OPTIONS IN PDFMAKER-SUPPORTED PROGRAMS

1. Open the program whose conversion options you want to change.

2. Click the **Adobe PDF** menu, and click **Change Conversion Settings**.

   –Or–

   In the case of Internet Explorer, click the **Convert Current Web Page** button on the Adobe PDF toolbar, and click **Preferences**. (You only have a limited number of options available to you in the Preferences dialog box. See "Change Web Page Settings" later in this chapter for more options.)

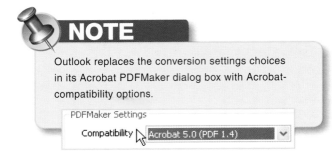

NOTE

Outlook replaces the conversion settings choices in its Acrobat PDFMaker dialog box with Acrobat-compatibility options.

3. In the Adobe PDFMaker dialog box, shown for Word in Figure 3-15, the Settings tab provides:

- A Conversion Settings drop-down list where you can choose a default or custom set of core conversion values (see "Change Core PDF Conversion Settings" later in the chapter) for those programs that support it.

- Several options (the exact number depends on the program) that are tuned for that particular program.

4. Select the options you want, and click **OK**.

CHANGE FILE TYPE OPTIONS IN ACROBAT

1. Click the **Edit** menu, click **Preferences**, and in the Preferences dialog box, click the **Convert To PDF** category.

2. In the Converting To PDF list box, click the file type whose options you want to change, and click the **Edit Settings** button. An Adobe PDF Settings dialog box appears with options pertaining to the file type:

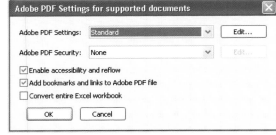

Click here to view default and custom settings files

Click here to change the settings in a settings file

- Document-related file types also provide an Adobe PDF Settings drop-down list where you can choose a default or custom settings file.

- Most image-related file types have a limited number of conversion settings you can change (see Figure 3-16), typically related to the color scheme used and the level of compression, if supported.

  Several more options exist that you can change to fine-tune your conversions. See "Change Core PDF Conversion Settings" later in the chapter.

3. Make any changes and click **OK** twice to close the Adobe PDF Settings and Preferences dialog boxes.

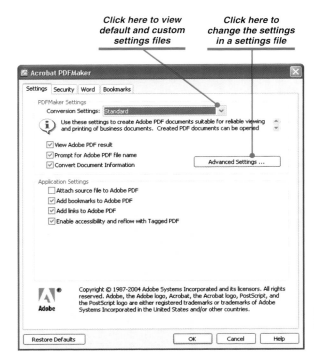

Figure 3-15: Each program has a similar Adobe PDFMaker dialog box with tailored options.

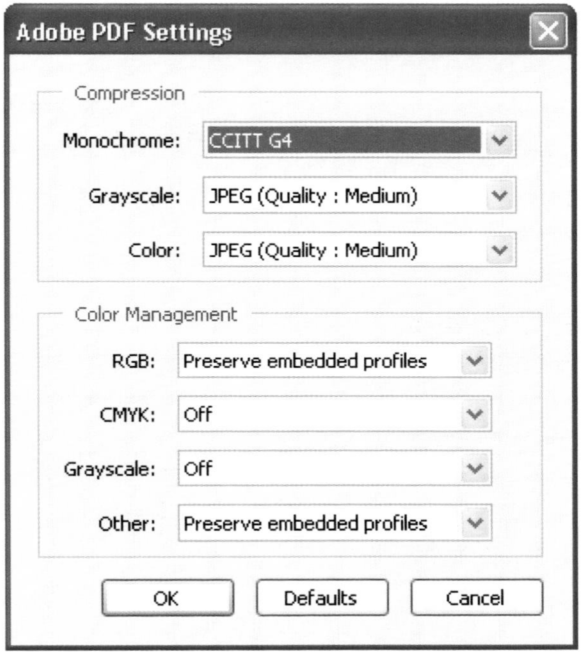

Adobe PDF Settings   ☒

Compression

Monochrome: | CCITT G4 | ∨ |

Grayscale: | JPEG (Quality : Medium) | ∨ |

Color: | JPEG (Quality : Medium) | ∨ |

Color Management

RGB: | Preserve embedded profiles | ∨ |

CMYK: | Off | ∨ |

Grayscale: | Off | ∨ |

Other: | Preserve embedded profiles | ∨ |

[OK]   [Defaults]   [Cancel]

Figure 3-16: You can choose compression and color management for TIFF images.

NOTE

Changes made to the Adobe PDF printer driver are program-specific; that is, changes made in one program do not transfer to the Adobe PDF printer driver in other programs.

Figure 3-17: Conversion settings for the Adobe PDF printer driver are accessed by clicking the Properties or Options button in a program's Print dialog box.

CHANGE OPTIONS FOR THE ADOBE PDF PRINTER DRIVER

You can change certain options in a program's Print dialog box that affect how a PDF is converted when using the Adobe PDF printer driver.

1. Open the program whose Adobe PDF printer driver options you want to change. Open a file you want to convert, or open a report (as in QuickBooks).

2. Click the **File** menu and click **Print**. In the program's Print dialog box, change the printer to **Adobe PDF**, and click the **Properties** or **Options** button.

3. In the Adobe PDF Document Properties dialog box, click the **Adobe PDF Settings** tab, shown in Figure 3-17. Make any changes to the available options. The Default Settings drop-down list lets you choose a default or custom set of core conversion values (see the "Change Core PDF Conversion Settings" section next).

4. Click **OK** when finished to close the Adobe PDF Document Properties dialog box. Select any additional printing options in the Print dialog box, and click **OK** to convert or "print" the file or document.

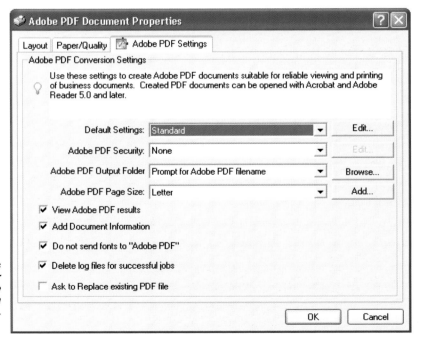

UNDERSTANDING SETTINGS FILES

Core conversion settings for documents and images are located in six folders in the Abode PDF Settings dialog box, shown in Figure 3-18. Acrobat provides a starter kit of six default settings files (also referred to as *job options*) whose values are tuned for specific uses (for example, the High Quality Print settings file selects a PDF resolution of 2400 dpi, as compared to the Standard settings file (the predominate file used for common conversions) that converts at 600 dpi. You can add to this list of settings files by indicating the values you need and providing a new file name (see "Change Core PDF Conversion Settings"). The settings apply universally and can be selected when converting documents in Acrobat and PDFMaker-supported programs, and when using the Adobe PDF printer driver. The default settings are:

- **High Quality Print** sets values that provide higher-resolution printing than the values used for the Standard settings file. More information from the original document is retained.

- **PDF/A:Draft**, **PDF/X-1a:2001**, and **PDF/X-3: 2002** are predominately used by Distiller to check PostScript files for ISO (International Organization for Standardization) standards compliance (see Chapter 5 for more information on using Distiller to create and optimize PDFs).

- **Press Quality** sets values that satisfy most commercial digital printing needs. Typically, the company will provide you the values it requires and you will create a new settings file based on the press quality values and further modified by the printer's recommendations.

- **Smallest File Size** sets values that are most suitable for online viewing. File size is reduced by a combination of compression, downsampling, and lower resolution.

- **Standard** sets values appropriate for desktop printing, proofs, and other general uses. This is the "middle of the road" settings file that most users will find suitable for most uses.

Change Core PDF Conversion Settings

The core conversion settings for PDF documents allow for easy implementation of settings for specific tasks. You can choose from several default files, or you can make changes and save the full set of six settings folders with a new file name that you can choose for future use (see the QuickFacts "Understanding Settings Files"). You can change which settings file is currently in use and make changes to values in the Adobe PDF Settings dialog box (see Figure 3-18) or the Adobe PDF Settings tab (used by the Adobe PDF printer driver; see Figure 3-17).

To access the Adobe PDF Settings dialog box or tab:

- In Acrobat, click the **Edit** menu, click **Preferences**, click the **Convert To PDF** category, click the pertinent file type, and click the **Edit Settings** button.

- In supported Microsoft products, click the **Adobe PDF** menu, and click **Change Conversion Settings**.

- When using the Adobe PDF printer driver, click the **Properties** or **Options** button in the Print dialog box, click the **Adobe PDF Settings** tab, and click the **Edit** button next to the Default Settings drop-down box.

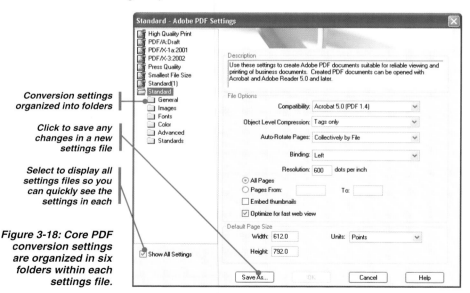

Conversion settings organized into folders

Click to save any changes in a new settings file

Select to display all settings files so you can quickly see the settings in each

Figure 3-18: Core PDF conversion settings are organized in six folders within each settings file.

NOTE

If you change the settings file in an Adobe PDF Settings dialog box or tab (used by the Adobe PDF printer driver), all subsequent conversions for that particular program or printer driver will use that settings file until you change it again. However, changing the settings file for one program or its printer driver doesn't affect conversions elsewhere. In other words, you can have different settings files in effect concurrently—High Quality Print in Word, Smallest File Size in Publisher, a custom file in Illustrator, and Press Quality in Acrobat.

TIP

Custom settings files become available in the Conversion Settings drop-down lists in all supported programs.

CHANGE THE ACTIVE SETTINGS FILE

1. Open the Adobe Settings dialog box or tab in the program (or printer driver) whose conversion settings file you want to change.

2. Click the **Conversion Settings** down arrow, and click the name of the default or custom settings file whose values you want to use (the drop-down list may be labeled differently in some programs; for example, it's named Default Settings for the Adobe PDF printer driver).

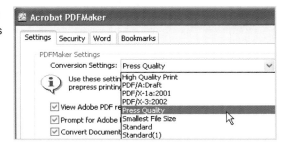

3. Click **OK**.

CREATE A CUSTOM SETTINGS FILE

1. Use the instructions in "Change the Active Settings File" to change to the settings file in the program or file type that most closely matches the custom file you want to create. For example, if all you want to do is change which fonts are embedded during the conversion, start with the Standard settings file as your base file, and just change the font-related settings.

2. Depending on the program, click the **Edit** or **Advanced** settings button associated with its conversion settings. An Adobe PDF Settings dialog box appears (see Figure 3-18) with the core conversion settings for that settings file organized into six folders (see Chapter 5 for detailed information on each folder).

3. Make any changes and click **Save As** to create a new settings file (you cannot change any of the default settings files; you can only create new files based on them).

   –Or–

   Click **OK** to save changes to an existing custom settings file. The dialog box closes.

4. In the Save Adobe PDF Settings As dialog box, change the file name and then click **Save** (if you save the settings file in a different folder, the settings file will not display in the Conversion Settings drop-down list box). The file is saved with a .joboptions file extension.

5. Click **OK** to close any open dialog boxes.

Change Web Page Settings

You can change several web page attributes when converting a web page in Acrobat.

1. Open Acrobat and click **Create PDF From Web Page** on the File toolbar.

2. In the Create PDF From Web Page dialog box, click the **Settings** button.

3. In the Web Page Conversion Settings dialog box:

   - Select the options you want in the converted content from the PDF Settings area.

   - Under File Type Settings, click the **HTML** file type, and click **Settings**. Change options in the HTML Conversion Settings dialog box, shown in Figure 3-19, and click **OK**.

4. Click **OK** to close the Web Page Conversion Settings dialog box.

5. Click **Create** to convert the web

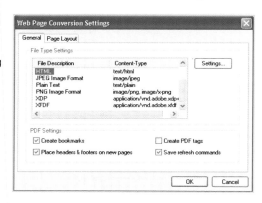

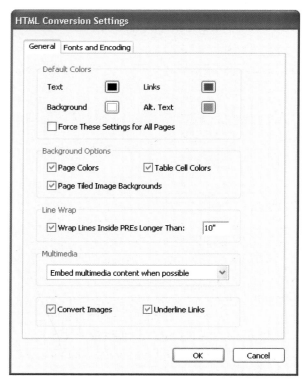

Figure 3-19: Several options unique to HTML pages can be modified to satisfy specific needs.

NOTE

See Chapter 5 for more information on the individual settings used in the default and custom settings files to convert files to PDFs.

Chapter 4

Editing PDF Files

Acrobat provides several features you can use to modify a PDF. In this chapter you will learn how to work with the pages in a PDF document; how to add headers, footers, and watermarks; and how to number and trim pages. You will also see how to copy, change, and add text to a PDF. Finally, you will learn how to enhance readers' use and breadth of a PDF document by adding articles and attachments.

Work with Pages

You can change the composition of a PDF file by adding and removing pages to create a new document that doesn't resemble the original file. For example, you can stitch together a document from several sources, including Word documents, web pages, and Excel spreadsheets, inserting and removing pages as needed. You also can alter the appearance of a page by changing the page size, or alter the margins to show less content. To support a PDF that might no longer look like the original document (or documents), Acrobat provides features such as page numbering, headers, footers, and backgrounds that allow you to re-create a unified appearance.

Add and Remove Pages

You can alter the structure of a PDF document by adding pages from other PDF documents and removing pages you don't want.

INSERT ANOTHER PDF

1. In Acrobat, open the PDF document to which you want to add pages from another PDF document.

2. Click the **Document** menu and click **Insert Pages**.

   –Or–

   Click the **Pages** tab in the navigation pane; right-click a page and click **Insert Pages**.

3. In the Select File To Insert dialog box, open the folder that contains the PDF you want to add, click the file, and click **Select**.

4. In the Insert Pages dialog box, click the **Location** down arrow to establish whether the inserted pages will be inserted before or after the page you select.

5. In the Page area, select the first, last, or other page in the current document where you want the pages added (if you navigated to the page where you wanted the new pages added, its page number will appear in the Page text box).

6. Click **OK** when finished. The new pages are placed in the current document.

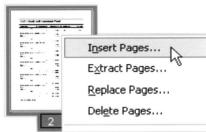

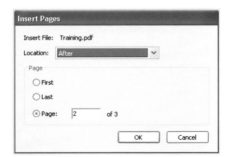

REPLACE PAGES

You can replace a series of pages in a PDF with an equal number of pages in a series from another PDF document.

1. In Acrobat, open the PDF document in which you want to replace pages with those from another PDF document.

2. Click the **Document** menu and click **Replace Pages**.

   –Or–

   Click the **Pages** tab in the navigation pane. Right-click a page and click **Replace Pages**.

3. In the Select File With New Pages dialog box, open the folder containing the PDF with the replacement pages you want, click the file, and click **Select**.

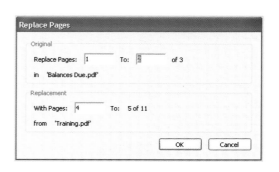

4. In the Replace Pages dialog box, in the Original area, type the page or page series in the Replace Pages text box. (If replacing more than one page, the pages must be in a consecutive series, for example, 7 to 9.)

5. In the Replacement area, type the starting page in the replacement PDF in the With Pages text box. Acrobat completes the series for you by the number of pages in the series you chose in step 3.

6. Click **OK** when finished and click **Yes** to confirm the action. The replacement pages are added to the current document.

REMOVE PAGES

1. In Acrobat, open the PDF document that contains the pages you want to delete.

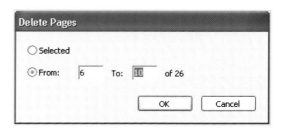

2. Click the **Document** menu and click **Delete Pages**. In the Delete Pages dialog box, type the series of pages you want deleted in the From text boxes.

   –Or–

   Click the **Pages** tab in the navigation pane. Press and hold **CTRL** while clicking as many pages as you want deleted, or press and hold **SHIFT** while clicking the first and last pages in a series to select all the pages in the series. Right-click a selected page and click **Delete Pages**. The Delete Pages dialog box appears with the **Selected** option selected by default.

3. Click **OK** to delete the pages you entered or selected, and click **OK** again to confirm you want to delete the pages.

QUICKSTEPS

USING PDFS FOR PRESENTATIONS

In Chapter 2, we described how to view and navigate a PDF in Full Screen view to maximize the amount of the screen used for viewing your PDFs. You can enhance Full Screen view with page transitions to give your PDFs a presentation quality similar to a PowerPoint slide show (see *Microsoft PowerPoint 2003 QuickSteps*, published by McGraw-Hill/Osborne, for more information on using PowerPoint to create presentations and slide shows).

SET UP FULL SCREEN AS THE INITIAL VIEW

You can display a PDF in Full Screen view when the document is first opened so your users will receive the presentation experience right from the start.

1. In Acrobat, open the PDF that you want to display similar to a PowerPoint presentation.
2. Click the **File** menu, click **Document Properties**, and click the **Initial View** tab. In the Window Options area, click the **Open In Full Screen Mode** check box. Click **OK**.

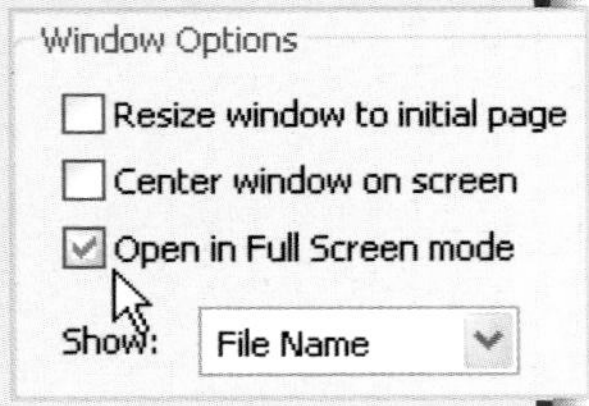
Window Options
Resize window to initial page
Center window on screen
Open in Full Screen mode
Show:
File Name

3. Save the PDF. The next time the PDF is opened, it will open in Full Screen view (you can return to the standard Acrobat view by pressing **ESC**).

CHOOSE A TRANSITION

1. Click the **Document** menu and click **Set Page Transitions**.

   –Or–

   In the Pages tab in the navigation pane, select the pages to which you want to apply the transition, right-click a page, and click **Set Page Transitions**. (In step 4 of this procedure, you'll see how you can change the pages you want to receive a transition.)

Continued...

Trim Unwanted Content on a Page

You can adjust the margins surrounding a rectangular area of content that's displayed on a page (or *crop* the page), thereby eliminating any content outside a defined area.

1. In Acrobat, navigate to the page in the document whose margins you want to adjust.
2. Click the **Tools** menu, click **Advanced Editing**, and click **Crop Tool**. Drag a rectangular marquee using the crosshair mouse pointer over the area on the page that you want to retain. Adjust the area by dragging the corner sizing handles (see Figure 4-1). Double-click within the marquee or press **ENTER** to open the Crop Pages dialog box.

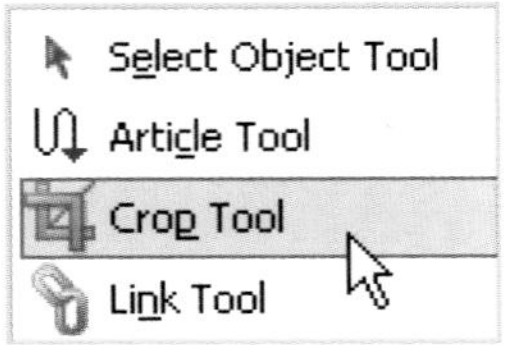
Select Object Tool
Article Tool
Crop Tool
Link Tool

Figure 4-1: The area outside the marquee is removed using the Crop tool.

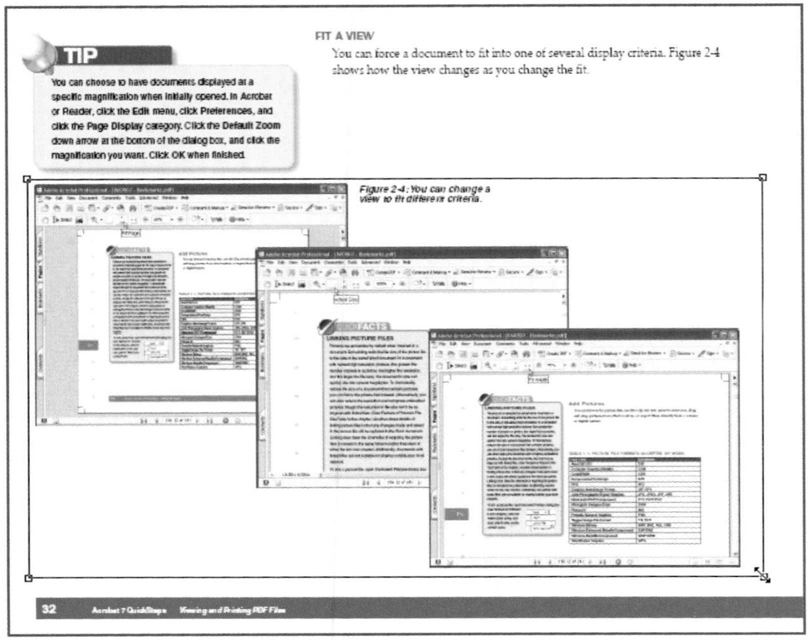
TIP
You can choose to have documents displayed at a specific magnification when initially opened. In Acrobat or Reader, click the Edit menu, click Preferences, and click the Page Display category. Click the Default Zoom down arrow at the bottom of the dialog box, and click the magnification you want. Click OK when finished.
FIT A VIEW
You can force a document to fit into one of several display criteria. Figure 2-4 shows how the view changes as you change the fit.
Figure 2-4: You can change a view to fit different criteria.
32 Acrobat 7 QuickSteps Viewing and Printing PDF Files

USING PDFS FOR PRESENTATIONS
(Continued)

2. In the Set Transitions dialog box, shown in Figure 4-2, in the Page Transition area, click the **Effect** down arrow, and select the type of transition you want to occur. Click the **Speed** down arrow, and choose how fast you want the transition to occur.

3. Click the **Auto Flip** check box if you want the pages to automatically change. In the After text box, type the number of seconds before a page moves to the next page, or click the **After** down arrow, and select one of the predefined durations.

4. In the Page Range area, select the pages in the PDF that you want to receive the transition.

5. Click **OK** when finished.

Figure 4-2: *You can "wow" your readers with snazzy transitions between pages shown in Full Screen view.*

3. In the Margin Controls area, you can make precise adjustments to margins by using the respective margin spinners or by typing a value. Changes are reflected in the preview area, as shown in Figure 4-3.

4. Click **OK** when finished. The page size is reduced to the dimensions of the area of the cropping marquee and displays that way in the document pane.

NOTE

When printing cropped pages in a PDF, by default, the cropped areas will print centered on the paper at the dimensions they were cropped. You can expand the content on cropped pages to fill the paper to the standard margins. Open the Print dialog box by pressing **CTRL+P** (see Chapter 2 for more information on printing a PDF), click the **Page Scaling** down arrow, and click **Fit To Printer Margins**. Select other printing options and click **OK**. All pages in the PDF containing content reduced by cropping will have their content expanded to fit the paper size.

Page Scaling: | Fit to Printer Margins

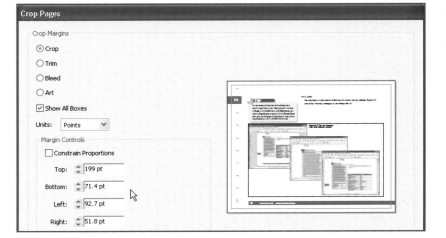

Figure 4-3: *You can set cropping values and see the effect on the preview page.*

TIP

If you are preparing PDF documents for a commercial printer, you might need to adjust various boundary boxes that determine page spacing for trimming, folding, and other production details. To display boxes created in layout programs, such as Adobe InDesign, in the document pane, click the **Edit** menu, click **Preferences**, and click the **Page Display** category. In the Page Display area, click the **Display Art, Trim, Bleed Boxes** check box, and click **OK**. Additional commercial layout techniques are beyond the scope of this book.

☑ Display art, trim, bleed boxes
☑ Display large images

TIP

To create a header or footer that displays different information on odd and even pages, you will need to set up two instances of the header or footer. In the Add Headers & Footers dialog box, in the Page Options area, click the **Alternation** down arrow, and choose the first set of pages you want to work on. Use the procedures in "Add Headers and Footers" to set up the first set, click **OK**, and then repeat to set up the other set of pages. See the QuickSteps "Working with Headers and Footers" for information on how to remove or change existing settings.

Alternation:	Do not alternate ∨
	Do not alternate
	Even Pages Only
	Odd Pages Only

Add Headers and Footers

Often, after stitching a PDF together from multiple sources (see Chapter 3 for information on creating PDFs), you will want to give the document a consistent theme. An easy and effective technique is to use headers and footers to provide the reader with a similar set of information on each page, such as the document title, author, and page numbers. You can type text and/or use automated features that insert the current date and page number (see "Add Page Numbers" later in this chapter for more information). You can even create separate headers and footers for odd and even pages.

1. Open the document in Acrobat, click the **Document** menu, and click **Add Headers & Footers**.

2. In the Add Headers & Footers dialog box, click the **Header** or **Footer** tab, depending on which you want to use. Each tab displays an identical set of tools that allows you to build the content and appearance you want, as shown in Figure 4-4.

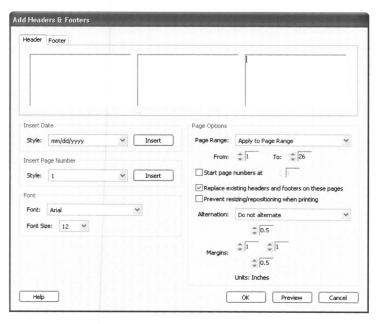

Figure 4-4: The Header and Footer tabs provide identical tools to set up a consistent appearance across pages.

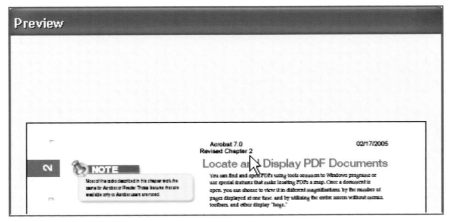

3. Click the left-, center-, or right-alignment text box at the top of the dialog box, and type the information you want to display in each area of the page. For example, if you want the document title to appear centered on the page and the date to be right-aligned, you would type the title in the center-alignment box and insert the date code in the right-alignment box. Use one or more of the following options:

- To insert the current date, place your insertion point in the applicable alignment box, before or after any text that might be in the box. In the Insert Date area, click the **Style** down arrow, click the date style you want, and click **Insert**. A set of double less than/greater than (<< >>) characters identify the date style you chose.

- To change the typeface and size for all text in the header or footer, in the Font area, click the **Font** and **Font Size** down arrows, and select the font attributes you want.

- To apply the header or footer to a page range, in the Page Options area, click the **Page Range** down arrow, click **Apply To Page Range**, and set the range in the From and To boxes.

- To adjust the position of the header or footer on the page, use the applicable **Margin** spinner; or select the current margin value, and type a new value.

4. Click **Preview** to see how your text appears on the pages in the PDF, as shown in Figure 4-5. Click **OK** to return to the original dialog box, make any adjustments, and click **OK** when finished.

Figure 4-5: A custom header or footer can add details to a PDF that are not integral to the original document.

WORKING WITH HEADERS AND FOOTERS

You can modify and remove headers or footers after you've added them (see "Add Headers and Footers").

CHANGE HEADERS AND FOOTERS

1. Click the **Document** menu, click **Add Headers & Footers**, and click the **Header** or **Footer** tab to display details of the most recently created header or footer (there may be up to three instances of a header or footer: one that affects all pages, one for odd pages, and one for even pages):

   - To retain existing header or footer information with any new changes, deselect the **Replace Existing Headers And Footers On These Pages** check box.

   ☐ Replace existing headers and footers on these pages
   ☐ Prevent resizing/repositioning when printing

   - To remove all header or footer information and replace it with your new changes, click the **Replace Existing Headers And Footers On These Pages** check box.

2. Click **OK** when finished and click **OK** again to confirm you want to replace the existing headers and footers.

REMOVE HEADERS AND FOOTERS

Click the **Document** menu, click **Add Headers & Footers**, and click the **Header** or **Footer** tab to display the details of the most recently created header or footer. Delete all text from the three alignment boxes, click the **Replace Existing Headers And Footers On These Pages** check box, click **OK**, and click **OK** again to confirm you want to replace the existing headers and footers.

–Or–

Click the **Edit** menu and click **Undo Headers/Footers** to remove the most recently created header or footer.

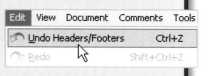

Add Page Numbers

You can add page numbers to a PDF in a couple of ways. One way only displays the page numbers when the document is opened in Acrobat or Reader, and then only in the Pages tab and in the navigation bar at the bottom of the document pane. The other method allows you to add page numbers in the header or footer, and they become a saved element in the document that will appear when printed.

ADD NAVIGATION PANE AND NAVIGATION BAR PAGE NUMBERS

You can change how Acrobat and Reader display the page numbering of the current PDF shown in the document pane. The numbers only appear in the Pages tab and in the navigation bar—they do not affect any numbering scheme in the content of the PDF nor are they printed.

You have several numbering formats you can use to segregate a PDF into sections. For example, you can use upper- or lowercase letters or roman numerals to identify the table of contents and other front matter in a book layout (similar to the page numbering in this book) while using cardinal numbers for content pages. Additionally, you can add prefixes, such as 1-1, 1-2 and 2-1, 2-2, and so forth, to individually number chapters, appendixes, and similar divisions of content.

1. Open the document in Acrobat, and click the **Pages** tab in the navigation pane. You can select the range of pages that you want to add numbers to at this point, or you can wait and assign them in a few steps.

2. Click **Options** in the navigation pane toolbar, and click **Number Pages**.

3. In the Page Numbering dialog box, shown in Figure 4-6, in the Pages area, select the pages you want to number (if you selected pages in the Pages tab, the **Selected** option is selected by default).

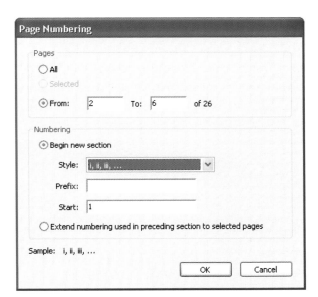

Figure 4-6: You can subdivide a PDF into numbered sections that are only available when viewing a PDF.

NOTE

If you choose None as the numbering style in the Page Numbering dialog box, the page numbers for the selected or identified pages will not be displayed.

4. In the Numbering area, click **Begin New Section**, click the **Style** down arrow, and select the numbering style you want. If you want a prefix, type it in the Prefix text box. In the Start text box, type the number where you want the numbering to start.

   –Or–

   Click **Extend Numbering Used In Preceding Section To Selected Pages** if you are continuing a numbering scheme from a section you previously set up.

5. Click **OK** when finished. The page numbers display in the affected pages in the Pages tab and in the page number box in the navigation bar.

   ⏮ ◀ | iii (4 of 26) | ▶ ⏭

ADD DOCUMENT PAGE NUMBERS

See "Add Headers and Footers" for more information on the general procedures to set up headers and footers.

1. Open the document to which you want to add page numbers in Acrobat, click the **Document** menu, and click **Add Headers & Footers**.

2. In the Add Headers & Footers dialog box, click the **Header** or **Footer** tab to determine whether to place the numbers at the top or bottom of the page.

3. Click the left-, center-, or right-alignment text box where you want the page number to appear. The insertion point appears in the box.

4. In the Insert Page Number area, click the **Style** down arrow, and click the numbering style you want (styles with "n" add the number of total pages in the PDF along with the current page number), and click **Insert**. A set of double less than/greater than characters (<< >>) identify the page numbering style.

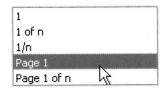

5. Type any text that you want, either preceding or following the coded numbering style. For example, you could type the title of the document followed by the <<Page 1 of n >> style.

6. In the Font area, select a typeface and size for the numbering and text.

7. In the Page Options area, choose a page range to which the page numbering applies. If you want to start at a number other than 1, click the **Start Page Numbers At** check box, and use the spinner; or type the number at which you want the numbering to start.

8. Add any other information or options you want to the header or footer, and click **OK** when finished.

Add a Background or Watermark

Backgrounds and watermarks are text or images you add behind or on top of existing PDF content, respectively. For example, you could include a faded logo behind a page of plain text, or superimpose a watermark of "Sold" on top of a listing showing houses for sale. You can choose when to show the effect (on-screen and/or on paper), where on a page it's positioned and its size, its opacity (or lack of transparency), and on which pages you want it to appear.

1. Open the document to which you want to add a background or watermark in Acrobat, click the **Document** menu, and click **Add Watermark & Background**.

2. In the Add Watermark & Background dialog box, shown in Figure 4-7, in the Type area, select whether you want to add a background or watermark and whether to display it on-screen, on printed output, or both.

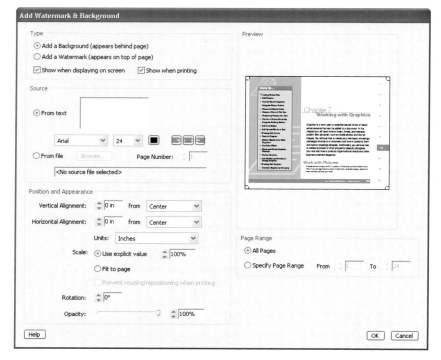

Figure 4-7: You can underlay or superimpose text and images on selected pages in a PDF using backgrounds and watermarks.

3. In the Source area, determine whether you want text or an image file to provide the desired effect:

   - Click **From Text** and type the text in the text box. Use the typeface and font size drop-down lists, the text color button and palette, and alignment buttons to change the appearance of typed text. Your changes appear in the Preview area.

   - Click **From File**, click **Browse**, and locate and select the image file (.pdf, .jpg, and .bmp file types only) that you want. Click **OK**. The image is displayed on the preview page on the right side of the dialog box. In the case of a PDF document, use the **Page Number** spinner to find the page you want to use.

4. In the Position And Appearance area, change how and where on a page the effect is displayed (changes are reflected in the Preview area):

   - Use the **Vertical** and **Horizontal** distance spinners and reference drop-down lists to determine how far the effect is from the top, center, or bottom of a page. In the Units drop-down list box, change the units of measurement from the default amount to a percentage of the page.

● Click **Use Explicit Value** and use the percentage spinner to set a resize value, or click **Fit To Page**. In the case of watermarks, click the **Prevent Resizing/Repositioning When Printing** check box to lock the effect in place when printing.

● Use the **Rotation** spinner to turn the effect at an angle (positive numbers turn the effect counterclockwise; negative numbers turn it clockwise).

● Use the **Opacity** slider or spinner to set the transparency of the background or watermark, determining how much the effect blocks out the content on the PDF.

5. In the Page Range area, choose to display the effect on all pages in the PDF, or click **Specify Page Range** and use the **From** and **To** spinners to determine a consecutive set of pages on which the effect is displayed.

6. Click **OK** when you are finished. Figure 4-8 shows an image background under a text-based watermark.

Figure 4-8: Both a background and a watermark can be utilized in a PDF.

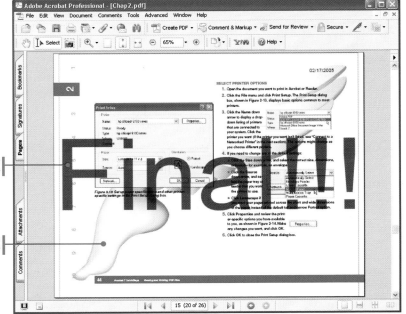

Text used as a watermark on top of content

Background image under content

UNDERSTANDING TEXT IN ACROBAT

At first glance, it can be quite confusing when working with text in Acrobat because there are tools, toolbars, and references that deal with both *content* text and *markup/comment* text. Content text, covered in this chapter, is included in the source document and became part of the PDF document during the conversion process. You work with content text using the Select and TouchUp Text tools, and changes you make become integral to the PDF document's content. Markup and comment text are comprised of notes and text boxes, as well as several markup tools that point out actions and emphasize text that you want others to see, such as crossouts and suggested replacement text. These comments and markups reside "on top" of the content text and can be easily removed or hidden. Chapter 7 describes how to add comments and work with markup tools.

TIP

You can look up the meanings and pronunciations of words using a free online reference site. Click the **Select** tool, right-click the word in the PDF displayed in the document pane, and click **Look Up "*yourword*"** to connect to the Reference.com web site. A thesaurus and Google search of the word is also available at this site.

Edit Text

Never a threat to Microsoft Word as a premier word processor, Acrobat provides basic editing functions you can use to make minor changes to text in a PDF, copy text to other documents, and add new text. The editing limitations in Acrobat quickly will become apparent, and you might find it easier, faster, and less frustrating to make anything but minor changes in the source document and reconvert it to a PDF.

Copy Text Using the Select Tool

You can copy selected text in a PDF document for use in other applications, such as Word or Excel (as well as into comments and bookmarks; see Chapters 7 and 9, respectively). You can use either the Select tool or the TouchUp Text tool to select the text you want to copy (see "Modify Text in Acrobat" later in the chapter for information on using the TouchUp Text tool), although the Select tool provides the most flexibility in selecting text and offers additional copy options.

1. Open the document in Acrobat, and select the text you want to copy (see the Quick-Steps "Selecting Text with the Select Tool").

2. Place your mouse pointer in the selection, wait a moment, and then point to the text selection icon 🔲 to display a menu of options:

   - Click **Copy To Clipboard** to copy the selected text as paragraph text.

   - Click **Copy As Table** to copy the selected text in a row-and-column configuration. (If the text is not in a table in the PDF, the text will appear in the other document as a single cell.)

3. Open the destination document and position the insertion point where you want the copied text to be inserted.

4. Click the program's **Edit** menu, and click **Paste** (or **Paste Special** for other inserting options, if available).

   –Or–

   Press **CTRL+V**.

CAUTION

You cannot add or replace text, including text that contains *embedded* fonts (font definitions that are a part of the PDF file) unless the font used is installed on your computer. However, you can change text properties, such as the font size and character spacing, for text that uses embedded fonts (see "Change Text Properties" later in this chapter and see Chapter 5 for more information on working with embedded and system fonts).

In either case, the copied text is added to the destination document. (If the characters don't look the same as they did in the PDF, the font used in the PDF was not available on the system used by the destination document and a substitution font was used. Add the missing font to the other system to correct the mismatch. See *Windows XP QuickSteps*, published by McGraw-Hill/Osborne, for more information on working with your operating system.)

Modify Text in Acrobat

The TouchUp toolbar contains tools used to make minor changes to existing text in a PDF and to add and position new blocks of text.

1. Click the **Tools** menu, click **Advanced Editing**, and click **Show TouchUp Toolbar**.

2. Drag the TouchUp toolbar from its position in the toolbar area to a more convenient place in the Acrobat window.

CHANGE EXISTING TEXT

1. In Acrobat, open the PDF document and navigate to the page where you want to modify text.

2. Click the **TouchUp Text** tool on the TouchUp toolbar, and click in the text near where you want to make changes. A blue border outlines a bounding box of editable text, as shown in Figure 4-9.

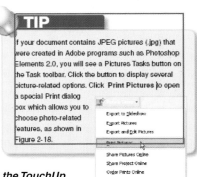

Figure 4-9: When using the TouchUp Text tool, editable text is identified by a blue-bordered bounding box.

SELECTING TEXT WITH THE SELECT TOOL

The Select tool is used to identify and select text that you can copy to other programs or to which you can add comments and markups (see Chapter 7).

Click the **Select** tool on the Basic toolbar, and use one of the following techniques to select paragraph text. Pointers will appear at the starting and ending points of the highlighted text:

I► Select

The Page Handling area

- Drag the I-beam mouse pointer across the text you want selected.
- Click at the start of your selection. Press and hold **SHIFT** and click at the end of the text you want selected.
- To select a word, double-click it.
- To select a line of text, triple-click it.
- To select all text on a page, click the **Edit** menu and click **Select All**; click paragraph text anywhere on the page, and press **CTRL+A**; or click text anywhere on the page four times.

EXTEND A SELECTION

Drag one of the pointers identifying the start or end of a selection to increase or decrease the characters selected.

SELECT TEXT AS A COLUMN

To transfer the same line endings in the PDF to the destination document and retain a columnar layout, you need to select the text in column mode.

1. Move the mouse pointer into one of the margins surrounding the columnar text you want to select. The mouse pointer changes to an I-beam on top of a small, rectangular marquee.

   ⌶ 1. Use the Copies text b
   increase or decrease

2. Drag the marquee over the text you want to select. The text is highlighted without any starting and ending pointers.

3. You can use several common word-processing techniques to add and remove characters, copy and paste text, and start new lines. For example:

   - Drag over text to select it, or press and hold **SHIFT** and use the arrow keys; click outside the selection to deselect it.
   - Replace text by selecting it and typing new text or pasting text from the Clipboard (click the **Edit** menu and click **Paste**, or press **CTRL+V**).
   - Remove text by selecting it and pressing **DELETE** or by clicking **Delete** or **Cut** on the Edit menu.
   - Insert text by clicking to establish your insertion point (a blinking vertical line) and typing to insert characters.
   - Add a new line by pressing **ENTER**.

4. Change text properties (see "Change Text Properties" later in the chapter).

ADD NEW TEXT ELEMENTS

You can add text contained in its own bounding box as a separate element from existing text.

1. In Acrobat, open the PDF document and navigate to the page where you want to modify text.

2. Click the **TouchUp Text** tool, press and hold **CTRL**, and click near where you want the new text.

3. In the New Text Font dialog box, choose the font you want and whether to orient the text in a standard horizontal or vertical mode (the font must be installed on your local computer, and many common fonts do not have vertical mode capability). Click **OK**. A small bounding box with the words "New Text" appears where you clicked.

   New Text Font
   Choose the text font and writing mode
   Font: Arial
   Mode: Horizontal
   OK   Cancel

   New Text

4. Type the new text you want. The bounding box expands to fit the text you added.

5. Use the editing techniques described in the previous section and see "Change Text Properties" later in the chapter to add bolding and other attributes and to reposition the bounding box (see the next section).

You can use a few programs to edit the text from a PDF page and then have the changes reflected in the PDF. For example, if you have Adobe Illustrator installed on your system, click the **TouchUp Object** tool, and right-click the bounding box(es) you want to edit. Click **Edit Object** and the text will open in Illustrator (right-click the page outside a bounding box, and click **Edit Page** to open the full page in the editing program). Make your edits and save the page in Illustrator. Switch back to Acrobat and the changes will be updated in the PDF. To choose an editing program, click the **Edit** menu, click **Preferences**, click the **TouchUp** category, and click the **Choose Page/Object Editor** button to locate the executable file for the program you want to use. | Choose Page/Object Editor... |

You can quickly add an em dash (—) to text in a PDF. Using the TouchUp Text tool, position the insertion point in the text where you want the em dash, right-click, click **Insert**, and then click **Em Dash**.

Making anything but minor text changes in Acrobat can cause major changes to the alignment, flow, and position of text in the PDF. After making any changes, review the PDF to ensure everything is in place.

REPOSITION TEXT

Acrobat divides selected elements in a PDF, including text, into separate bounding boxes that you can move by dragging them on a page to a new location.

1. In Acrobat, open the PDF document and navigate to the page where you want to move text.

2. Click the **TouchUp Object** tool, and click the text you want to move. A bounding box surrounds a portion of the text (Acrobat may subdivide a bounding box into smaller bounding boxes).

–Or–

Drag the mouse pointer over several elements to select their bounding boxes, and move them together as a unit.

–Or–

Click the **Edit** menu and click **Select All**, or right-click the page and click **Select All**, to select all elements on a page. Figure 4-10 shows a collection of selected elements on a page.

3. Point in the bounding box(es), and drag to a new location on the page (you cannot drag elements to other pages).

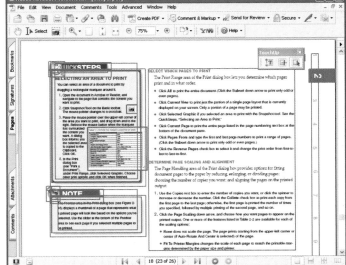

Figure 4-10:
Elements surrounded
by bounding boxes
can be moved, deleted,
and manipulated using
the TouchUp Object

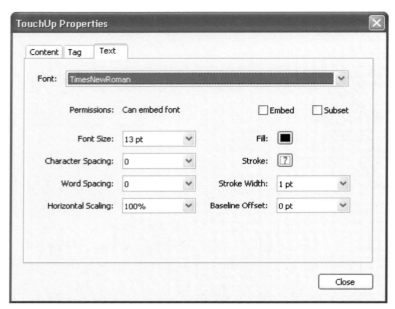

Figure 4-11: You can change several properties of selected text using the TouchUp Text tool and its properties dialog box.

Change Text Properties

You can change several properties of selected text using the TouchUp Text tool.

1. In Acrobat, open the PDF document and navigate to the page where you want to modify text properties.

2. Click the **Tools** menu, click **Advanced Editing**, and click **TouchUp Text Tool**.

   –Or–

   Click the **TouchUp Text** tool on the TouchUp toolbar.

3. Drag across the text you want to change, right-click the selection, and click **Properties**.

4. In the TouchUp Properties dialog box, shown in Figure 4-11, click the **Text** tab (if it is not already displayed), and change one or more properties, as shown in Table 4-1 (as you change a property, you can see the effect on the selected text).

5. Click **Close** when finished.

TABLE 4-1: TEXT ATTRIBUTES

USE THIS ATTRIBUTE...	TO...
Font	Select the font you want. Fonts embedded in the PDF document are listed first; fonts available on your system are listed below the divider.
Embed (if available)	Add the full font definition to the PDF file; click **Subset** if you want only a portion of the font definition added (see Chapter 5 for more information on fonts).
Font Size	Type or select a different size for the text.
Character Spacing	Type or select a value that adjusts the spacing between selected characters.
Word Spacing	Type or select a value that adjusts the spacing between selected words.
Horizontal Scaling	Type or select a value that adjusts the proportion between the height and width of selected text.
Baseline Offset	Type or select a value that adjusts the distance between selected text and the reference baseline on which it resides.
Fill	Change the color of the text.
Stroke and Stroke Width	Change the color and thickness of the text.

QUICKSTEPS

WORKING WITH IMAGES

Images, like text, can be edited in source programs and returned to a PDF. You can also reposition images using the TouchUp Object tool.

EDIT IMAGES

1. In Acrobat, click the **TouchUp Object** tool, right-click the image, and click **Edit Image**. Your selected image editing program will open with the image displayed in its window.

2. Edit and save the image.

3. Switch back to Acrobat. The changes are reflected in the image in the PDF.

REPOSITION IMAGES

1. In Acrobat, click the **TouchUp Object** tool, and click an image. A blue bounding box surrounds it.

2. Drag the image to where you want it on the page.

REMOVE, COPY, AND PASTE IMAGES

In Acrobat, right-click the image and click the option you want from the top of the context menu:

Cut
Copy
Paste
Delete

- Click **Cut** to remove the image and make it available for pasting to other pages in the current PDF or other PDF documents.

- Click **Copy** to retain the image in the PDF and make it available for pasting to other pages in the current PDF or other PDF documents.

- Click **Delete** to remove the image from the PDF.

- Click **Paste** after navigating to the page where you want to place a cut or copied image.

Add Articles and Attachments

Acrobat has several features that allow you to make your PDF more convenient for readers to use and provide more robust content beyond the actual PDF. Articles and attachments offer each of these enhancements (see Chapter 9 for information on other enhancements you can add, such as links, bookmarks, and multimedia).

Use Articles

Articles are used to provide the readers of your PDF with a guided tour through a topic in the document. Think of newspapers or magazines, where you often have to flip across columns and noncontiguous pages to finish a story. Using articles, you can tie each of those disparate locations together so the reader "hops" over other PDF elements and sees one continuous thread of information.

CREATE AN ARTICLE

To create an article, use the Article tool to identify the content you want to stitch together into one reading thread.

1. In Acrobat, open the PDF document and navigate to the page where the content you want included in an article starts.

2. Click the **Tools** menu, click **Advanced Editing**, and click **Article Tool**.

TIP

When you select a graphics program to be the default image editor, be sure and select the actual program and not a shortcut. In Acrobat, click the **Edit** menu, click **Preferences**, click the **TouchUp** category, and click the **Choose Image Editor** button. (See *Photoshop CS QuickSteps* or *Photoshop Elements 3 QuickSteps*, both published by McGraw-Hill/Osborne, for information on editing images).

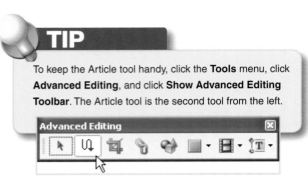

To keep the Article tool handy, click the **Tools** menu, click **Advanced Editing**, and click **Show Advanced Editing Toolbar**. The Article tool is the second tool from the left.

3. Drag the crosshair pointer over the first block of text, images, or other elements you want in the article. Release the mouse button. A bounding box with eight sizing handles and a reference number surrounds the content, as shown in Figure 4-12.

4. Navigate to the next block of content you want in the article, and drag the article pointer across that content. A similar bounding box surrounds the second content, with the reference number incremented by one. For example, each block of content in the first article in a PDF is referenced as 1-1, 1-2, and so on. The second article in the PDF is referenced as 2-1, 2-2, and so forth.

5. Repeat step 4 until all content in the article is identified.

6. Press **ENTER** to finish the article. In the Article Properties dialog box, title the article, add other identifiers as needed, and click **OK**. See the QuickSteps "Editing Articles" for more information on using articles.

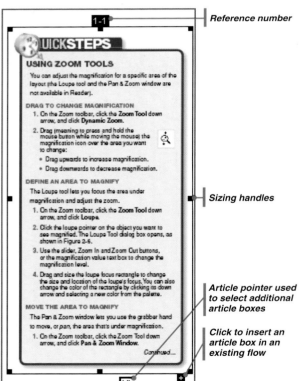

Figure 4-12: An article box is identified by a sequence number and a bounding box with sizing handles.

Reference number

Sizing handles

Article pointer used to select additional article boxes

Click to insert an article box in an existing flow

READ ARTICLES

1. In Acrobat or Reader, open the PDF document, click the **View** menu, click **Navigation Tabs**, and click **Articles**.

2. In the floating tab window, right-click the article you want to view, and click **Read Article**. The first block of the article content displays at the top of the document pane. (You can close the tab window after making your article selection, or dock it on the navigation pane by clicking the **View** menu, clicking **Navigation Tabs**, and clicking **Dock All Tabs**.)

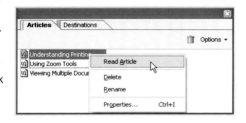

3. Hover the **Hand** tool over the article (the Hand tool pointer shows a downward-pointing arrow when placed over content in the article), and click to jump to the next block of content in the article.

4. Repeat step 3 to cycle through all article content in the PDF. When finished viewing the article, re-zoom as necessary to see a full-page view, and use the Pages tab or navigation bar to display the next page you want to view.

EDITING ARTICLES

You can insert a new article box into the flow of an existing article; combine articles; and move, resize, and delete articles.

MOVE OR RESIZE AN ARTICLE

Before you can move or resize an article box, you need to end the article.

In Acrobat, click the **Article** tool and click the article box you want to move or resize:

- Point anywhere in the box, and drag the box to move it.
- Point to one of the sizing handles, and drag the double-headed arrow pointer to resize the box.

ADD AN ARTICLE BOX TO AN EXISTING ARTICLE

1. In Acrobat, click the **Article** tool and click the article box after which you want to insert a new box.

2. Click the plus (+) sign in the lower-right corner of the bounding box (see Figure 4-12). Click **OK**. In the message box that appears, click **OK** to confirm that you want to add a new article box.

3. Navigate to the content that will be in the new article box, and drag across it using the Article tool. The bounding box is numbered in sequence to the article flow, and all other article boxes are renumbered accordingly.

COMBINE ARTICLES

1. In Acrobat, click the **Article** tool and click any article box in the article that you want read first.

2. Click the plus (+) sign in the lower-right corner of the bounding box. Click **OK**. In the message box that appears, click **OK** to confirm that you want to add a new article box.

3. Press and hold **CTRL** and click an article box in the article you want added to the end of the first article. The two articles are combined and renumbered into one article.

Continued...

Add Attachments

Attachments expand the scope of information that you can include with a PDF document. Much like the attachments we use in e-mail, attachments in Acrobat are separate files—whether PDF or other file formats—that are available to the reader for ancillary information.

1. In Acrobat, open the PDF to which you want to add an attachment.

2. Click the **Attach A File** down arrow on the File toolbar, and click **Attach A File**.

   –Or–

   Click the **Document** menu and click **Attach A File**.

3. In either case, in the Add Attachment dialog box, locate and open the folder that contains the file(s) you want to attach to the PDF. Select the file you want. To add multiple files, press and hold **CTRL** while clicking noncontiguous files; or click the first file in a contiguous series of files, press **SHIFT**, and click the last file in the series. Click **Open** when finished. The Attachments tab is displayed below the document pane. Figure 4-13 shows a tab with several attachments. The file(s) are listed in a columnar format, and a paper clip icon is displayed on the left end of the Acrobat status bar at the bottom of the Acrobat or Reader window to indicate the PDF has attached files.

TIP

You can display the Attachments tab (without inserting a file) by clicking the **Attachments** tab in the navigation pane or by clicking the **View** menu, clicking **Navigation Tabs**, and clicking **Attachments**.

EDITING ARTICLES *(Continued)*

DELETE AN ARTICLE

You can delete an entire article or individual bounding boxes in an article.

1. Right-click within an article bounding box using the Article tool, and click **Delete**.

2. Click **Article** to delete the entire article, or click **Box** to just remove the content within the bounding box from the article. In the latter case, the remaining bounding boxes will be renumbered.

4. The Attachment tab toolbar provides several features used when working with attachments:

- **Add** allows you to add additional files.

- **Open** displays the selected attachment in Acrobat (if it's a PDF) or in its parent program (assuming the program is installed on the computer). Changes made to open, attached PDF documents are automatically updated in the attachment. Changes made to non-PDF open attachments in their parent programs are not reflected in the attached file. You need to reattach the updated file to the PDF.

- **Save** allows the reader to save selected attachments as files on his or her computer.

- **Delete** removes selected attachments from the PDF.

- **Search** allows the reader to search for words or phrases in the selected attachment(s) using the Search PDF pane (see Chapter 6).

- **Options** duplicates the actions available from the other attachment tools and provides a way to add amplifying information about an attachment. Select the attachment in the Attachments tab, click **Options**, and click **Edit Description**. In the Edit Attachment Description dialog box, type a description and click **OK**. The text appears next to the attachment name in the Description column.

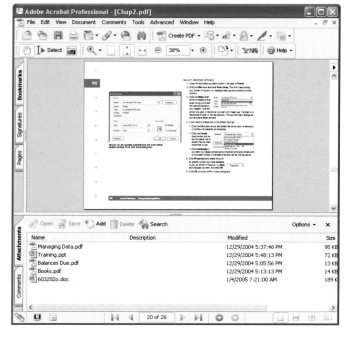

Figure 4-13: You add and view the attachments in a PDF in the Attachments tab at the bottom of the Acrobat window.

Chapter 5

Using Acrobat Distiller and Preflight

Acrobat Distiller is a separate program that comes with Acrobat Professional and converts PostScript files (.ps) and Encapsulated PostScript files (.eps) to PDF files. PS and EPS files are created by drawing programs and desktop publishing programs, such as Adobe Illustrator and InDesign, and by saving a document or image file created when printing to a PostScript printer. An independent program is used for this process because it produces high-quality PDF files that can be used in commercial printing.

Preflight is a process within Acrobat Professional that allows you to check a PDF file for errors that can cause problems when the file is used in commercial printing. Among the areas that Preflight checks are color, image resolution, and fonts.

Both Distiller and Preflight are advanced tools meant for producing professional-quality PDF files used in commercial printing. This chapter will introduce you to both products and describe how they are used.

Use Acrobat Distiller

Chapter 3 describes in detail how to convert many different commonly used files to PDF files. Two file types not discussed in Chapter 3 are PS and EPS files. Converting these files to PDFs is the job of Acrobat Distiller. In converting the files, Distiller gives you a high degree of control to produce exactly the file that you want. This control is obtained through the large number of settings that can be made and then saved, so the same settings can be easily and repeatedly used.

After starting Distiller, you should review the preferences that are to be used with it, select the settings that will control the conversion, and then choose the files to be converted. You can customize the Distiller settings to meet your needs and save them with a unique name so they can be used in the future, both by you and by others to whom you give the settings, for example, on a CD.

Start Acrobat Distiller

You can start Acrobat Distiller either from within Acrobat or directly from the Start menu.

Within Acrobat, click the **Advanced** menu and click **Acrobat Distiller**.

–Or–

From Windows, click the **Start** menu, click **All Programs**, and click **Acrobat Distiller 7.0**.

In both cases, Acrobat Distiller opens, as shown in Figure 5-1.

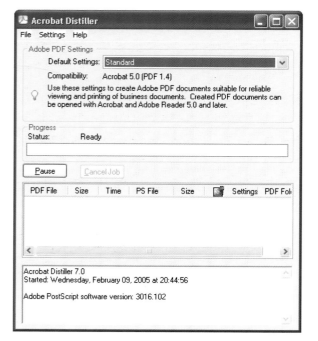

Figure 5-1: Acrobat Distiller can convert several files at a time.

UNDERSTANDING POSTSCRIPT

PostScript is a language developed by Adobe to describe a page of text and graphics. Many printers, especially high-resolution laser printers, image setters, and commercial printing presses, can directly use a PostScript file to produce a high-quality printed image (these printers are considered "PostScript printers"). Most desktop publishing applications and graphics programs can directly produce encapsulated PostScript (EPS) files independent of how they print. If a PostScript printer is installed on your network or on your computer, most programs in general (not just desktop publishing and graphics programs) can use the PostScript printer driver to create an image file that can be printed on a physical PostScript printer or used by Distiller to create a PDF.

PostScript is the first high-level printer language (in comparison to most early print streams, which were just a series of characters with formatting commands) to describe an entire page with its images, fonts, graphics (such as borders and shading), and many other subtle characteristics. PostScript is therefore called a page description language (PDL) and supports high-quality printing on a printer that can interpret it.

Because of its ability to provide a detailed description of a page, PostScript is also used to transfer information between programs. It is in this way that Acrobat Distiller comes into use and greatly enhances this function, because so many more programs can use PDF files than can use PostScript files.

Set Distiller Preferences

As with most parts of Acrobat, you can set a number of preferences in Distiller.

1. In Distiller, click the **File** menu and click **Preferences**. The Preferences – Acrobat Distiller dialog box appears.

2. In the Startup Alerts section, choose whether to keep the following options selected by default:

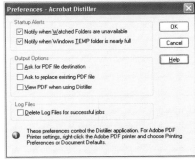

- **Notify When Watched Folders Are Unavailable** tells you when a folder that you have set up to automatically convert all PostScript files put in that folder is unavailable. See "Use Watched Folders" later in this chapter.

- **Notify When Windows TEMP Folder Is Nearly Full** tells you when the hard drive used by your Windows Temp folder, which Distiller also uses, has less than 1 MB left. You need approximately double the size of a PostScript file to convert it to a PDF.

3. In the Output Options section, click one or more of the following options (not selected by default):

- **Ask For PDF File Destination** requests a path and file name when you drag a PostScript file into Distiller. Otherwise, the original path and file name are used.

- **Ask To Replace Existing PDF File** warns you before replacing an existing PDF file with a file with the same name. Otherwise, the file is replaced without notice.

- **View PDF When Using Distiller** opens the PDF file in Acrobat after it is converted.

4. In the Log Files section, click **Delete Log Files For Successful Jobs** to keep the log entries only for jobs that failed to be converted. The log file, which you can scroll through in the bottom of the Distiller window, is stored in a file named Messages.log in the C:\Documents and Settings*user name*\Application Data\Adobe\Acrobat\Distiller 7\ folder.

5. When you are done setting the preferences you want, click **OK**.

Select Distiller Settings

After opening Distiller and before starting to convert files, choose the setting you want to use when converting a file.

Click the **Default Settings** down arrow, and choose from the following:

- **High Quality Print** creates high-quality PDF files for printing on desktop printers. This setting can produce large files and is commonly used for producing documents with photographic images.

- **PDF/A:Draft** creates files that meet international standards for archiving electronic documents. These files cannot contain scripts or encryption.

- **PDF/X-1a:2001** creates files that meet international standards for graphic content exchange. All fonts are embedded in the files, and colors must be CMYK or spot colors or both.

- **PDF/X-3:2002** creates files that meet international standards for graphic content exchange. All fonts are embedded and may use device-independent color and color management.

- **Press Quality** creates high-quality files that you can send to a commercial printer for digital printing but that are not compliant with the PDF/X international standards. All information required for printing is kept in the file, including fonts and images.

- **Smallest File Size** creates lower-resolution files to use on a web site or to send via e-mail. Fonts are not embedded, and higher compression is used, as well as lower-resolution images.

- **Standard** creates files that provide reasonable quality on desktop printers while also keeping the file size to a middle range. Subsets of the fonts are embedded, and moderate levels of both compression and resolution are used.

Convert PostScript Files

When you have chosen the settings to control the conversion of PostScript to PDF files, you can start the actual conversion in several ways.

DRAG AND DROP A POSTSCRIPT FILE INTO DISTILLER

1. Start Windows Explorer and open the folder that contains the PostScript file. Drag the Explorer window to the left side of the screen.

2. Start Distiller (see "Start Acrobat Distiller" earlier in this chapter), and select the default settings you want to use. Drag Distiller to the right side of the screen.

3. From Windows Explorer, drag the PostScript file (either .ps or .eps) to the right anywhere within the Distiller window. The conversion process begins, as shown in Figure 5-2.

DOUBLE-CLICK A POSTSCRIPT FILE

If you are working on a computer with Acrobat installed, it is likely that files with .ps and .eps file extensions have been defined in such a way that when you double-click one of those files, the file will open in Distiller and be converted. Distiller does not need to be running.

Open Windows Explorer, open the folder containing the PostScript file to be converted, and double-click that file.

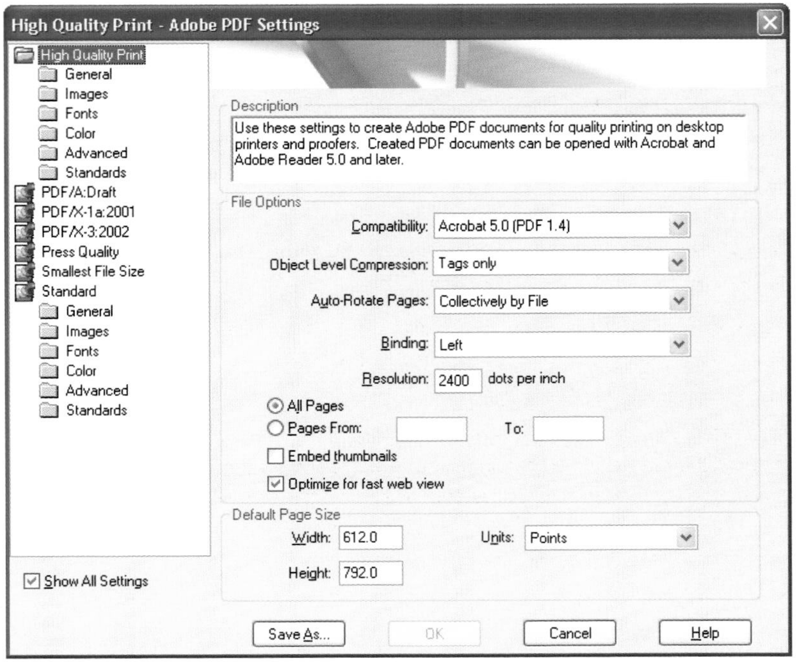

High Quality Print - Adobe PDF Settings

- High Quality Print
  - General
  - Images
  - Fonts
  - Color
  - Advanced
  - Standards
- PDF/A:Draft
- PDF/X-1a:2001
- PDF/X-3:2002
- Press Quality
- Smallest File Size
- Standard
  - General
  - Images
  - Fonts
  - Color
  - Advanced
  - Standards

☑ Show All Settings

Description

Use these settings to create Adobe PDF documents for quality printing on desktop printers and proofers. Created PDF documents can be opened with Acrobat and Adobe Reader 5.0 and later.

File Options

Compatibility: Acrobat 5.0 (PDF 1.4)

Object Level Compression: Tags only

Auto-Rotate Pages: Collectively by File

Binding: Left

Resolution: 2400 dots per inch

⦿ All Pages
○ Pages From: ___ To: ___
☐ Embed thumbnails
☑ Optimize for fast web view

Default Page Size

Width: 612.0   Units: Points
Height: 792.0

Save As...   OK   Cancel   Help

Figure 5-2: Distiller shows you the progress and gives you information about a conversion that is underway.

OPEN A POSTSCRIPT FILE IN DISTILLER

1. Start Distiller, select the relevant default settings, click the **File** menu, and click **Open**.

2. In the Acrobat Distiller – Open PostScript File dialog box, open the folder that contains the PostScript file(s) you want to convert.

3. If the files are .ps files, they will be displayed. If you want to convert .eps files, click the **Files Of Type** down arrow, and click **EPS Files (*.eps)**.

4. Click the file you want to convert. If you want to convert more than one file, press CTRL and click noncontiguous files; or click the first file in a list, press SHIFT, and click the last file to select a contiguous set of files (see Figure 5-3).

5. When you have selected the files you want to convert, click **Open**. The files are converted.

Control the Distiller Conversion

While a conversion is underway, you can do several things to control the process.

1. With Distiller open, start the conversion of a series of files as described in "Convert PostScript Files" earlier in this chapter.

2. To temporarily stop the upcoming conversion of files that are in the queue, click **Pause** or right-click the file entry and click **Pause**.

3. To resume the conversion of files in a paused queue, click **Resume** or right-click the file entry and click **Resume**.

4. To permanently stop a running conversion, click **Cancel Job** or right-click the file entry and click **Cancel Job(s)**.

5. To open a converted file in Acrobat, right-click the file entry and click **View**.

6. To open the folder from which a file originated, right-click the file entry and click **Explore**.

7. To remove the converted file entries from the list in Distiller, right-click any file entry and click **Clear History**.

8. To save the list of converted file entries, right-click any file entry and click **Save List**.

Figure 5-3: You can open as many files as you want at the same time in Distiller.

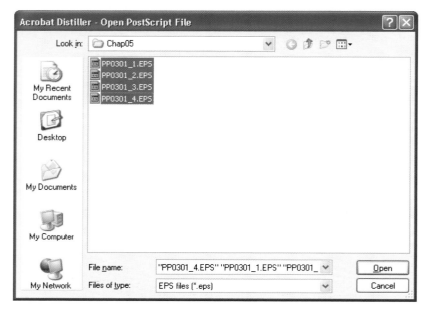

"PRINTING" THROUGH THE DISTILLER

Chapter 3 describes how in almost all programs you can use the Adobe PDF printer driver to create a PDF file. This process is, in effect, "printing" through the Distiller to produce a highly tailored PDF file.

1. Start the program from which you want to create a PDF file. Click the **File** menu and click **Print**. The Print dialog box appears.

2. Click the **Printer Name** down arrow, and click **Adobe PDF**.

3. Click **Properties**. The Adobe PDF Document Properties dialog box appears with the Adobe PDF Settings tab displayed, as shown in Figure 5-4.

4. Click the **Default Settings** down arrow, and select the settings you want to use. These are the same settings described in "Select Distiller Settings" earlier in this chapter.

5. Review and adjust the other options as desired, many of which are similar to the Distiller preferences.

6. When finished, click **OK** twice to transfer the printed output of the program to a PDF file.

Customize Distiller Settings

The Distiller settings, which are the same settings used by Acrobat, as discussed in Chapter 3, allow you to control the quality, size, and characteristics of the PDF file that is created. Acrobat and Distiller come with seven predefined groups of settings, as described in "Select Distiller Settings" earlier in this chapter. You can start with any of these groups, modify anything in the six folders of settings, and then save the settings under a new name so that it can be used in future conversions.

To create a custom group of settings:

1. From Distiller, click the **Settings** menu and then click **Edit Adobe PDF Settings**. The Adobe PDF Settings dialog box for the currently selected default settings group appears.

Figure 5-4: Looking at the Adobe PDF properties dialog box, it is obvious that the Distiller is being used in this process.

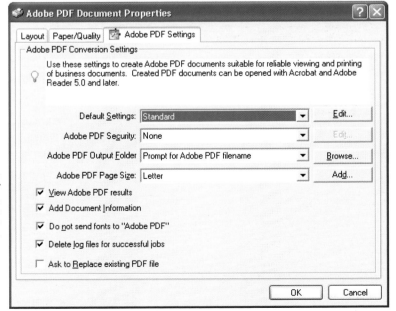

NOTE

The custom settings that you create in Distiller are available in Acrobat (click the **Edit** menu, click **Preferences**, click **Convert To PDF**, click **Edit Settings**, select the setting to use, and click **OK**); in the Acrobat PDFMaker dialog box in Microsoft Office applications, click **Conversion Settings** and click **OK**; and in the Adobe PDF printer driver in other programs (from the Print dialog box), click **Properties**, click **Default Settings**, and click **OK**.

2. If you want to work with another group of settings, click **Show All Settings** and click the group you want to work with, as shown in Figure 5-5.

3. Work through the settings in each of the folders, as described in the following sections, to obtain the results you want. The defaults that you see when you first open a folder are the optimum for the particular settings group that you have chosen.

4. When you are finished, click **OK** to save the file with the existing name (if you are changing one of the original groups of settings, the file name will be numerically incremented, for example "Standard(1)"), or click **Save As** to give the file a new name.

GENERAL FOLDER

The General folder allows you to enter a description, determine the compatibility, and set the overall file appearance, resolution, and page size:

- **Compatibility** should be set to the latest version that you believe the majority of your readers will have. "Acrobat 5.0 (PDF 1.4)" is a good choice.

- **Object Level Compression** should be set to "Off" for the highest quality files and for use with Acrobat 5 and earlier versions. Set it to "Tags Only" for smaller files that will be used by Acrobat 6 or 7.

- **Auto-Rotate Pages** should be set to "Collectively By File" to display the entire file in either portrait or landscape orientation, depending on the orientation of the majority of pages. "Individually" causes each page to be displayed based on its orientation. "Off" causes no rotation to take place.

- **Binding** determines how facing pages are displayed.

- **Resolution** allows you to emulate on the screen what you will see on a printed page. The higher the resolution, which can go from 72 to 4000, the larger the file and the longer it will take to load.

- **Pages** specifies the pages to be converted. If the To field is left blank, pages beginning with the From page to the end of the document are converted.

- **Embed Thumbnails** includes a thumbnail image of each page in the PDF. Since Acrobat 5 and later versions automatically generate a thumbnail, this setting is only needed for earlier versions.

- **Optimize For Fast Web View** increases the speed of downloading and viewing a PDF over an intranet or the Internet, if that is the intent of the file.

- **Default Page Size** allows you to specify a size if it was not done previously.

Figure 5-5: Adobe PDF settings control how a file is converted to a PDF in both Distiller and Acrobat.

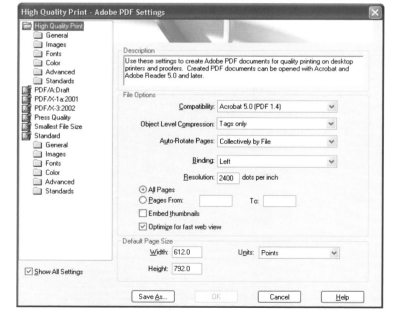

IMAGES FOLDER

The Images folder allows you to control downsampling, compression, and image quality for color, grayscale, and monochrome images (see Figure 5-6):

- **Downsampling** combines pixels to reduce the resolution of an image. See the "Choosing a Resolution" QuickFacts to determine which resolution to use. You have a choice of three types of downsampling:

  - **Average** determines the average color in an area and replaces the entire area with it.

  - **Subsampling** makes an entire area the color of a pixel in the center of the area.

  - **Bicubic** determines a weighted average color in an area and replaces the entire area with that color. This produces the best results, but it is also the slowest method.

  - **Compression** and **Image Quality** let you choose the type and degree of compression. You are given three choices of compression with color and grayscale images and an Acrobat 5.0 (PDF 1.4) compatibility (see the Tip about Acrobat 6.0 (PDF 1.5)):

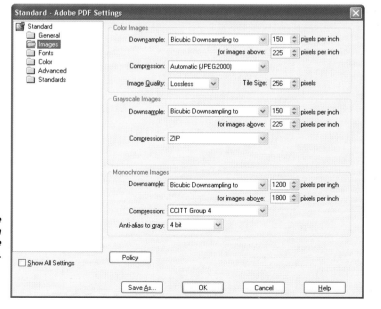

Figure 5-6: The Images folder is the primary means by which you can control the size and quality of the PDF files you create.

NOTE

OpenType fonts can only be embedded if Acrobat 7.0 (PDF 1.6) compatibility has been selected in the General folder.

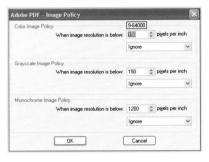

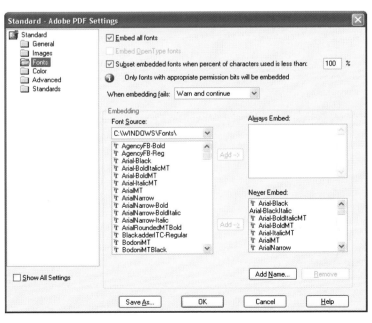

- **ZIP** compression—which should be used with black-and-white images, text, simple images with repeating patterns, and large blocks of repeating colors—is a lossless compression in which no information about the image is lost during compression. You have no choice of image quality with ZIP compression.

- **JPEG** compression—which should be used with color or grayscale photographs and complex page layouts with color—is a lossy compression in which some information about the image is lost during compression. You can choose an image quality, from minimum (for the highest compression) to maximum (for the lowest compression).

- **Automatic (JPEG)** combines JPEG compression with an automatic determination of the best quality for a particular image.

- **Anti-Alias To Gray** is used with monochrome images to smooth jagged edges. You have a choice of 2 bit, 4 bit, and 8 bit, which will give you 4, 16, or 256 shades of gray.

- **Policy** lets you determine what to do with images that come into the PDF conversion process below the resolution you have specified.

FONTS FOLDER

The Fonts folder lets you determine the fonts included in a PDF file (if fonts are not embedded, they must be downloaded to the system viewing the PDF):

- **Embed All Fonts** specifies that all fonts in a document be embedded when a PDF is created.

- **Subset Embedded Fonts** allows you to embed all or only a subset of the characters within the font if the number of different characters used falls below a stated percentage.

- **Embedding** allows you to choose the fonts you want to embed if you don't embed all fonts, as well as those you don't want to embed. If a font is not in the Font Source list, you can add its name, or you can remove a font as well (see Figure 5-7).

Figure 5-7: By embedding the fonts in a PDF, you ensure that when the file is viewed or printed it appears as you intended.

CHOOSING A RESOLUTION

Your choice of a conversion resolution, in pixels per inch (ppi), should be based on the resolution, in dots per inch (dpi), of the output device used to print the document being converted. Color and grayscale have one relationship, while monochrome has another, as shown in the following table.

OUTPUT DEVICE RESOLUTION	COLOR & GRAYSCALE RESOLUTION	MONOCHROME RESOLUTION
300 dpi	120 ppi	300 ppi
600 dpi	170 ppi	600 ppi
1200 dpi	240 ppi	1200 ppi
2400 dpi	300 ppi	1500 ppi

Monochrome resolution should be the same as the output device, up to 1500 dpi or ppi. Above 1500 ppi or dpi, there is no noticeable improvement in quality, although the file size continues to grow.

COLOR FOLDER

The Color folder lets you determine how color is handled when a PDF is created:

- **Settings File** allows you to select an existing color settings file, for example, one that is used with other graphics programs, such as Photoshop. If you select such a file, other settings in the folder, except Device-Dependent Data, are changed to the settings in the file and cannot be changed.

- **Color Management Policies** and **Working Spaces** allow you to specify which objects will undergo color management or conversion to a particular color scheme and the particular formula used to do that.

- **Document Rendering Intent** lets you choose the method by which color gets mapped between color spaces.

- **Device-Dependent Data** lets you set how color will be treated when the document is printed and control the amount of ink used by colors that are eventually covered up by other colors.

ADVANCED FOLDER

The Advanced folder, shown in Figure 5-8, allows you to specify the degree to which PostScript settings and conventions are carried over to a PDF file created from a PostScript file:

- **Options** lets you create settings and PostScript code (XObjects) in a PostScript file and have them carried over to and take precedence in a PDF file.

- **Document Structure Conventions (DCS)** allows you to bring PostScript information, such as warnings, comments, document title, and creation date, into a PDF file.

Standard - Adobe PDF Settings

Standard
- General
- Images
- Fonts
- Color
- Advanced
- Standards

Options
- ☑ Allow PostScript file to override Adobe PDF settings
- ☑ Allow PostScript XObjects
- ☑ Convert gradients to smooth shades
- ☑ Convert smooth lines to curves
- ☑ Preserve Level 2 copypage semantics
- ☑ Preserve overprint settings
  - ☑ Overprinting default is nonzero overprinting
- ☐ Save Adobe PDF settings inside PDF file
- ☑ Save original JPEG images in PDF if possible
- ☐ Save Portable Job Ticket inside PDF file
- ☐ Use Prologue.ps and Epilogue.ps
- ☐ Create Job Definition Format (JDF) file

Document Structuring Conventions (DSC)
- ☑ Process DSC comments
- ☐ Log DSC warnings
- ☐ Preserve EPS information from DSC
- ☐ Preserve OPI comments
- ☑ Preserve document information from DSC
- ☑ Resize page and center artwork for EPS files

☐ Show All Settings

[Save As...]   [OK]   [Cancel]   [Help]

Figure 5-8: The Advanced folder provides the means to preserve PostScript information after a file has been converted to PDF.

NOTE

The handling of color is a complex subject. The best approach is to use one of the settings files, such as one of the defaults, or, if you are going to use a commercial printer, let them tell you the settings to use.

TIP

You can also simply delete the settings file from the C:\Documents and Settings\All Users\Documents\Adobe PDF\Settings folder.

Figure 5-9: Adobe PDF settings files have the extension .joboptions.

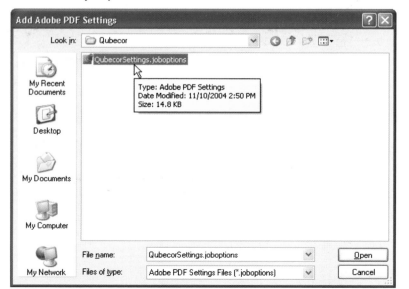

STANDARDS FOLDER

The Standards folder allows you to check how well a PostScript file meets a given standard and what to do when it doesn't meet that standard:

- **Compliance Standard** lets you select the standard to use when checking compliance.
- **When Not Compliant** allows you to either continue with the conversion or cancel it.
- **If Neither TrimBox Nor ArtBox Are Specified** lets you either report that fact as an error or set the TrimBox (the dimensions to which a page will be trimmed) to the MediaBox (the physical page size) minus any offset.
- **If BleedBox Is Not Specified** lets you either set the BleedBox (the outer edge of a bleed) equal to the MediaBox or equal to the MediaBox minus any offset.
- **Default Values If Not Specified In The Document** lets you specify default values for fields required in various standards.

Add and Remove a Settings File

If you are given a PDF settings file by, for example, a commercial printer, you can easily add it to the list of default settings.

1. Start Distiller, as described earlier in this chapter. Click the **Settings** menu and click **Add Adobe PDF Settings**. The Add Adobe PDF Settings dialog box appears.

2. Locate the folder in which you have stored the new settings file. Click that file, as shown in Figure 5-9, and click **Open**. The file is designated as the default settings file and is available for future selection from the Default Settings drop-down list.

–Or–

1. Start Distiller, as described earlier in this chapter. Drag the Distiller window to the right side of the screen.

2. Start Windows Explorer. Drag it to the left side of the screen.

3. In Windows Explorer, locate the folder in which you have stored the new settings file.

4. Drag the file from Windows Explorer to Distiller. The file is designated as the default settings file and is available for future selection from the Default Settings drop-down list.

When you are finished using a settings file, you can also easily remove it.

1. Start Distiller. Click the **Settings** menu and click **Remove Adobe PDF Settings**. The Remove Adobe PDF settings dialog box appears.

2. Click the file you want removed, and click **Remove**. Click **Close** to close the dialog box.

Handle Fonts

When a PostScript file is converted to PDF, the fonts used in the file must be available to Distiller so they can potentially be embedded in the PDF. In some cases, the fonts are embedded in the PostScript file and are immediately available to Distiller. In other cases, only the font names are in the PostScript file, and Distiller must look in folders to locate the fonts. It is therefore important that Distiller know where the font files are.

On a computer running Windows with Acrobat installed, at least two folders contain fonts by default:

- C:\Program Files\Adobe\Acrobat 7.0\Resource\Font (see Figure 5-10)
- C:\Windows\Fonts

TIP

In the Font Locations dialog box, if the fonts folder icon is not visible or has an X through it, the folder is not available and you must reestablish the connection. The easiest way to do that is to remove the folder and re-add it in the dialog box.

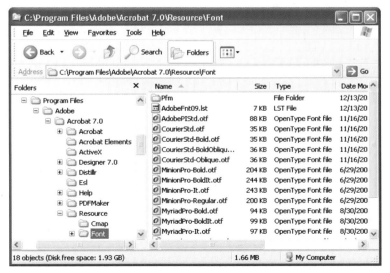

Figure 5-10: When you install Acrobat, it creates a fonts folder with a few default fonts.

EMBEDDING AND SUBSTITUTING FONTS

Embedding all the fonts in a document is a good practice because it ensures that the reader of the document or the printer will have all the fonts available. On the downside, however, embedding fonts increases the file size, makes the document load more slowly, and may be unnecessary if the fonts are common and on most computers, such as Arial and Times Roman. Also, some fonts are prevented from being embedded by the font manufacturer.

When fonts are not embedded and Acrobat tries to display or print a file, it first tries to locate the font on the computer on which Acrobat is running. If it is unsuccessful in this, Acrobat will generate a substitution for the font. The substitution is created using a Multiple Master typeface in either a serif font (similar to Times Roman) or a sans serif font (similar to Arial). This font can be stretched or condensed as needed so the line and page endings remain the same.

If fonts or individual characters are unique, for example, script fonts, the substituted font will not look anything like the original. Also, in the case of very special characters, no substitution may be found, and Acrobat will use a bullet character (•) of the correct size in its place.

You can turn off the use of fonts on the local computer and force the use of either embedded fonts, if they exist, or substituted fonts.

In Acrobat, click the **Advanced** menu and deselect **Use Local Fonts**. (Use Local Fonts is selected by default.)

| ✔ | Use Local Fonts | Shift+Ctrl+Y |

If you wish, you can add or remove fonts folders.

1. Start Distiller, as described earlier in this chapter. Click the **Settings** menu and click **Font Locations**. The Adobe Distiller – Font Locations dialog box appears.

2. Click **Add**. In the Browse For Folder dialog box that appears, locate the folder you want, and click **OK**.

3. If you want to use only PostScript fonts when you have both TrueType and PostScript versions of the same font, click **Ignore TrueType Versions Of Standard PostScript Fonts**.

4. To remove a fonts folder, select the folder path and click **Remove**.

5. When you have finished using the Font Locations dialog box, click **OK**.

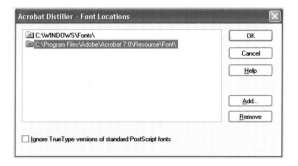

TIP

It is a good practice to embed fonts from within the program that originally created the PostScript file and not in Distiller. This way, you know that what you see in the authoring program is what is in the PDF file.

Use Watched Folders

Distiller provides a way to automatically convert PostScript files to PDF files by setting up one or more (up to 100) folders, called *watched folders*, that Distiller periodically reviews. Any PostScript files that it finds are converted unless a PostScript file is marked read-only. You can create separate PDF conversion and security settings for a watched folder, and you can specify that an existing group of PDF conversion settings be used with it. (Security settings will be discussed in Chapter 10.)

To create and use watched folders:

1. Open Windows Explorer and create a folder for use as a watched folder.

2. Start Distiller, click the **Settings** menu, and click **Watched Folders**. The Watched Folder dialog box appears.

3. Click **Add Folder**. Locate the folder you just created, and click **OK**. The folder is added to the list in the Watched Folders dialog box, as shown in Figure 5-11.

4. In the list, click the new watched folder, and then click **Edit Settings**. The same six settings folders described earlier in "Customize Distiller Settings" are displayed within a new grouping called "Folder." You can edit these settings, as discussed earlier in the "Customize Distiller Settings" section. When you are finished, click **OK**. The PDF Settings dialog box closes, and a Settings icon is displayed next to the Watched Folder icon.

5. If you want to attach an existing settings group to a watched folder, click the watched folder and click **Load Settings**. Click the settings group you want to use, and click **Load**. Again, the Settings icon is displayed next to the Watched Folder icon.

6. To remove the settings group from a watched folder, click the watched folder and click **Clear Settings**.

7. To remove a folder from the Watched Folders list, click the watched folder and click **Remove Folder**. This does not delete the folder or even the In and Out folders, it just removes it from Distiller's watch list.

8. When you are finished establishing settings for watched folders, click

Figure 5-11: If you create a lot of PostScript files and convert them to PDF files, set up a watched folder to automatically handle the conversion.

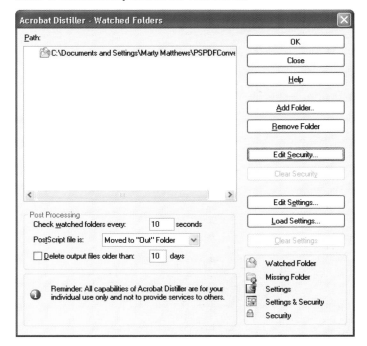

NOTE

If you use the Load Settings command after using the Edit Settings command, the loaded settings file replaces all of the previous settings made during editing. In other words, the settings are not cumulative.

NOTE

When you tell Acrobat that a particular folder is a watched folder by placing it in the Watched Folder list, Acrobat creates two subsidiary folders, In and Out, under the new watched folder. You must put the files you want to create in the In folder, and when the file is converted, Acrobat will put both the original PostScript file and the new PDF file in the Out folder.

NOTE

When Distiller finishes a conversion, a log file, which can be opened in Notepad, is created, showing any problems, such as font substitutions and incorrect color types. (You can also see this information in the Distiller window.)

NOTE

Distiller has several security features that allow you to add encryption and passwords and restrict what can be done with a file. Chapter 10 describes these features in detail.

OK. If you reopen Windows Explorer and look at the folder you created for PostScript conversions, you will see that it now has two subfolders, In and Out, as well as a Folder settings group.

9. In Windows Explorer, place a PostScript file in the In subfolder; or, from another program, save a PostScript file to the In subfolder. In Windows Explorer, open the **Out** subfolder and wait. In short order (depending on the size of the file), you will see both the new PDF file and the original PostScript file appear.

Use Preflight

Preflight allows you to look at and test a PDF file to see if it meets a user-defined set of criteria (Preflight profiles) needed for commercial printing. Preflight is a way of making sure that when you use a PDF file to print several to many thousand copies, they will turn out satisfactory. Preflight is primarily used by graphics professionals to review files that have been submitted for commercial printing. It can also be used to gather information about a PDF, such as whether all graphics use the same color scheme, and whether all needed fonts are embedded.

In this section we'll take a brief look at Preflight and what you can quickly do with it. We will not look at how profiles are created and edited, and we will only examine the summary information that Preflight generates.

Start Preflight

Preflight works on a PDF file already open in Acrobat.

1. Start Acrobat and load the desired PDF file.
2. Click the **Advanced** menu and click **Preflight**.

   –Or–

   Click the **Preflight** tool on the Print Production toolbar.

In either case, the Preflight dialog box appears, as shown in Figure 5-12.

Select and Execute a Profile

In the top of the Preflight dialog box is a list of profiles. If you scroll down the list, you will see that the first 16 are comprehensive profiles that test a number of features needed for commercial printing. Below this are a number of tests that look at specific things, such as compatibility with a given version of Acrobat and images that are not CMYK (a four-color color scheme based on cyan, magenta, yellow, and black). To select and execute a profile:

1. Click **Preflight Only Pages** and enter a range of pages.
2. Scroll through the list of profiles until you find the one you want.
3. Click that profile and click **Execute**.

   –Or–

   Double-click the profile.

Review Results

The results depend on the profile and what Preflight finds. If you select one of the simple single-function profiles, you will get commensurate results. For example, if you select "List Images Not CMYK," you will get a corresponding list.

Figure 5-12: Preflight tests how well a PDF file compares to a given profile.

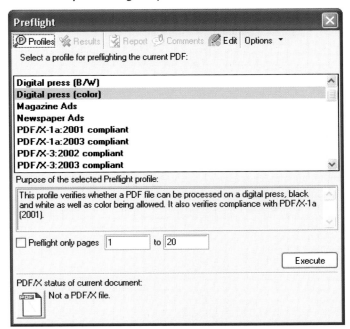

QUICKSTEPS

USING PDF OPTIMIZER

PDF Optimizer is another tool frequently used by graphics professionals. It provides a number of ways in which the size of PDF files can be reduced. Start out by analyzing a file's space usage and then run Optimizer and examine the results.

Like Distiller and Preflight, Optimizer has a large number of settings that you can customize. This QuickSteps will only review what you can quickly do with Optimizer. The default settings work in many situations to produce efficient files.

ANALYZE SPACE USAGE

1. In Acrobat, with the file you want optimized open, click the **Advanced** menu and click **PDF Optimizer**. The PDF Optimizer dialog box appears.
2. Click **Audit Space Usage** in the upper-right corner. The Audit Space Usage dialog box appears and displays the space usage in various areas.

RUN OPTIMIZER

1. In Acrobat, with the file you want optimized open, click the **Advanced** menu and click **PDF Optimizer**. The PDF Optimizer dialog box appears.
2. Review the six pages of settings by clicking each page in the list on the left.
3. When you are ready, click **OK** in the lower-right corner. In the Save Optimized As dialog box, locate the folder and enter the name to use with the optimized file. Click **Save**. The file is optimized and saved.
4. Click the **Audit Space Usage** command again and see the difference.

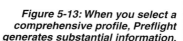

If you select one of the more complex profiles, you will get more comprehensive results, as shown in Figure 5-13. These results can be expanded and displayed in context using comments on a PDF page.

1. Click the plus sign (+) next to a summary item to display additional details.
2. Double-click a detail item to have it identified with a dotted red border on the PDF page.
3. Click **Show Detail Information About Document** at the bottom of the dialog box, and scroll to the bottom.
4. Click **Comments** in the toolbar to place comments in the PDF file. When the process is complete, point at the comments with your mouse cursor to read them. If you want to remove the comments, click **Options** and click **Remove Preflight Comments**.
5. Select a detail item and click **Show Selected Page Element In Snap View**. If the item can be displayed in Snap View (not all can), a small Snap View dialog box will appear, displaying the item.
6. Click **Report** in the toolbar to have a comprehensive report produced in a PDF. The Save As dialog box appears, providing you with the opportunity to locate and name the file. When finished, click **Save**. The report is opened in Acrobat.
7. When done with Preflight, click the **Close** button.

NOTE

Most of the tasks described in this chapter work the same for Acrobat or Reader. Those features that are available only to Acrobat users are noted.

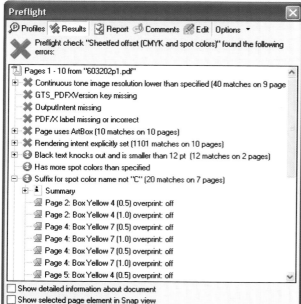

Figure 5-13: When you select a comprehensive profile, Preflight generates substantial information.

How to...

- *Using the Search PDF Pane or the Find Toolbar*
- *Search a PDF File with the Find Toolbar*
- *Search Multiple PDF Files with the Search PDF Pane*
- *Refining a Multidocument Search*
- *Do an Advanced Search*
- *Use Boolean Search Operators*
- *Search PDF Files on the Internet*
- *Setting Search Preferences*
- *Prepare for Indexing*
- *Creating Appropriate File Names*
- *Build an Index*
- *Customize an Index*
- *Search Using an Index*
- *Rebuild and Update an Index*

Chapter 6

Searching and Indexing PDF Files

A great benefit of being able to put many different types of documents into a common format, such as the Portable Data Format (PDF), is that you can then easily search and index them. In this chapter you'll see how to set up and perform a search on one or more PDF files and how to prepare, build, search, and customize an index of PDF files.

Search PDF Files

In earlier chapters, especially in Chapter 3, you can see how to create PDF files from many different sources and locations, including the Internet; the description of the Organizer in Chapter 2 shows how files can be grouped into collections. Acrobat allows you to search a particular PDF file or a file system drive of PDF files. You can search on a local drive, on a network drive, or on the Internet. You can search the textual part of the file, as well as search attachments, comments, bookmarks, digital signatures, form fields, object data, document properties, metadata, and structure.

USING THE SEARCH PDF PANE OR THE FIND TOOLBAR

You can search a single PDF file using either the Search PDF pane or the Find toolbar. In both cases you can search for a partial word, a whole word, or a series of words in the open file. Also, in both cases Acrobat will search the text, comments, bookmarks, form fields, digital signatures, and layers.

THE FIND TOOLBAR

The Find toolbar allows you to enter one or more words, and then click **Next** or **Previous** to search for that word or words in the PDF file that is open on the screen.

THE SEARCH PDF PANE

The Search PDF pane, in addition to the Find toolbar tasks, allows you to search multiple PDF files on local or network drives, or on the Internet; do complex searches including using Boolean expressions (search criteria statements connected with logical "ands" and "ors"); and search attachments, object data (for images and other objects), metadata (file properties), and PDF indexes.

Search a PDF File with the Find Toolbar

For a simple search of the PDF file that is currently open, the Find toolbar is probably the quickest and easiest method.

1. If it isn't already running, start Acrobat and open the PDF file you want to search.

2. Click the **View** menu, click **Toolbars**, and click **Find**.

   –Or–

   Right-click any toolbar and click **Find**. The Find toolbar will open.

3. Type the word or words in the Find text box.

4. Click the **Find** down arrow to review the available search options:

   - **Whole Words Only** will ignore instances in which the word you entered is a part of another word.

   - **Case-Sensitive** will ignore instances in which the capitalization is different from what you entered.

   - **Include Bookmarks** will search bookmarks for your search word(s).

   - **Include Comments** will search comments for your search word(s).

   - **Open Full Acrobat Search** will open the Search PDF pane.

5. Select the options that you want, and then click **Next** to search in a forward direction in the document, or click **Previous** to search in a backward direction. When an instance of the word or words is found, it is highlighted.

6. Continue to click **Next** or **Previous** to successively highlight your word or words in the document.

7. When you are done, click **Close** in the Find toolbar.

   –Or–

   With the Find toolbar selected, press **ESC**.

2. The contents of the insertion point.

USE THE **CLIPBOARD**

The *Clipboard* is a loca

NOTE

In earlier versions of Acrobat, PDF files had to be indexed before they could be searched. More recent versions no longer require indexing.

TIP

Some of the searching described here can also be done in Adobe Reader 7.

TIP

To remove the highlight from a word that is selected, click anywhere else in the document pane.

NOTE

If you use the Find toolbar a lot, you can dock it with the other toolbars at the top of the Acrobat window by simply dragging it to an empty space.

Search Multiple PDF Files with the Search PDF Pane

For a more comprehensive search tool that allows you to search a number of files or documents at one time, use the Search PDF pane.

1. Click the **Search** tool in the File toolbar.

   –Or–

   Press **SHIFT+CTRL+F** to open the Search PDF pane.

2. Type the word or words in the text box for which you want to search.

3. Click **All PDF Documents In,** and click the down arrow below it to open a drop-down menu of areas to search on your computer or the network to which you are attached.

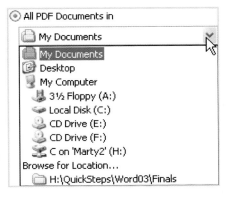

4. If you would like to identify a particular folder or folders to search, click **Browse For Location** to open the Browse For Folder dialog box.

5. Click the **plus sign** on the left of the computer, network, drive, or parent folder, as necessary, to identify the folder(s) you want to search.

6. Click the search option you want to use:

   - **Whole Words Only** will ignore instances in which the word you entered is a part of another word.

   - **Case-Sensitive** will ignore instances in which the capitalization is different from what you entered.

   - **Include Bookmarks** will search bookmarks for your search word(s).

   - **Include Comments** will search comments for your search word(s).

Search PDF

Finished searching for:
document

Finished searching in:
\\Marty2\c\QuickSteps\Word03\Finals

Documents found:
12

Total instances found:
908

➡ New Search

Results:

⊞ 📄 860801.indd
⊞ 📄 860802.indd
⊞ 📄 860803.indd
⊞ 📄 860804.indd
⊞ 📄 860805.indd
⊞ 📄 860806.indd
⊞ 📄 860807.indd
⊞ 📄 860809.indd

Sort by: Relevance Ranking ▾
☑ Collapse file paths

➡ Refine Search Results

➡ Done

➡ **Find a word in the current PDF document**

Figure 6-1: The initial response to a multidocument search is to list the documents where a match was found.

7. Click **Search**. The Search PDF pane will display the results of the search, as you can see in Figure 6-1.

8. If the results of your search lists two or more files, as does Figure 6-1, open those files by clicking the **plus sign** on the left of the file name to display all of the instances where the sought-after word or words appears.

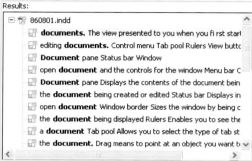

9. You can choose to sort the Results list by the relevance ranking (how close the result is to the search criteria), the date modified, the file name, or the location.

10. Click one of the results to open the document and specific page in the document pane. Initially the found words may not be tagged and a dialog box will appear asking if you want to do that; the dialog box will also ask the order in which you want to read the file.

11. If your entries were not tagged, click **Start** to prepare to tag the file. If you closed the Search PDF pane, click **Search** in the File toolbar to reopen it, and then click one of the results in the document you just tagged. The page will open with the word or words tagged, as shown in Figure 6-2.

12. When you have your search results as needed, click **Done** at the bottom of the Search PDF pane, and close the open PDF file if needed.

TIP

While you are working through the results of a search, you can click **Hide** to close the Search PDF pane and get a larger view of the PDF file. You can then reopen the pane and see the same search results by clicking the **Search** tool in the File toolbar. After you click **Done** in the Search PDF pane, this ability goes away.

REFINING A MULTIDOCUMENT SEARCH

After doing a multidocument search, you may find that you have more results than you want. You can help this situation by refining your search. In essence, doing a search within your previous search results.

1. In the Search results view of the Search PDF pane, click **Refine Search Results** at the bottom of the pane. A slightly modified Advanced search pane opens.

2. Enter additional search criteria using the fields and techniques described in "Do an Advanced Search."

3. Click **Refine Search Results**.

4. Repeat steps 1 through 3 as many times as you wish to further refine the search.

5. When you have completed your search, click **Done**.

Do an Advanced Search

If you need to do a sophisticated search with more complex criteria than is available with the basic search, you can do so with Acrobat's Advanced Search Options.

1. Click the **Search** tool in the File toolbar.

2. Click **Use Advanced Search Options** at the bottom of the Search PDF pane. The Search PDF pane will change to display a more detailed set of criteria-selection features, as shown in Figure 6-3.

3. Type in the top text box the word or words for which you want to search.

4. Click the **Return Results Containing** down arrow to open the drop-down list. Click the way you want your search words used (some of these options are available only with multidocument searches):

   - **Match Exact Word Or Phrase** identifies the exact matches to everything in the search-for text box.

Figure 6-2: The ability to search multiple PDF documents can be very important in changing any large document, such as a book.

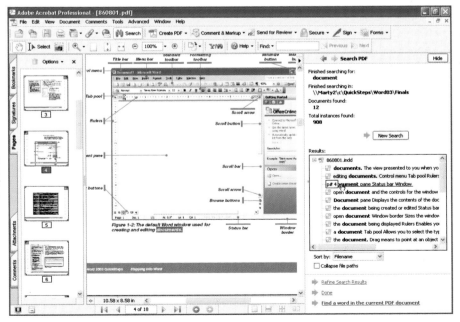

Figure 6-3: Acrobat's advanced search features allow you to specify a sophisticated set of criteria.

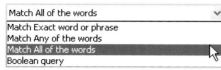

- **Match Any Of the Words** identifies the matches to any one or more of the words in the search-for text box.

- **Match All Of The Words** identifies the matches in which all of the words in the search text box appear, but not necessarily in the same sequence or together.

- **Boolean Query** identifies the matches to a Boolean expression (see "Use Boolean Search Criteria" later in this chapter).

5. Click the **Look In** down arrow, and click the folder, index, or drive you want to search. To select a particular folder, click **Browse For Location** and click the **plus sign** on the left of the computer, network, drive, or parent folder, as necessary, to identify the folder(s) you want to search.

6. If you wish, click the **Use These Additional Criteria** down arrow for the left drop-down list. This displays a set of file attributes that can be compared to the criteria that you supply.

7. If you are using the Additional Criteria, click the file attribute you want to use, click the relational value, and enter the criteria.

8. Click the search options you want to use:

- **Whole Words Only** will ignore instances in which the word you entered is a part of another word.

- **Case-Sensitive** will ignore instances in which the capitalization is different from what you entered.

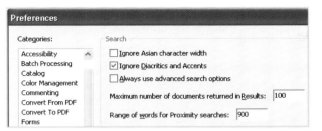

- **Proximity** identifies the matches where two or more words are within a certain number of words of each other, which you specify by clicking the **Edit** menu, clicking **Preferences**, and clicking **Search**. For example, if you search for "advanced search" and "proximity" and leave the default 900 words for the proximity preference, you'll get back all instances where "advanced search" and "proximity" are within 900 words of each other.

- **Stemming** identifies the matches that stem from the word you provide. For example, if you search for "quick," you'll get back instances of "quickly," "quicker," "QuickSteps," and "Quicken."

- **Include Bookmarks** will search bookmarks for your search word(s).

- **Include Comments** will search comments for your search word(s).

9. Click **Search**. The Search PDF pane will display the results of the search.

See "Search Multiple PDF Files with the Search PDF Pane" and the "Refining a Multidocument Search" QuickSteps for handling the results of a search.

Use Boolean Search Operators

Boolean operators allow you to limit or expand your search by including these operators in the phrase for which you are searching. Boolean operators include:

- **AND** (you can also use **&**) has the same effect as using Match All Of The Words, which limits the search by requiring the words or phrases on both sides of AND be present in order for a match to occur. For example, if you search for water AND mountains, you will get only the matches that contain both "water" and "mountains."

- **OR** (you can also use I) has the same effect as using Match Any Of The Words, which expands the search by allowing a match if the words or phrases on either side of OR are present. For example, if you search for water OR mountains, you will get only the matches that contain "water" or "mountains" or both.

- **Exclusive OR**, which uses ^, finds a match if the words or phrases on either side of ^ are present—but both words and phrases cannot be present. For example, if you search for water ^ mountains, you will get only the matches that contain either "water" or "mountains"; you will not get matches that contain both "water" and "mountains."

- **NOT** (you can also use !) limits the search by excluding the cases that contain the word or phrase following NOT. For example, if you search for `NOT mountains`, you will get only the matches that do not contain "mountains."

- **Quotation marks** around a phrase have the same effect as using Match Exact Word Or Phrase, so if you want to use one of the Boolean operators as a search word and not as an operator, you can put quotes around it or the entire phrase. For example, if you search for `"mountains and water"` you will get only matches to the exact phrase "mountains and water."

- **Parentheses** around a phrase specify that it should be evaluated before the remainder of the search-for text. For example, if you search for `"moderate climate" & (mountains | water)`, matches with "mountains" or "water" will be found first and then from those results, "moderate climate" matches will be found.

To perform a Boolean search:

1. Click the **Search** tool in the File toolbar, and click **Use Advanced Search Options** at the bottom of the Search PDF pane.

2. Type in the top text box the Boolean phrase for which you want to search (see the previous examples).

3. Click the **Return Results Containing** down arrow to open the drop-down list, and click **Boolean Query**.

4. Click the **Look In** down arrow, and click the folder, index, or drive you want to search. To select a particular folder, click **Browse For Location** and click the **plus sign** on the left of the computer, network, drive, or parent folder, as necessary, to identify the folder(s) you want to search.

5. If you wish, use the Additional Criteria; click the search options you want to use, as described in "Do an Advanced Search" earlier in this chapter.

6. Click **Search**. The Search PDF pane will display the results of the search.

See "Search Multiple PDF Files with the Search PDF Pane" and the "Refining a Multidocument Search" QuickSteps for handling the results of a search.

NOTE

Acrobat does not support using wildcards, such as * and ?, in its searches.

Search PDF Files on the Internet

PDF and other files on the Internet can be searched for a particular word or phrase.

1. Click the **Search** tool in the File toolbar, and click **Search The Internet Using Yahoo!** at the bottom of the Search PDF pane. The Internet version of the Search PDF pane will open.

2. Type in the top text box the word or phrase for which you want to search.

3. Click the **How Precise Would You Like To Make Your Search** down arrow, and click one of the options:

   - **Match Exact Word Or Phrase** identifies the exact matches to everything in the search-for text box.

   - **Match Any Of the Words** identifies the matches to one or more of the words in the search-for text box.

   - **Match All Of The Words** identifies the matches in which all of the words in the search-for text box appear, but not necessarily in the same sequence or together.

4. If you wish, click **Search Only In PDF files**, and then click **Search The Internet**. Your Internet browser will open with some of the search results that were found, as shown in Figure 6-4.

5. Click any of the entries to open and read them, and/or click **Next** at the bottom of the window to view the next set of entries.

6. When you are finished, close your browser.

TIP

If you use the Search The Internet pane a lot, you can include it with your toolbars and directly open the pane with a single click. If the toolbar is not displayed, click the **View** menu, click **Toolbars**, and click **Search The Internet**.

QUICKSTEPS

SETTING SEARCH PREFERENCES

There are several overall search preferences that you can set to tailor Acrobat's searching to your tastes.

1. Click the **Edit** menu, click **Preferences**, and in the Categories list, click **Search**. The Search option of the Preferences dialog box will open, as you can see in Figure 6-5.

2. Click to check or uncheck the options that are correct for you:

- **Ignore Asian Character Width** will treat both full- and half-width Asian characters as the same.

- **Ignore Diacritics And Accents** will treat both plain characters and the same characters with diacritics and accents as the same.

- **Always Use Advanced Search Options** will cause the Advanced Search options to be immediately displayed when you open the Search PDF pane.

- **Maximum Number Of Documents Returned In Results** allows you to enter the maximum number, from 1 to 10,000, of documents that will be returned from a search.

- **Range Of Words For Proximity Searches** allows you to enter a number of words, from 1 to 10,000, that will be the maximum number of words separating the searched-for items in a proximity search.

- **Enable Fast Find** will store information on your hard disk about frequently accessed PDF files so they can be searched faster.

- **Maximum Cache Size** allows you to enter the maximum number, from 5 to 10,000, of megabytes of disk space that will be used to store PDF information that will be used for fast searching.

- **Purge Cache Contents** will delete the temporary information stored on your hard disk and used to speed up searching PDF files.

3. When you are finished, click **OK**.

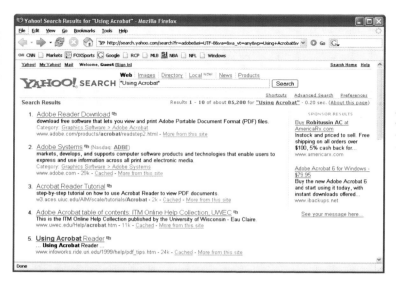

*Figure 6-4:
The results
from an Acrobat
Internet search
can be extensive
unless you limit
the search.*

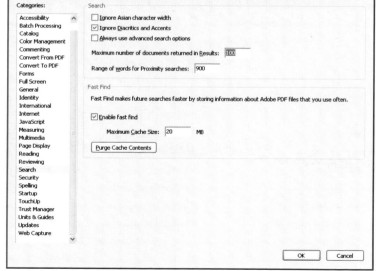

*Figure 6-5:
Search
preferences let
you structure
how Acrobat
will perform
searches.*

NOTE

An *index*, as it is used here with PDF files, is an alphabetical list of all the words, numbers, and objects (graphics and nontextual items) contained in one or more files. Each PDF file is searched for content and properties, and the results are cataloged in one or more index files (.idx). The set of index files are managed by and accessed through a .pdx file with the same name as the folder that contains the .idx files.

TIP

If a file that you want to index was brought into a computer using a scanner, make sure that the scanned image was converted to searchable text. See Chapter 3 for a discussion of this.

TIP

A complex or deeply nested folder structure will slow down the searching.

NOTE

While you could use the existing folder structure that currently contains the files on your disk, it is recommended that you create a new folder or folder structure. You can then copy the files to it, package the files with the index, possibly put it on a CD, and make the search process more efficient.

Index PDF Files

While Acrobat has a powerful search capability, it is often more efficient to create an index of a set of PDF files, enabling a high-speed search using that index. The creation of a PDF index is done with Acrobat's Catalog feature, which is applied to a specific group or collection of PDF files.

Prepare for Indexing

To prepare a set of PDF files for indexing:

1. Create a folder or simple folder structure to hold the files to be indexed.
2. Divide large files into smaller logical sections to improve the search speed.
3. Review each of the files as you move them into the folder structure and make sure:

   - The file name can be read by all of the types of computers that will use the file. See the "Creating Appropriate Files Names" QuickFacts in this chapter.
   - The file's properties have all the searchable information you want. See "Set File Properties for Searching" later in this chapter.
   - The files are the latest versions and are complete.

PREPARE FOLDERS

An index is best kept with the files that it indexes. Create and use a folder or a simple folder structure to contain both the PDF files and the index.

1. Click **Start** to open the Start menu, and click **My Computer**. Click **Folders** on the toolbar to open the Folders pane.
2. In the Folders pane, click the **plus signs** on the left of the necessary drives and folders until you have opened the folder that you want to use for indexing.
3. Right-click in the right detail pane, click **New**, and then click **Folder**. Type a name for the new folder. Double-click the new folder to open it.
4. Repeat step 3 to create the full folder structure you want. For example, Figure 6-6 shows the folder structure used to hold the PDF files for some of the QuickSteps books.

DIVIDE FILES

Large files take more time to search and provide less efficient indexing. If you have a large document that has logical breaks, it makes sense to divide the document into those segments so that the file you open is closer to what you are looking for. To divide a large file:

1. In Windows Explorer locate the PDF file you want to divide, and double-click it to start Acrobat and load the file.

2. Locate the first group of pages that you want in a separate file. Click the **Document** menu, click **Extract Pages**, and enter the **From** and **To** page numbers in the Extract Pages dialog box.

3. Click **OK**. A new document will open in Acrobat with just the pages you selected. Review that file to make sure it has what you want.

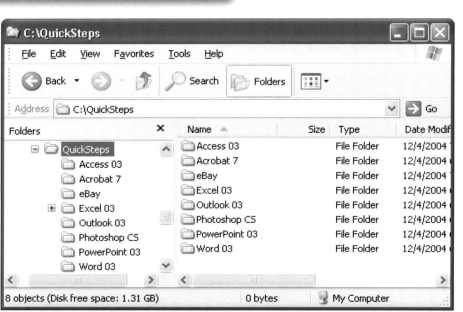

Figure 6-6: The folder structure used to index a set of PDF files should not be more than three levels deep.

CREATING APPROPRIATE FILE NAMES

As you prepare PDF files for indexing, it is important that the names you give the files be readable in all environments in which they will be used. The first step is to determine where the files and index will be opened.

If it is likely that a wide variety of systems will use the file, then the DOS file naming system of an eight-character file name and a three-character extension should be used for files, and an eight-character name should be used for folders. For example, MyFile01.pdf.

If you are using the files and index exclusively on either Mac or Windows systems, then you can, of course, use the conventions for that system. If your files and index will be used on both Mac and Windows, then use the Windows conventions because the Mac is more forgiving.

If you are going to put the files and index on a CD, then you need to consider which CD file system you will use: Joliet, UDF, and ISO 9660 are three that are in common use:

- **ISO 9660** is the original international file-system standard for CDs and is readable on most systems, including Windows, Mac, DOS, UNIX, and Linux. While there are some extensions to the basic ISO 9660 standard (Joliet is one of them), when the ISO 9660 standard is used to refer to a CD file system it implies DOS naming conventions of eight-character file names with three-character extensions and eight-character folder names.

- **Joliet** is a frequently used CD file system on Windows-based systems with file names of up to 64 characters, including spaces. It also has a secondary DOS 8.3 name convention usable on a Mac.

- **UDF** (Universal Disk Format) is compatible with DVD devices and is used to incrementally write only a portion of a CD at a time, such as DirectCD. UDF allows file names up to 127 characters, but most CD writing systems limit UDF to 64 characters for compatibility with Joliet.

4. Click **File** and click **Save As**. Locate the new folder you created for indexing (see "Pre-pare Folders" earlier in this chapter) in the Save As dialog box that opens.

5. Enter the file name that you want to use (see the "Creating Appropriate File Names" QuickFacts in this chapter), and click **Save**.

Leave the new file open so you can set file properties for searching next.

SET FILE PROPERTIES FOR SEARCHING

A PDF file's properties provide the opportunity to enter selected information about a file that can be easily indexed and searched. This information is called *metadata*: data that defines other data—a file's worth in this case. To set file properties:

1. With the file whose properties you want to set open in Acrobat, click the **File** menu and click **Document Properties**. The Document Properties dialog box will open.

TIP

You can open and change a PDF file's properties directly from Windows Explorer without opening the document. In Windows Explorer, right-click the file, click **Properties**, and click the **PDF** tab. While this dialog box looks different, it is the same information as in the Properties dialog box opened from Acrobat.

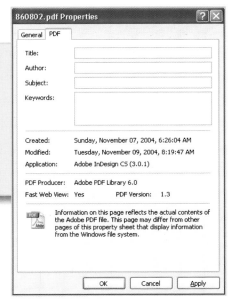

2. Fill in the Title, Author, and Subject fields in a consistent manner with other documents in the set of files you are planning to index.

3. Fill in the Keywords field with words you want indexed in the document, as shown in Figure 6-7. Place either commas or semicolons between the keywords. Acrobat will automatically change commas to semicolons.

4. Click **Additional Metadata**. You will see the document's descriptive information you entered in the preceding steps. Below that you can enter additional copyright information, which is valuable in many circumstances.

The Advanced information, opened by clicking **Advanced** in the left column, is a means for programs that create PDF files to add advanced indexing information and is beyond the scope of this book.

5. When finished, click **OK** twice to close both Properties dialog boxes. Save and close your Acrobat file.

Document Properties

Description | Security | Fonts | Initial View | Custom | Advanced

Description

File: 860802.pdf

Title: Microsoft Office Word 03 QuickSteps Chapter 2

Author: Marty Matthews

Subject: Working with Documents

Keywords: start a document; Templates; Wizards; enter text; delete text; copy text; move text; find text; replace text; check spelling; check grammer; save a document; close a document

Created: 11/7/2004 6:26:04 AM

Modified: 12/20/2004 11:20:58 AM

Application: Adobe InDesign CS (3.0.1)

[Additional Metadata...]

Advanced

PDF Producer: Adobe PDF Library 6.0

PDF Version: 1.3 (Acrobat 4.x)

Location: H:\QuickSteps\Word03\Finals\

File Size: 5.64 MB (5,916,518 Bytes)

Page Size: 10.58 x 8.58 in   Number of Pages: 28

Tagged PDF: No   Fast Web View: Yes

Help   OK   Cancel

Figure 6-7: A PDF file's properties provide a way to make certain important information gets indexed.

Build an Index

Once you have collected copies of all the PDF files in a folder or folder structure (see "Prepare Folders" and "Divide Files" earlier in this chapter), prepared the files by giving them appropriate names (see the "Creating Appropriate File Names" QuickFacts in this chapter), updated the file properties (see "Set File Properties for Searching" earlier in this chapter), and made sure the files are complete and the most recent versions, you can begin the actual process of indexing.

1. In Acrobat click the **Advanced** menu, click **Catalog**, and click **New Index**. The New Index Definition dialog box opens.

2. Enter the title and description for the documents that you are indexing.

3. Click **Options** and select the custom features and properties that you want to use as described in "Customize an Index," next in this chapter.

4. Under Include These Directories, click **Add**, open the drive and folders needed to locate the folder or parent folder containing the files to be indexed, and click **OK**.

5. Under Exclude These Subdirectories, click **Add**, open the drive and folders needed to locate the folders containing the files you do not want indexed, and click **OK**.

6. When you have selected the folders and entered the text you want (see Figure 6-8), click **Build** to begin the process of building an index.

Figure 6-8: You can build an index from any number of folders on your disk or any disk in a network.

7. Select the folder where you want the index stored. Under almost all circumstances you want this to be the folder or parent folder containing the files being indexed, which should already be selected. When you are ready, click **Save**. During the index-building process, you will be shown the progress and what files are being processed, as you can see in Figure 6-9.

8. When the index is complete, click **Close**.

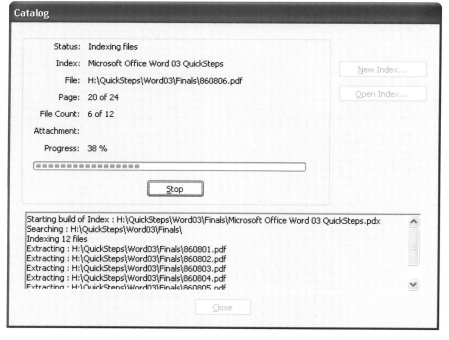

Figure 6-9: Acrobat shows you the progress of building an index.

Customize an Index

Acrobat gives you a number of ways that you can customize building an index through the New Index Definition Options button and Options dialog box.

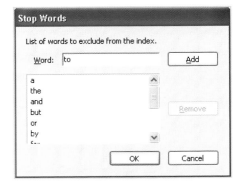

1. From the New Index Definition dialog box (see "Build an Index" immediately above), click the **Options** button to open the Options dialog box.

2. Select the following options that are appropriate for the index that you are building:

   - **Do Not Include Numbers** allows you to exclude numbers from the index, which may remove a number of entries and speed up searching.

   - **Add IDs To Adobe PDF v1.0 Files** updates Acrobat version 1.0 files with identification numbers that are needed if the file names are shortened to the 8.3 DOS naming convention. Later versions of Acrobat files have IDs by default.

   - **Do Not Warn For Changed Document When Searching** will turn off the automatic warning that appears when a file is searched and it has changed since it was indexed.

3. Click **Custom Properties** to include in the indexing custom file properties that have already been added to the PDF files. Custom file properties sometimes come from other applications, such as Microsoft Office, but in all cases are beyond the scope of this book.

4. Click **XMP Fields** to include in the indexing custom XMP (Extensible Metadata Platform) fields that you enter. Enter an XMP field you want to include, and click **Add**. When you are done, click **OK**. XMP fields are a document's metadata (the contents of its Properties dialog box; see "Set File Properties for Searching" earlier in this chapter) in XML (Extensible Markup Language) format. Creating and using XMP fields and XML are beyond the scope of this book.

5. Click **Stop Words** to exclude from the indexing up to 500 words that you enter. Enter a word to exclude, and click **Add**. When you are done, click **OK**.

6. Click **Structure Tags** to include in the indexing tags that you enter. Enter a tag you want to include, and click **Add**. When you are done, click **OK**.

7. When you have completed the index customization that you want, click **OK** again.

NOTE

If you exclude numbers or certain words, it is a good idea to tell users of this in a Readme file that accompanies the index and files since they will not be able to search on these items.

Search Using an Index

After you have created an index, as described earlier in this chapter, you can use that index to greatly speed up the searching of a set of PDF files.

1. Click the **Search** tool in the File toolbar.
2. Click **Use Advanced Search Options** at the bottom of the Search PDF pane. The Search PDF pane will change to display a more detailed set of criteria-selection features.
3. Type in the top text box the word or words for which you want to search.
4. Click the **Return Results Containing** down arrow to open the drop-down list. Click the way you want your search words used.
5. Click the **Look In** down arrow, and click **Select Index**. The Index Selection dialog box will open. Click **Add**. The Open Index File dialog box will open, as shown in Figure 6-10.

Figure 6-10: An Acrobat .pdx index file is a small file that directs Acrobat to open a folder of the same name, which contains the actual indices.

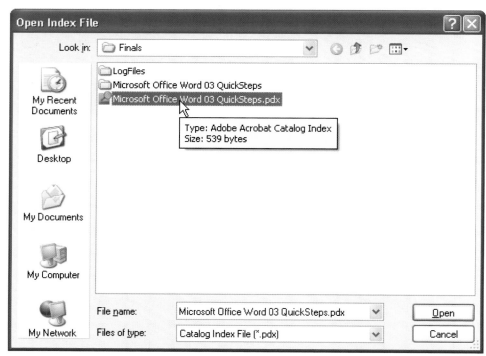

6. Locate and click the index file you want to use, and click **Open**. You are returned to the Index Selection dialog box. Make sure the index you want to use is checked and others are not.

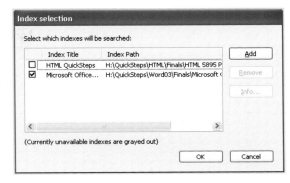

7. Click the index you want to use (not its check box), and click **Info** to look at the information that was entered for that index. Click **Close** when you are done looking at it.

8. When you have selected the index you want to use for the search, click **OK**.

9. Complete the remainder of the Search PDF pane as described in "Do an Advanced Search" earlier in this chapter. Click **Search**. The Search PDF pane will display the results of the search.

   See "Search Multiple PDF Files with the Search PDF Pane" and the "Refining a Multi-document Search" QuickSteps for handling the results of a search.

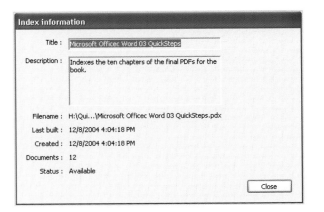

Rebuild and Update an Index

As files change and new files are added to a set of PDF files, you will want to revise the index you have created for that set.

1. In Acrobat click the **Advanced** menu, click **Catalog**, and click **Open Index**. The Open Index File dialog box opens.

2. Locate and double-click the index (.pdx file) you want to revise. The Index Definition dialog box opens, as shown in Figure 6-11.

3. As desired, change the title, description, and directories that are included or excluded.

4. Click one of the following buttons at the bottom of the dialog box to perform the actions described:

   - **Build** to update the existing index by adding new entries and marking deleted entries as being invalid.

   - **Rebuild** to completely replace the existing index with a new one.

   - **Purge** to delete the existing index but not the .pdx file.

5. The index will be updated, rebuilt, or purged as you requested. Click **Close**.

Figure 6-11: An existing index can be updated, rebuilt, or purged.

Chapter 7
Collaborating with Acrobat

Capitalizing on the ubiquity of PDF as the "view anywhere, by anyone" file format, Acrobat includes a number of tools and features that support collaborative computing among PDF users, including those using Adobe Reader 7. Documents can be quickly set up for review among teams using browsers or e-mail, and can be easily tracked within Acrobat. Commenting tools (referred to as *annotation* tools in early Acrobat versions) allow you to identify text edits you want performed in a document; add notes, text highlights, and professional-looking stamps; and even record verbal remarks. You can further mark up a document by drawing your own graphic objects. Comments in PDF documents are conveniently organized and managed using the Comments tab. You can also summarize comments and compare versions of a document to identify differences between them.

If you want to send a document as an attachment to an e-mail and solicit comments and markups, you can use the PDFMaker toolbar and menu options in Office programs and in Internet Explorer to convert a document or web page, and e-mail it in one step. Open the document in its parent program, click **Convert To Adobe PDF And Email** (in Internet Explorer, click **Convert Web Page And Email**) from the Abode PDF menu or toolbar, and select where you want the PDF saved. After the document is converted and saved, the PDF is attached to a new e-mail message (see Figure 7-1).

Convert Web Page to PDF...
Add Web Page to Existing PDF...
Print Web Page...
Convert Web Page and Email...

Set Up and Track Reviews

Reviews allow all parties interested in providing input on a document to do so in an efficient, organized, and largely automated manner. Using a review, you can invite people to comment on a PDF document and track the responses received. You can set up a review with only the standard e-mail program, browser, and Internet connections you already have. Reviews can be *e-mail-based* or *browser-based*, or you can simply attach a PDF document to an e-mail and ask the recipient to add comments (this latter method does not work with Tracker, a tracking feature described later in the chapter).

Set Up an E-Mail-Based Review

An e-mail-based PDF document review is a four-part process:

- **Send An Invitation** starts the process by sending the PDF file as an e-mail attachment to one or more reviewers.

- **Review And Return Comments** allows reviewers to use Acrobat or Reader (if commenting is enabled) to add comments, mark up a PDF, and return the PDF to either the originator or to someone designated by the originator.

- **Integrate Comments** allows the recipient of the reviewer's comments to consolidate them into one master PDF document.

- **Track Reviews** provides the comments consolidator with a tool to assist him or her in organizing reviewed PDFs (see "Track Reviews" later in the chapter).

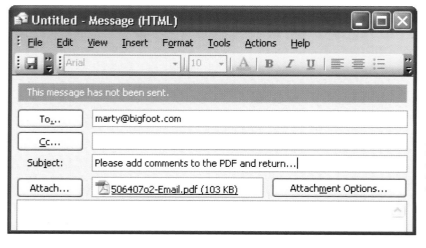

Figure 7-1: Converting an Office document or web page to a PDF, e-mailing it as an attachment, and inviting comments can be accomplished in a few clicks.

NOTE

Documents used in an e-mail-based review are tracked by Acrobat 7 and Reader 7. If you change the location of the tracked (master) PDF or make a copy using Save As, the new document becomes the tracked document and the original PDF becomes untracked. Opened, untracked documents do not display a Send Comments option on the File menu, nor is a Send Comments button displayed on the Commenting toolbar. In Adobe Reader 7, only tracked documents that have commenting enabled display any commenting and markup tools.

NOTE

E-mail- and browser-based reviewers must use Acrobat 6.0 or later, or, if you choose, Adobe Reader 7.0.

TIP

You can change the identity information that you pass to reviewers in e-mail- and browser-based reviews. Click the **Edit** menu, click **Preferences**, and click the **Identity** category. Make any changes and click **OK**.

SEND AN INVITATION

The review process starts by using a wizard to identify reviewers, identify who will receive comments (this is optional; by default, the person who sends a PDF for review is the person who receives the reviewed versions), and determine whether Adobe Reader can be used and which commenting tools can be used.

1. Click the **File** menu, click **Send For Review**, and click **Send By Email For Review**.

–Or–

Click **Send For Review** on the Tasks toolbar, and click **Send By Email For Review**.

In either case, first-time use displays the Identify Setup dialog box, where you establish your identity information to prospective reviewers. Fill out the form (see Figure 7-2), and click **Complete**.

Figure 7-2: Establish your identity as you want it displayed in the e-mail invitations received by reviewers.

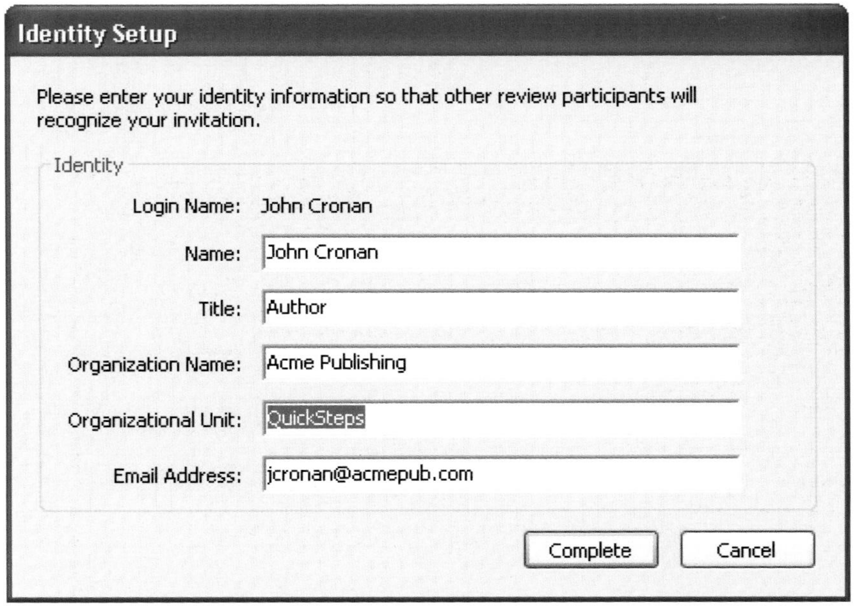

Identity Setup

Please enter your identity information so that other review participants will recognize your invitation.

Identity

Login Name:	John Cronan
Name:	John Cronan
Title:	Author
Organization Name:	Acme Publishing
Organizational Unit:	QuickSteps
Email Address:	jcronan@acmepub.com

Complete   Cancel

2. In the first step of the Send By Email For Review Wizard, select the PDF file you want to send for review. If you have a PDF displayed in the document pane, its name appears in the Specify A PDF File To Send drop-down list box.

–Or–

Click the **Specify A PDF File To Send** down arrow to select any opened PDF.

–Or–

Click **Browse** and locate and select the PDF you want to be reviewed. Click **Open**.

In all cases, click **Next**.

3. In the second step of the wizard, you invite reviewers and select reviewing options:

- Type reviewer e-mail addresses in the text box, separating entries by pressing ENTER; or click **Address Book** and double-click the e-mail addresses of the reviewers you want from your e-mail address book. Click **OK** to close the address book.

- Click **Customize Review Options** to determine who will receive the reviewers' comments (typically, you), whether you want to display the Drawing MarkUp toolbar for their use (see "Use Drawing Tools" later in the chapter), and whether Adobe Reader 7.0 users can add comments. Click **OK** when finished.

4. Click **Next**. The third and final step provides a boilerplate e-mail subject line that includes the PDF file name and a message telling the reviewer what to do (see Figure 7-3). Edit the text as needed, and click **Send Invitation** when done. The Outgoing Message Notification dialog box appears, informing you that the e-mail and attached PDF will be automatically sent (if configured) or that you can send it manually. Click **OK**.

Figure 7-3: Use standard reviewing instructions or add your own.

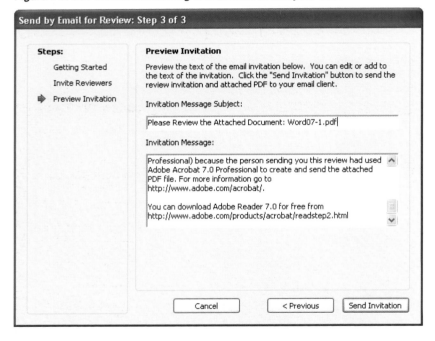

NOTE

Depending on how the originator sets up the review, a reviewer may or may not see the Commenting toolbar and How To pane. Whether or not these features appear can be set by clicking the **Comments** menu, clicking **Commenting Preferences**, and clicking the **Reviewing** category.

Recipients make comments (using the tools described later in this chapter) and click the **Send Comments** button in the toolbar of the PDF to return the comments by e-mail to the originator (or to the e-mail address designated in the Send By Email For Review Wizard).

1. Open the e-mail invitation, shown in Figure 7-4, review the instructions, and then open the attached PDF document in Acrobat or Reader 7 (if Reader was selected by the originator).

2. Click **Save** on the File toolbar, and save the PDF to your local system.

3. In the Acrobat/Reader window (see Figure 7-5), use the Commenting toolbar and other available commenting tools to make comments or mark up the document (see "Add Comments and Markups" later in the chapter). The How To pane provides additional information on the selected commenting tool.

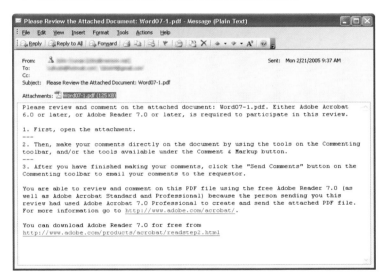

Figure 7-4: A prospective reviewer receives the PDF as an e-mail attachment along with boilerplate or custom instructions.

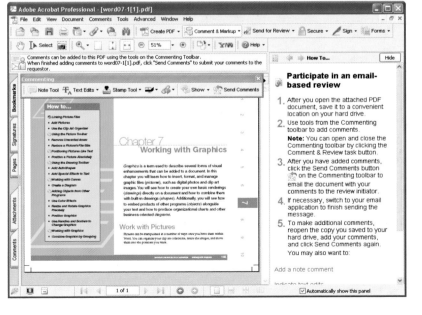

Figure 7-5: A received PDF document for review opens with the tools you need to add comments and relevant instructions.

NOTE

FDF files contain only the comments in a PDF, not the content. They have a much smaller file size than the related PDF file and are often used to import and export comments instead of transferring the entire PDF (see "Import and Export Comments" later in the chapter). Also, documents reviewed by Acrobat 6 users return an FDF file to the originator instead of a PDF.

NOTE

You might receive a security warning from a firewall program, such as the one included with Windows XP Service Pack 2, when you attempt to open reviewed documents. You will need to unblock access to Acrobat for the review process to continue.

TIP

You can merge comments from reviewed PDF documents into the master PDF at any time. With the PDF containing the reviewer's comments open, click the **Comments** menu and click **Merge Comments Onto Master PDF**. You will receive confirmation of the merge.

---

4. When finished, click **Send Comments** on the Commenting toolbar or on the File menu. In the Send Comments dialog box, you can:

   - Add or remove e-mail addresses to determine who receives the PDF with your comments. Type new e-mail addresses (separate each with a semicolon), or click **Address Book** and select names from your e-mail program's contacts list.

   - Edit the boilerplate subject line and message text if you want.

5. Click **Send** when complete and click **OK** after being notified that the message has been given to your default e-mail application.

INTEGRATE COMMENTS

The recipient of a reviewer's comments receives an e-mail with an attached PDF or FDF (file data format) file containing the comments.

1. Open the reviewer's e-mail, look for any changes to the boilerplate message text, and open the attached FDF or PDF file.

2. In the Merge Comments dialog box, click **Yes** to merge the reviewer's comments with the master document on your system. You will receive a confirmation that the comments were added successfully. Click **OK**.

   –Or–

   Click **No, Open This Copy Only** to open the file and view the comments without adding them to your original document.

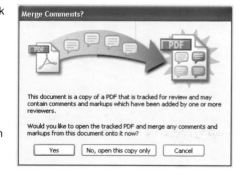

   In either case, a version of the original PDF opens and you will see the reviewer's comments. (If you merged the comments, they may be included with comments from previous reviewer(s).) Figure 7-6 shows an example of a reviewed PDF document by multiple reviewers.

Pencil markup

Text replacement comment

Note comment

Pop-up comment window

How To pane tailored to selected tool

Text insertion comment

ScreenTip-style box shows comment text and other information

Comments listed in the Comments tab

Adobe Acrobat Professional - [Word07-1.pdf]

File   Edit   View   Document   Comments   Tools   Advanced   Window   Help

Search   Create PDF   Comment & Markup   Send for Review   Secure   Sign   Forms

Select   80%   Help

Commenting

Note Tool   Text Edits   Stamp Tool   Show   Send Comments

How to...

- Linking Picture Files
- Add Pictures
- Use the Clip Art Organizer
- Using the Picture Toolbar
- Remove Unwanted Areas
- Reduce a Picture's File Size
- Positioning Pictures Like Text
- Position a Picture Absolutely
- Using the Drawing Toolbar
- Add AutoShapes
- Add Special Effects to Text
- Working with Curves
- Create a Diagram
- Adding Objects from Other Programs
- Use Color Effects
- Resize and Rotate Graphics Precisely
- Position Graphics
- Use Handles and Borders to Change Graphics
- Working with Graphics
- Combine Graphics by Grouping

DRAFT

Chapter 7
Working with Graphics

2/21/2005 10:35:04 AM
default   Options
I like the new title

Graphics is a term used to describe several forms of enhancements that can be added to a document. In this chapter you will learn how to insert, format, and manage graphic files (*pictures*), such as digital photos and clip art images. You will see how to create your own basic renderings (*drawings*) directly on a document and how to combine them with built-in drawings (*shapes*). Additionally, you will see how to embed products of other programs (*objects*) alongside your text and how to produce organizational charts and other business-oriented *diagrams*.

Work with Pictures

Pictures can be manipulated in a number of ways once you have them within Word. You can organize your clip art col...ages, and move them into the positions you want.

John Cronan
and Images

Microsoft Office Word 2003 QuickSteps   Working with Graphics   155

Expand All   Collapse All   Next   Previous   Reply   Delete   Set Status   Checkmark   Show   Sort By   Search   Print Comments   Options

John Cronan   Using

default   I like the new title

default   There has got to be a better word for this!

default

1 of 1

Automatically show this panel

Receive comments from an email-based review

Reviewers send their comments to you in an email attachment. When you open this attachment, a dialog box appears, asking if you want to merge the comments to your tracked PDF document. If you click Yes, your copy of the PDF document opens and the reviewer's comments are placed onto it. If you click No, Open This Copy Only, the reviewer's copy opens.

To manage comments more easily, merge the reviewer's comments to your tracked PDF document. If you later decide that you don't want to include the comments in your copy, you can easily hide or delete them by using options in the Comments List.

This feature is not available if you use Acrobat or Adobe Reader in a browser window.

You may also want to:

Show and hide comments

Print comments and markups

Comment and Markup

How To...   Hide

Figure 7-6: Comments in a reviewed PDF can be seen in several configurations.

QUICKSTEPS

SETTING UP A BROWSER-BASED REVIEW

Unlike an e-mail-based review, which can be set up by anyone with a common e-mail program and Internet connectivity and which retains the master PDF copy on a local system, a browser-based review requires a WebDAV (Web-based Distributed Authoring and Versioning) server to retain the PDF file and comments so all reviewers can access it. (The steps required to establish the WebDAV server and a comments repository are beyond the scope of this book.)

Once properly configured, a browser-based review works similarly to an e-mail-based review (see "Set Up an E-Mail-Based Review"). The primary differences in conducting the two reviews are that in a browser-based review, a reviewer opens the PDF in a browser instead of in Acrobat or Reader, and the reviewed comments are uploaded to an online comments repository instead of being e-mailed back to the originator.

1. Start a browser-based review by opening the PDF to be reviewed in Acrobat.

2. Click **Send For Review** on the File or Tasks menus, and click **Upload For Browser-Based Review**. Complete the Initiate An On-Line Review Wizard to send the document to the server and to send invitations by e-mail for others to review it.

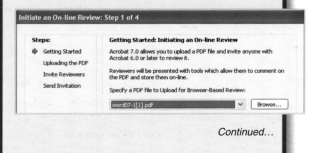

Continued…

Track Reviews

It's easy to become quickly overwhelmed by the various reviews you initiate or participate in. To help you organize and manage your reviews, Acrobat provides Tracker, a tool that monitors and categorizes reviewed content.

VIEW REVIEWED PDFS

1. Click **Send For Review** on the Tasks toolbar, and click **Tracker**. The Tracker window opens, as shown in Figure 7-7, and lists three categories of reviews in which you have documents involved:

   - **My Reviews** lists PDF documents for which you initiated the review.

   - **Participant Review** lists PDF documents someone sent you to be reviewed.

   - **Offline Documents** lists PDF documents you have downloaded from a browser-based review and stored on your local system.

Figure 7-7: Tracker lists your PDF documents involved in a review process and lets you manage and organize them.

NOTE

You can only drag a file into a folder if the file is not open.

2. To view or hide the documents in a review category, select the category in the left pane, and click **Expand** or **Collapse** on the Tracker toolbar.

–Or–

Click the plus (+) or minus (-) signs next to the review category name.

3. To see details for a PDF, click the file.
Information, such as whether it's browser- or e-mail-based and to whom and when it was sent, is displayed in the right pane.

4. Open any document listed in the left pane in Acrobat by clicking the document and clicking **Open** on the Tracker toolbar or by double-clicking the document.

ORGANIZE AND MANAGE REVIEWED PDFS

Use the Tracker toolbar (see Figure 7-7) to organize PDFs into folders, remove documents from Tracker, send reminders to reviewers, and add new reviews.

1. To add folders and move PDFs to them, click the review category to which you want to move the folder, and click **New Folder** on the Tracker toolbar. In the New Folder dialog box, type the folder name and click **OK**. Drag a PDF file directly under the new folder to add the PDF to the folder.

2. To remove a file or folder from Tracker, click it and click **Remove** on the Tracker toolbar.

3. To send e-mail reminders to reviewers, click the PDF, click **Manage** on the Tracker toolbar, and click **Email All Reviewers** to add your own comments to an e-mail message.

–Or–

Click **Send Review Reminder** to send a boilerplate reminder to reviewers.

4. To add new reviewers to a PDF, click the file, click **Manage**, and click **Invite Additional Reviewers**. Depending on the type of review the PDF is a part of, the Send By Email For Review Wizard or Initiate An On-Line Review Wizard opens, where you can add more e-mail addresses (see "Send An Invitation" earlier in the chapter).

Add Comments and Markups

Acrobat provides several groupings of tools that let you annotate (or otherwise explain, comment on, emphasize, or add your two cents to) a PDF document.

Work with Comments and Markups

The tools you use to make comments and markups share a common "comment and comment window" design. The *comment* (for example, a note icon, text highlight, rectangle, or stamp) displays in the PDF to provide a visual indication to the reader what the comment is about and where it's located. The *comment window* is a small pop-up window related to the comment where you can add text that, for example, explains the note, provides replacement text for crossed-out text, or provides amplifying information, such as review status and a reply flow. Figure 7-8 shows several examples of comments and comment windows.

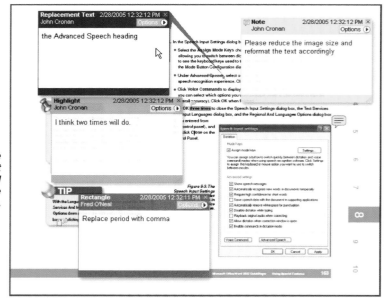

Figure 7-8: Comments are associated with pop-up comment windows in a matching color and with the comment type in the title bar of the comment window.

When working with several comments, you might find it easier to display the Properties bar, which provides one-click access to the most common properties for a particular comment type (or click **More** on the bar to open its Properties dialog box). To display the Properties bar, click the **View** menu, click **Toolbars**, and click **Properties Bar**. Click a comment to see the tailored Properties bar that is displayed.

VIEW COMMENT TEXT

You can view text in comment windows where they are located in the PDF document, or you can see all comments and markups at once in the document using the Comments tab (see "Manage Comments" later in the chapter for more information on the Comments tab):

- To view the text of the comment window without opening it, hover your mouse pointer over the comment. A ScreenTip-style box displays the originator's name, a review status (if applicable), and the text of the note (if there is no text in the comment window, the screen display doesn't appear).

- To open a comment in its own window, double-click the comment. The comment window opens near the comment surrounded by a colored border.

CHANGE COMMENT OPTIONS

You can display a review status, establish a reply thread, and perform other actions on comments.

1. Right-click a comment in the PDF.

   –Or–

   Open a comment window and click **Options** on the comment window toolbar.

   In either case, a menu of options is displayed (not all comments display the same options).

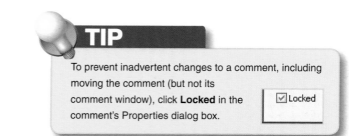

TIP

To prevent inadvertent changes to a comment, including moving the comment (but not its comment window), click **Locked** in the comment's Properties dialog box.

☑ Locked

Figure 7-9: You have several ways to change comments and customize their appearance.

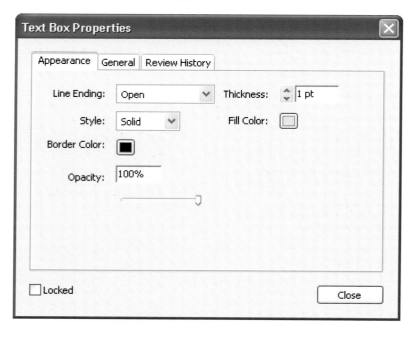

2. Select one or more of the following options:

- **Set Status** allows you to display several review or migration status terms with the comment. All reviewers can see this status. (*Migration* refers to importing comments to a previously revised PDF. See "Import and Export Comments" later in the chapter.)

- **Mark With Checkmark** displays a check mark ☑ with the comment in the Comments tab that only the originator sees.

- **Reset Pop-Up Note Location** returns the comment window to its default location in the PDF.

- **Delete** removes the note, but not necessarily all the components of the comment. For example, if you select some text, click **Replace**, and then click **Delete**, the note and insertion mark are deleted, but not the strikeout.

- **Reply** adds a "note within the note" to keep all related reviewer comments together in a single location.

- **Show Comments List** displays comments in the Comments tab.

- **Make Current Properties Default** applies the changes you make to one type of comment to all of your comments of the same type.

- **Properties** opens a Properties dialog box (a Note Properties dialog box is shown in Figure 7-9), where you can change the appearance of the icon used by the Note tool, change the author and comment subject, and view a history of reviews and migrations performed on the comment.

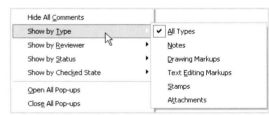

MOVE, SIZE, AND REMOVE COMMENTS

Use the Hand tool when moving, sizing, or removing comments:

- To move a comment (you cannot move text-edit comments, such as insertions or replacements), drag the comment where you want it.

- To move a comment window, click in the window's title bar, and drag it.

- To resize most comments, click the comment. If the comment is resizable, sizing handles will display in a bounding box or on the comment. Drag a sizing handle to resize the comment (a few drawing tools, such as the Polygon tool, don't display sizing handles, but can be resized by dragging a corner between line segments).

- To resize a comment window, drag the sizing handle in the lower-right corner of the window.

- To remove a comment, right-click it and click **Delete**, or select the comment and press **DELETE**.

SHOW AND HIDE COMMENTS

You can filter the comments you want to see, as well as open and close comment windows (pop-ups).

1. Click **Show** on the Commenting toolbar.

   –Or–

   Click the **Comments** menu and click **Show Comments And Markups** (Acrobat only).

   In either case, several options, which you can use to change the comments and comment windows you see, are displayed.

2. Click **Hide All Comments** to clear the document of comments, or click **Show All Comments** to return them to view. In either case, a message displays informing you that replies are hidden with original comments. Click **OK**.

3. Click **Show By** to filter the comments you want to see by one of four categories: type, reviewer, status, or checked state.

4. Click **Open All Pop-Ups** and then click **Close All Pop-Ups** to quickly show, then hide comment windows.

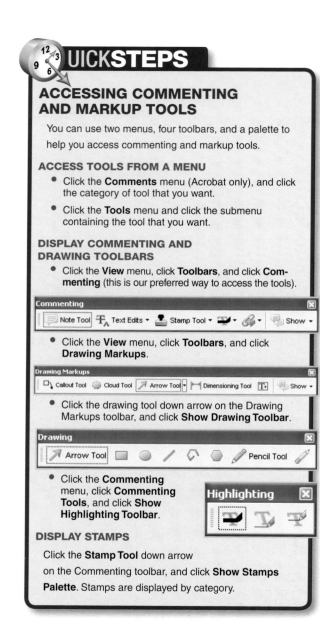

ACCESSING COMMENTING AND MARKUP TOOLS

You can use two menus, four toolbars, and a palette to help you access commenting and markup tools.

ACCESS TOOLS FROM A MENU

- Click the **Comments** menu (Acrobat only), and click the category of tool that you want.

- Click the **Tools** menu and click the submenu containing the tool that you want.

DISPLAY COMMENTING AND DRAWING TOOLBARS

- Click the **View** menu, click **Toolbars**, and click **Commenting** (this is our preferred way to access the tools).

- Click the **View** menu, click **Toolbars**, and click **Drawing Markups**.

- Click the drawing tool down arrow on the Drawing Markups toolbar, and click **Show Drawing Toolbar**.

- Click the **Commenting** menu, click **Commenting Tools**, and click **Show Highlighting Toolbar**.

DISPLAY STAMPS

Click the **Stamp Tool** down arrow on the Commenting toolbar, and click **Show Stamps Palette**. Stamps are displayed by category.

Add a Note

Notes are probably the most used commenting tool to add text comments during a review (you can also use the more limited Text Box tool, described in "Use Drawing Tools" later in the chapter). The Note tool provides a note icon to pinpoint where a note is directed and an associated pop-up comment window where you can add comments. You can change the note icon's appearance and several other properties.

1. In Acrobat 7 or Reader 7, open the PDF to which you want to add one or more notes.

2. On the Commenting toolbar, click **Note Tool**. The mouse pointer changes to a small note icon.

3. Click in the document where you want the note to be anchored. A default comment-style icon displays at that location, and the pop-up comment window is superimposed over it, showing your name and the date and time you created the note, as shown in Figure 7-10.

4. Type the body of the note in the text area of the comment window. The Properties bar displays several tools you can use to format your text.

5. When finished, close the comment window by clicking the **X** in the upper-right corner of the window or by clicking in the PDF outside the note.

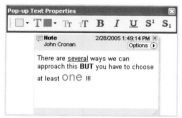

Figure 7-10: The Note comment and pop-up comment window illustrate the relationship between the two.

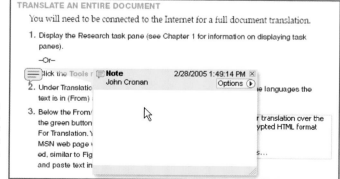

You can change the icon used to identify the note comment in a PDF. Press **CTRL+E** to display the Properties bar, and then select the note icon. Click the **Icon** down arrow, and click the appearance you want. The icon in the PDF reflects your changes.

Make Text Edits

The Text Edit tools let you identify text to be changed and provide alternative wording or comments without actually affecting the text in the PDF. See "Work with Comments and Markups" earlier in the chapter for information on how to use the comment window to display your suggested text or text you want to associate with the edit.

1. Open the PDF document to be reviewed in Acrobat or Reader.

2. For most text-editing tools, select the text that you want to change using the Select tool on the Basic toolbar (except for the Insert Text At Cursor tool, in which case you place the insertion point where you want the inserted text). See Chapter 4 for more information on selecting text in a PDF.

I▶ Select

3. Click **Text Edits** on the Commenting toolbar.

   –Or–

   Click the **Tools** menu, click **Commenting**, and click **Text Edits**.

   –Or–

   Click the **Comments** menu and click **Text Edits** (Acrobat only).

   In all cases, a menu of the Text Edit tools appears.

4. Click the tool whose text edit function you want. Table 7-1 describes the actions of the text-editing tools. Figure 7-11 shows how the comments appear in a PDF.

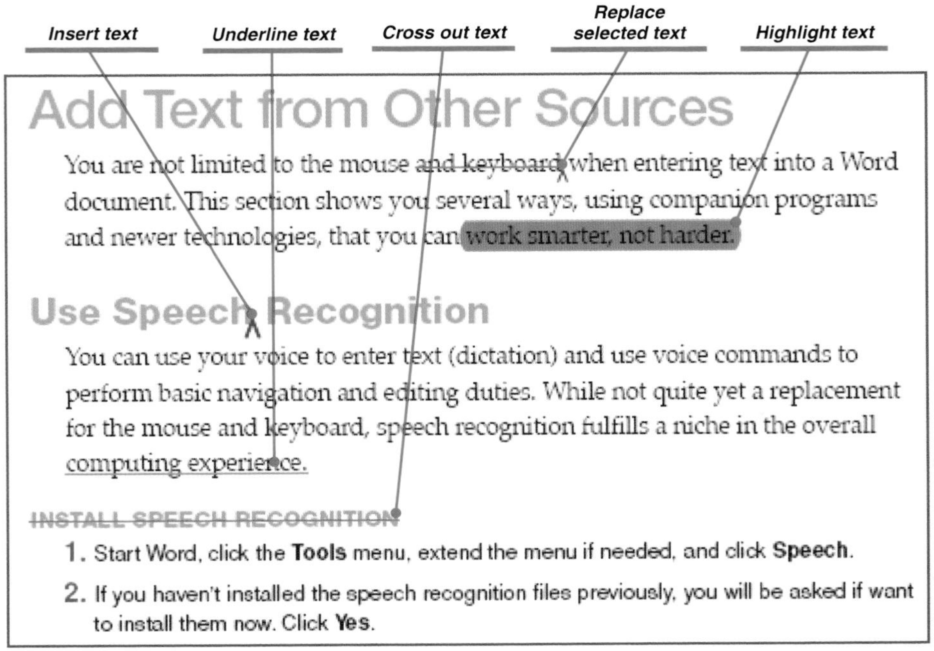

| Insert text | Underline text | Cross out text | Replace selected text | Highlight text |

Add Text from Other Sources

You are not limited to the mouse and keyboard when entering text into a Word document. This section shows you several ways, using companion programs and newer technologies, that you can work smarter, not harder.

Use Speech Recognition

You can use your voice to enter text (dictation) and use voice commands to perform basic navigation and editing duties. While not quite yet a replacement for the mouse and keyboard, speech recognition fulfills a niche in the overall computing experience.

INSTALL SPEECH RECOGNITION

1. Start Word, click the **Tools** menu, extend the menu if needed, and click **Speech**.

2. If you haven't installed the speech recognition files previously, you will be asked if want to install them now. Click **Yes**.

Figure 7-11: Text-editing comments are displayed similarly to the markups you would do with a pen and paper.

Use Highlighting Tools

The Highlighting tools are similar to the Highlight/Underline/Cross Out Selected tools described in Table 7-1, except that instead of first selecting text to highlight, you use the Highlighting tool to drag over the text you want selected. See "Work with Comments and Markups" earlier in the chapter for information on how to use the comment window to display text you want to associate with the highlight.

1. Open the PDF document to be reviewed in Acrobat or Reader.

2. Click the **Highlighting** tool on the Commenting toolbar.

   –Or–

   Click the **Tools** menu and click **Commenting**.

   –Or–

   Click the **Comments** menu, click **Commenting Tools**, and click **Highlighting**.

   In all cases, the three Highlighting tools are displayed.

3. Click **Show High-lighting Toolbar** (not shown on the Highlighting submenu) to keep the tools handy (see the "Accessing Commenting and Markup Tools" QuickSteps to view Commenting toolbars).

   > Show Highlighting Toolbar

4. Click the tool you want to use, and drag across the text you want to highlight.

5. Right-click the highlighted text and click **Open Pop-Up Note** to add text to a note window and/or use other options. See "Work with Comments and Markups" earlier in the chapter for information on using and changing comment windows.

TABLE 7-1: TEXT-EDITING TOOLS

TOOL	FUNCTION
⊤ₐ Replace Selected Text	Draws a line through the selected text, displays a caret (∧) at the end of the selection, and opens a comment window where you type replacement text. Point to the edited text to display a ToolTip-style box showing your name and your typed text, or click the caret to display the comment window.
T Highlight Selected Text	Highlights the selected text in the default color. Right-click the selection and click **Open Pop-Up Note** to add text to a comment window and/or use another option.
T Add Note To Selected Text	Attaches a comment window to the selected text.
Tₐ Insert Text At Cursor	Adds a caret (∧) where your insertion point was and opens a comment window where you can type text to be inserted. Point to the caret to display a ToolTip-style box showing your name and your typed text, or click the caret to display the comment window.
T Underline Selected Text	Underlines the selected text in the default color. Right-click the selection and click **Open Pop-Up Note** to add text to a comment window and/or use other options.
⊤ Cross Out Text for Deletion	Draws a line through the selected text. Right-click the selection and click **Open Pop-Up Note** to add text to a comment window and/or use other options.

ATTACHING FILES AND RECORDED COMMENTS

There is almost no end to what you can use as a comment. You can even attach files and audio recordings as comments.

ATTACH A FILE AS A COMMENT

1. Open the PDF in Acrobat.

2. Click the **Attach A File** down arrow on the File toolbar, and click **Attach A File As A Comment**. The mouse pointer changes to a pushpin.

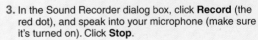

3. Click in the PDF where you want the comment, locate and select the file you want, and click **Select**.

4. In the File Attachment Properties dialog box, change the icon, color, or other attributes of the comment. Click **Close**.

5. Double-click the comment to open the file, or right-click the comment and click **Open File**. The attached file can be saved separate from the PDF by clicking **Save Embedded File To Disk** on the context menu.

ADD AN AUDIO COMMENT

1. Open the PDF in Acrobat.

2. Click **Comment And Markup** on the Task menu, click **Commenting Tools**, and click **Record Audio Comment**. The mouse pointer changes to a speaker. Click in the PDF where you want the comment to show.

3. In the Sound Recorder dialog box, click **Record** (the red dot), and speak into your microphone (make sure it's turned on). Click **Stop**.

   –Or–

   Click **Browse**, locate and select a prerecorded audio file, and click **Select**.

   In either case, click **OK** to close the Sound Recorder dialog box.

4. In the Sound Attachment Properties dialog box, change the icon, color, or other attributes of the comment.

5. To listen to an audio file, double-click the comment, or right-click the comment and click **Play File**.

Use Stamps

Stamps in Acrobat, are, well, stamps, albeit graphical representations of the rubber-and-ink stamps used for years to clearly identify documents and bring attention to details. Acrobat provides a collection of common stamps for reviewing, legal, and business purposes, as well as allowing you to create your own and organize them into categories. See "Work with Comments and Markups" earlier in the chapter for information on how to use the comment window to display text you want to associate with a stamp.

ADD A STAMP

1. Open the PDF document to be reviewed in Acrobat or Reader.

2. Click **Stamp Tool** on the Commenting toolbar, and click the category of stamp you want.

   –Or–

   Click **Show Stamps Palette** and click the down arrow at the top of the window to select a stamp category.

3. Click the stamp you want. Your mouse pointer becomes a semitransparent copy of the stamp.

4. Move the stamp into the position you want, and click. An opaque version of the stamp is displayed in the document.

CREATE A STAMP

You can use an image saved as a PDF to display as a stamp and add it to your stamp palette for future use.

1. Click **Stamp Tool** on the Commenting toolbar, and click **Create Custom Stamp**.

2. In the Select Image For Custom Stamp dialog box, click **Browse** and locate and select the image file you want to use (make sure the image is appropriately sized for the stamp you want). Click **Select** and then click **OK**.

3. In the Create Custom Stamp dialog box, shown in Figure 7-12, type a new category name; or click the **Category** down arrow, and click an existing category for the stamp. Type a name for the stamp. Leave **Down Sample Stamp To Reduce File Size** selected.

4. Accept the preview image for the stamp, or click **Select Image For Custom Setup**, and select a new image.

5. When finished, click **OK**. The stamp is added to the stamp category you selected or created, and it is available to be added to a PDF (see "Add a Stamp").

MANAGE CUSTOM STAMPS

1. Click **Stamp Tool** on the Commenting toolbar, and click **Manage Stamps**.

2. In the Manage Custom Stamps dialog box, you can add a new stamp; change a custom category name and change the category, name, and image used for a stamp; or delete a custom stamp (see "Create a Stamp" for information on creating and naming stamps).

Figure 7-12: You can create your own stamps from images saved as PDFs.

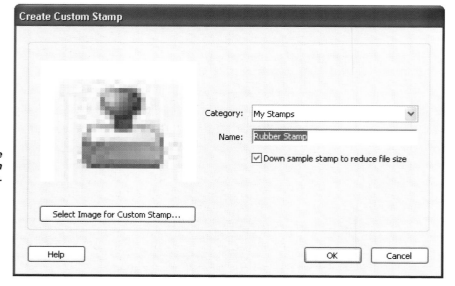

Use Drawing Tools

You can use many common drawing tools, such as rectangles, lines, and ovals, and some not-so-common tools, such as callouts, to add graphical comments to your PDF. The properties dialog boxes for drawing tools include options that are not available for other commenting tools. For example, you can adjust line thickness, style, and the type of line ending; change fill colors; and modify attributes of a particular tool. Each drawing tool is described in Table 7-2. See "Work with Comments and Markups" earlier in the chapter for information on how to use the comment window to display text you want to associate with a drawing tool.

TABLE 7-2: DRAWING TOOLS

TOOL	FUNCTION
Arrow	Provides a line that ends with an open arrowhead. Click where you want the line to start and end with an arrowhead. You can change the line ending from its Properties dialog box.
Callout	Provides a pointer connected to a text box. Click where you want the pointer to appear. You can move the pointer, mid-connector, and text box positions.
Cloud	Replaces a series of connected line segments with a cloud-like object. Click where you want to start and end the shape, and drag the line in the direction and length you want. Repeat with the other line segment, and close the shape. Click in the cloud and drag a line segment; the cloud will adjust accordingly.
Dimensioning	Provides a line with two closed arrowheads to indicate a distance between two points.
Line	Creates a straight line without endings. Click at the origin and drag to the end.
Oval	Creates a round object. Click near where you want the object, and drag to create the size and shape you want.
Pencil	Allows you to create freehand objects. Click to start the drawing, and drag continuously to create the shape you want. Release the mouse button to complete the drawing.
Pencil Eraser	Removes portions of an object created by the Pencil tool. Drag the mouse pointer over the segments of the drawing you want removed.
Polygon	Creates a closed shape consisting of three or more line segments. Click where you want to start and end the shape, and drag the line in the direction and length you want. Repeat with the other line segments, and close the shape.
Polygon Line	Creates a continuous shape consisting of line segments, not necessarily closed. Click where you want to start the shape, and drag the line in the direction and length you want. Repeat with the other line segments. Double-click to finish the drawing.
Rectangle	Creates a four-sided box. Click near where you want the object, and drag to create the size and shape you want.
Text Box	Creates a rectangular box into which you can type text. The box automatically resizes vertically as you add more text and can be resized to change the width of the box if needed. To edit text, double-click the box to place the insertion point in the text.

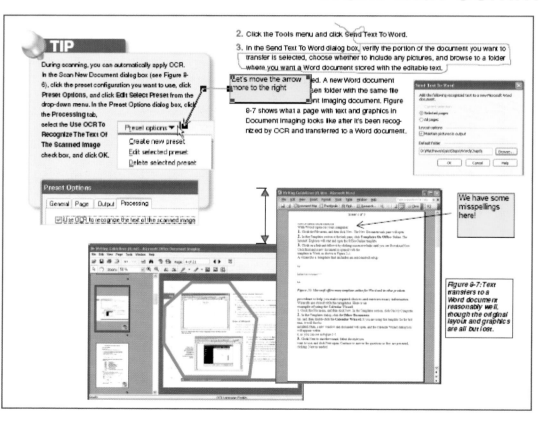

The drawing tools are available from the Tools and Commenting menus (Acrobat only) and from the Drawing Markups and Drawing toolbars (see the "Accessing Commenting and Markup Tools" QuickSteps earlier in the chapter). Drawing tools can be moved by dragging them and can be resized after making a selection by dragging a sizing handle (a few tools, such as the Polygon tool, do not display sizing handles and are resized by dragging a corner between line segments). Figure 7-13 shows several drawing tools used in a PDF.

Work with Comments in a PDF

Acrobat provides a number of features that you can use to manage the comments in a PDF. You can work with all the comments in a PDF from the Comments tab, import and export comments, and summarize them in various configurations.

Figure 7-13: Drawing markup tools add a lot of creativity to your comments.

Manage Comments

The Comments tab, shown in Figure 7-14, is the "Grand Central Station" for finding, viewing, sorting, printing, and otherwise working with the comments in a PDF.

1. Open the PDF document in Acrobat or Reader.

2. Click the **View** menu, click **Navigation Tabs**, and click **Comments**.

   –Or–

   Click the **Comments** tab on the navigation pane.

   In either case, the Comments tab opens under the document pane, listing comments by page.

3. Use the Comments tab toolbar to perform any of the available actions (see Figure 7-14).

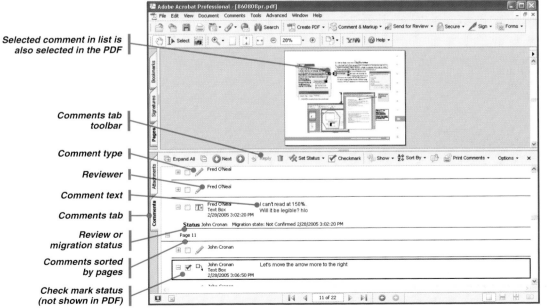

Figure 7-14: The Comments tab lists comments in a PDF and provides several management tools.

Selected comment in list is also selected in the PDF

Comments tab toolbar

Comment type

Reviewer

Comment text

Comments tab

Review or migration status

Comments sorted by pages

Check mark status (not shown in PDF)

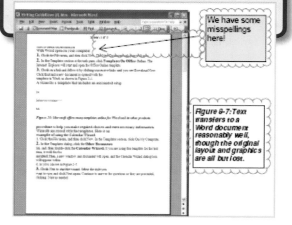

COMPARING PDF DOCUMENTS

When reviewing several documents, each with a number of revisions and stored in different locations, it's easy to lose track of comments. To ensure you have the most complete version of a document, you can compare other versions against your newest version. Acrobat will show you textual, graphic, and even formatting differences.

1. In Acrobat, click the **Document** menu and click **Compare Documents** (the two PDF documents do not have to be open).

2. In the Compare Documents dialog box, click the two **Choose** buttons to find and select the documents to compare.

3. In the Type Of Comparison area, select a visual or textual comparison, including the level of detail and color used to show differences (visual) and whether font information is identified (textual).

4. In the Choose Compare Report Type area, select the type of report you want. Click **OK** when finished. A visual report highlights differences in a colored "cloud."

Import and Export Comments

When using e-mail- or browser-based reviews, comments are easily merged into the master PDF document. However, in other cases, you might want to manually transfer comments between versions of the same document.

EXPORT ALL COMMENTS

1. In Acrobat or Reader (with commenting enabled), open the PDF containing the comments you want to export.

2. In Acrobat, click the **Comments** menu, click **Export Comments**, and click **To File**.

   –Or–

   In Reader, click the **Document** menu, click **Comments**, and click **Export Comments**.

3. In the Export Comments dialog box, locate where you want the FDF file stored, and name the file. Click **Save**.

4. Provide the FDF file to the holder of the PDF who will import your comments.

EXPORT SELECTED COMMENTS

1. In Acrobat or Reader (with commenting enabled), open the **Comments** tab (see "Manage Comments" earlier in the chapter).

2. Select the comment(s) you want to export. To select multiple comments, press and hold **CTRL** while clicking noncontiguous comments; or click the first comment in a series, press and hold **SHIFT**, and click the last comment in the series to select contiguous comments.

3. Click **Options** on the Commenting tab toolbar, and click **Export Selected Comments**. Locate where you want the FDF file stored, and name the file. Click **Save**.

4. Provide the FDF file to the holder of the PDF who will import your comments.

NOTE

You can export comments directly to the Word file that is the source document for the PDF. However, the PDF must have been tagged during the conversion process of the Word file. Click **To Word** from the Export Comments submenu to start the process.

NOTE

Exported comments will appear in the open PDF document in relation to where they were in the PDF. If the two documents differ in page numbering or layout, the comments might not be correctly positioned.

IMPORT COMMENTS

1. In Acrobat or Reader (with commenting enabled), open the PDF document that is to receive comments. (If you are importing comments to Word, open the Word document, click the **Acrobat Comments** menu, and click **Import Comments From Acrobat**.)

Acrobat Comments	
Import Comments from Acrobat...	

2. In the Import Comments dialog box, locate and select the file containing the comments. Click **Select**. The comments are added to the PDF.

Summarize Comments

Acrobat can provide a summary of the comments in a PDF document based on several criteria that you select.

1. In Acrobat, open the PDF containing the comments you want to summarize.

2. Click the **Comments** tab, click **Options**, and click **Summarize Comments**.

3. In the Summarize Options dialog box, select a layout, how you want the comments sorted, whether to include all or just displayed comments, and what font size to use.

4. Click **OK**. Either summary information is added to the current pages in the PDF or summary pages are added, depending on your choice in step 3. Figure 7-15 shows separate and same-page summaries.

5. Click **Save** on the File toolbar to save the summarized information as a new PDF.

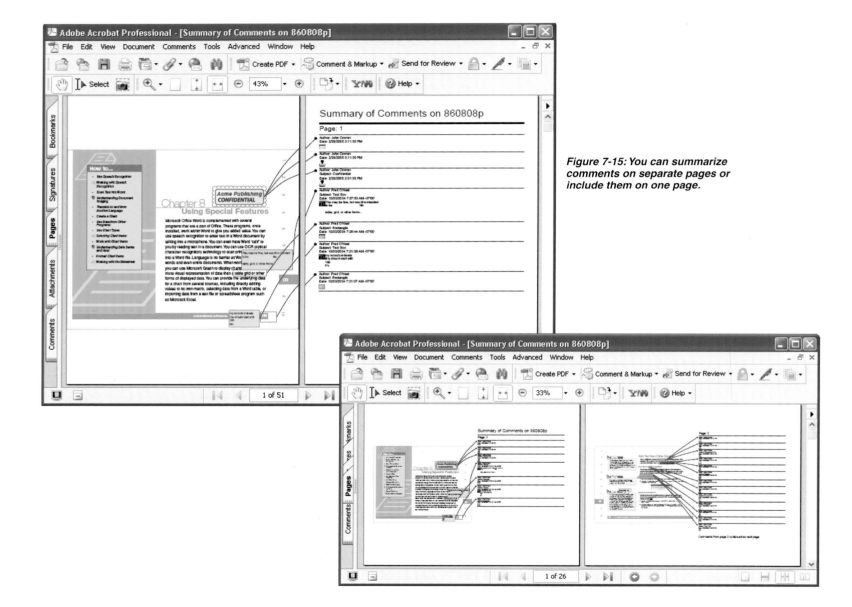

Figure 7-15: You can summarize comments on separate pages or include them on one page.

Chapter 8
Creating and Using Forms

Acrobat allows you to create forms either from scratch or from an existing form created in another application which can be converted to a PDF file or scanned into a PDF file. However a form is created, it can be filled out multiple ways: it can be printed and manually filled out (a *static* form); if its fields are created using special features available with Acrobat Professional, it can be filled out on a computer (an *interactive* form) using Acrobat Standard or Professional; or with special usage rights, it can be filled out using Adobe Reader. A filled-out form can be printed and stored as a paper form, saved on disk as an electronic document, or e-mailed as an electronic document; additionally, the data can be extracted and sent directly to a database or over the Internet.

A PDF form, at its simplest, is just like any other PDF document. It can be commented upon, transferred, viewed, and printed. With Adobe Designer, a separate program included with Acrobat Professional, you can design a form and add a number of interactive fields and controls. These fields can be used on a computer to fill in the form either directly or over the Internet.

In this chapter you will see how to design and create both static and interactive forms; how to use the various types of form fields, buttons, and templates; and how a PDF form can be filled out and its data collected in various ways.

Figure 8-1: You can start with a form in Word and convert it to PDF.

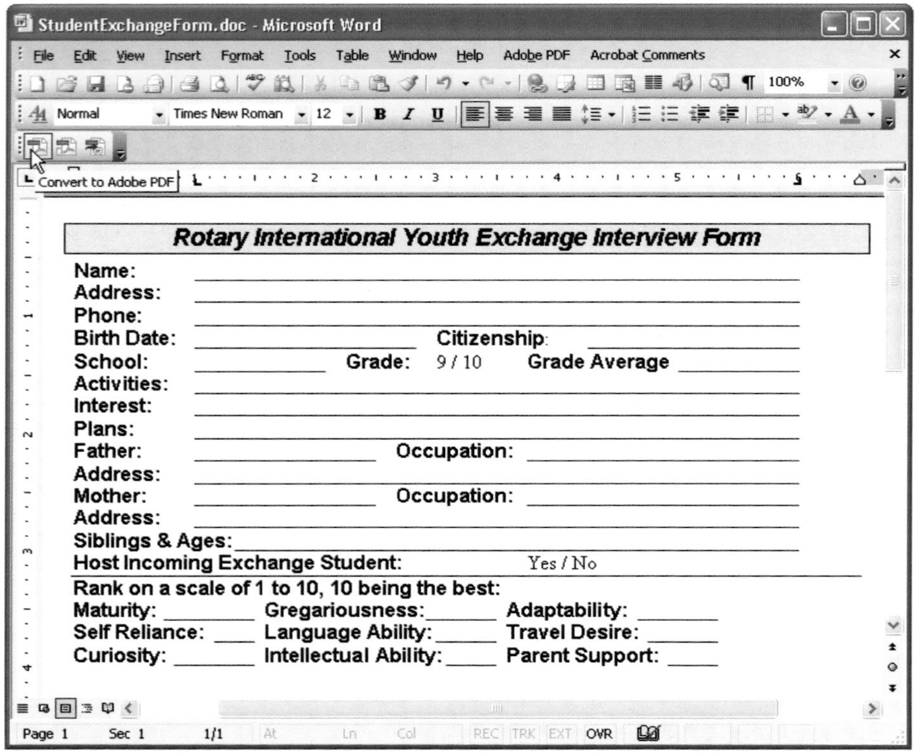

Create a PDF Form from an Existing Form

All types of existing forms can be turned into PDF forms, including ones that have been created in other applications–for example, forms created in Microsoft Word, forms in print form that are scanned into your computer, or forms downloaded from the Internet. Such forms can be static to be transmitted, viewed, and printed, or you can replace the static fields with interactive ones that can be filled in on a computer.

Transfer a Form from Word

If you have a form that has been created in Word on the same computer on which you have installed Acrobat, you should have a PDFMaker toolbar with a tool to convert a Word document to PDF, as shown in Figure 8-1.

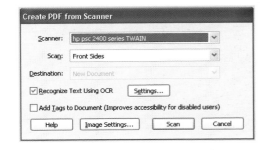

NOTE

If you don't have Word on the computer with Acrobat, or the copy of Word does not have the PDFMaker toolbar, you can still create a PDF in Word using Word's Print command with the Adobe PDF printer driver. You can also use other options to create a PDF, such as the Create PDF option in Acrobat's File menu (to convert a Word .doc file to PDF), as explained in Chapter 3.

1. Start Word and create or load the form you want to convert to PDF.

2. Click **Convert To Adobe PDF** in the PDFMaker toolbar. The Save Adobe PDF File As dialog box will open.

3. Select the file folder in which you want to save the PDF file, make any needed changes to the file name, and click **Save**. Several dialog boxes will appear informing you of the progress. Finally, Acrobat will open and display the new PDF file, as you can see in Figure 8-2.

Scan In a Printed Form

If you have a printed form that you would like to transfer into Acrobat to make either a static or interactive form, you can do so by scanning the form.

1. With a scanner properly set up and attached to the computer running Acrobat, load the form into the scanner.

2. Start Acrobat, click the **File** menu, click **Create PDF**, and click **From Scanner**. The Create PDF From Scanner dialog box will open.

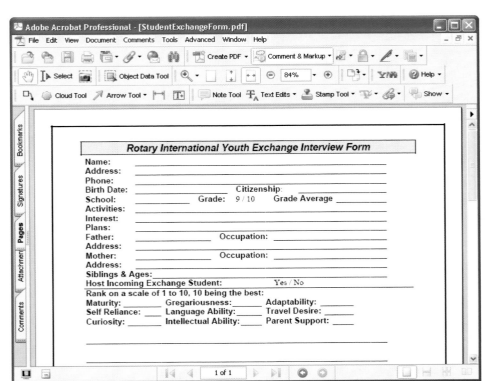

Figure 8-2: The exact same form appears in Acrobat and can be viewed and printed by anybody using the free Adobe Reader.

3. Click the **Scanner** drop-down list, and click the scanner you want to use. Click the **Scan** drop-down list, and click **Front Sides** or **Both Sides** depending on what you want to scan (with most scanners you will have to manually flip the pages).

4. If you want to search or change the text, you need to click **Recognize Text Using OCR**, and then click **Settings** to open the Recognize Text – Settings dialog box.

Figure 8-3: Any printed form can be scanned into a PDF file.

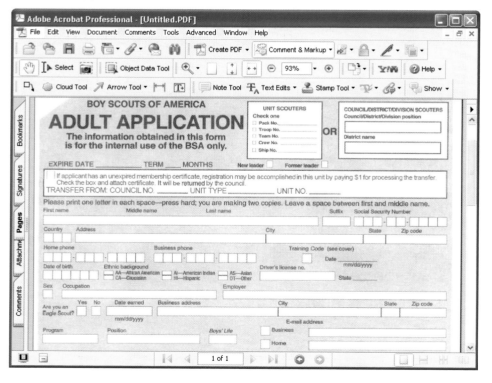

5. Select the language, output style (the difference is in how the PDF is constructed, as discussed in Chapter 3), and resolution that you want to use, and then click **OK**.

6. If you want to add tags to the new PDF file (see Chapter 3), click **Add Tags To Document**, and then click **Scan**. Your scanning software will start and show you the progress of the scanning. When scanning is done, the scanned document will open in Acrobat; it will look similar to what you see in Figure 8-3.

7. Click the **File** menu, click **Save**, select the file folder in which you want to save the PDF file, make any needed changes to the file name, and click **Save**.

Grab a Form from the Internet

A third way to bring a form into Acrobat is to download it from the Internet. Many companies and government agencies provide PDF forms on the Internet for your use, and all you have to do is download them. One of the most common agencies is the U.S. Internal Revenue Service, which has a myriad of PDF tax forms you can use.

1. Start your browser, such as Internet Explorer, type the URL of the site you want to go to (for example, http://www.irs.gov), and then press **ENTER**. Your requested web site should open.

2. Browse to the form you want to download, select the PDF format, make any other necessary detail selections, click the command needed to download the form (for IRS forms, you must first view the form), and click the drive and folder on your computer where you want to store the form.

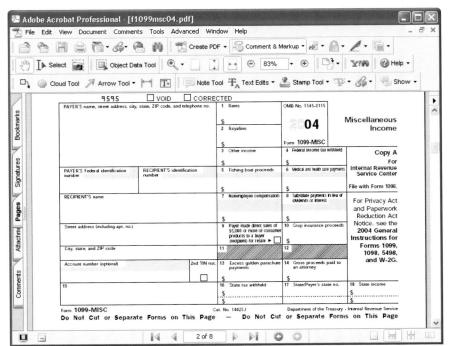

3. Start Acrobat, click the **File** menu, click **Open**, open the drive and folder(s) needed to locate the form, and click **Open** again. The downloaded form will open in Acrobat, as shown in Figure 8-4.

Figure 8-4: Numerous forms are available on the Internet.

QUICKSTEPS

SETTING PDF FORMS PREFERENCES

Acrobat provides a number of settings to control how forms behave when they are used, as well as several useful options to use when creating a form; these options are shown in Figure 8-5.

1. Click the **Edit** menu, click **Preferences**, and click **Forms** in the Categories list.

2. In the General area select:

   - **Automatically Calculate Field Values** to calculate field values as a user is doing the entry

   - **Show Focus Rectangle** to indicate which field is currently being worked on

   - **Keep Forms Data Temporarily Available On Disk** to allow the user to leave the form and return during a single session on the computer

   - **Show Text Field Overflow Indicator** to have a field display a plus sign (+) when more data has been entered into it than it can hold

   - **Always Hide Forms Document Message Bar** to hide the message bar when the form is opened

   - **Show Field Preview When Creating Or Editing Form Fields** to display how the field will look on the finished form

3. In the Highlight Color area, select:

   - **Show Border Hover Color For Fields** to place a border around a field when the mouse pointer passes over it

   - **Fields Highlight Color** to select the background color used when Highlight Fields is selected in the Document Message bar

   - **Required Fields Highlight Color** to select the color of the border that appears around required fields when an attempt is made to submit the form without those fields being filled in

4. When you have completed selecting your forms preferences, click **OK**.

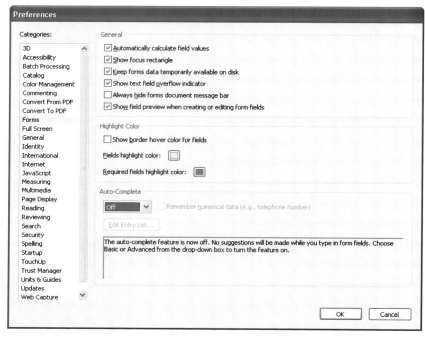

Figure 8-5: Forms preferences allow you to determine how forms will appear.

NOTE

Auto-Complete preferences, located in the Edit menu's Preferences dialog box, are discussed in the "Using Auto-Complete" QuickSteps toward the end of the chapter.

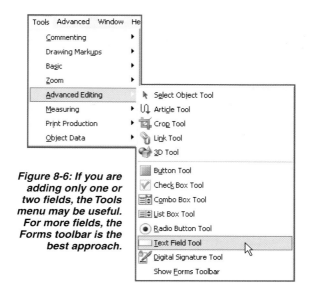

Figure 8-6: If you are adding only one or two fields, the Tools menu may be useful. For more fields, the Forms toolbar is the best approach.

Add Fields to an Existing PDF Form with Acrobat

Fields can be added to an existing PDF form in either Acrobat Professional, using a basic set of tools, or in Adobe Designer, with a much more comprehensive set of tools. To use Adobe Designer, see "Create an Interactive PDF Form with Adobe Designer" later in this chapter. In this section, the use of Acrobat's forms tools will be described.

Access a Form Tool in Acrobat

The form tools in Acrobat Professional are available from either the Tools menu or the Forms toolbar:

1. With Acrobat running and the form you want to make interactive open, click the **Tools** menu and click **Advanced Editing**.

2. Click one of the form field options (**Button** tool, **Check Box** tool, **Combo Box** tool, **List Box** tool, **Radio Button** tool, **Text Field** tool, or **Digital Signature** tool), as shown in Figure 8-6.

   –Or–

   Click **Show Forms Toolbar**. Click one of the form field tools in the toolbar. See Figure 8-7.

Button   Combo Box   Radio Button   Digital Signature

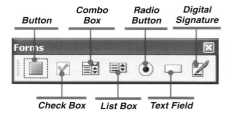

Check Box   List Box   Text Field

Figure 8-7: The floating Forms toolbar allows you to easily drag a form field to your form.

USING A GRID, GUIDES, AND RULERS TO ALIGN FIELDS

Acrobat provides an optional grid, custom guides, and rulers that help you align fields. These tools can be turned on or off, and you can set the grid's and rulers' properties.

1. With Acrobat running and the form you want to make interactive open, click the **View** menu and click **Grid**.

2. Click **Units & Guides** in the Categories list.

3. Adjust the settings that are correct for your form, and click **OK**.

4. Click the **View** menu and click **Rulers** to turn on rulers. Figure 8-8 shows a grid and rulers placed over a form created in Word and converted to a PDF.

5. Click the **View** menu and click **Guides**. With the Hand tool (the *grabber hand*) selected, move the mouse pointer to either the top or left ruler, and drag the guides you want to the form (you probably don't want both a grid and guides).

TIP

To help you align fields to a grid, click the **View** menu and click **Snap To Grid**. This gives the grid a magnetic quality so that when you are dragging fields to a form, they will be attracted ("snap") to the grid lines.

TIP

Using Points as the unit of measure gives you 72 gradations (points) per inch, which may be easier to align to an existing layout.

Use Acrobat Form Tools

The form tools available in Acrobat create interactive fields with the following functions:

- **Button** allows the form user to perform an action by clicking the button.
- **Check Box** allows the form user to indicate a nonexclusive choice, in which several items can be chosen.
- **Combo Box** allows the form user to open and choose an entry from a drop-down list of items.
- **List Box** allows the form user to choose from a displayed list of items.
- **Radio Button** allows the form user to indicate an exclusive choice, in which only one item can be chosen.
- **Text Field** allows the form user to type text.
- **Digital Signature** allows the form user to add a digital signature to a form and lock the data that they have added.

Figure 8-8: It is extremely difficult to get a grid to exactly match the spacing of an externally-created form.

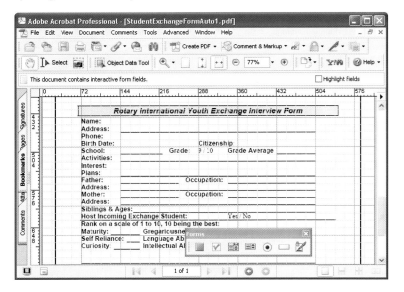

NOTE

A form field cannot be placed on top of a comment.

Once you have turned on the Forms toolbar (see "Access a Form Tool in Acrobat" earlier in this chapter), the grid, and possibly the rulers and Snap-To Grid (see the QuickSteps "Using a Grid, Guides, and Rulers to Align Fields"), you can begin to add fields to an existing form.

1. With the form on which you want to add fields, as well as the Forms toolbar, open in Acrobat Professional, click the tool you want to use in the Forms toolbar. The mouse pointer will turn into a crosshair.

2. Drag the **crosshair** from the upper-left corner of where you want the field to the lower-right corner.

   –Or–

   Double-click where you want a new field, and a field will be created using the defaults currently in effect for that type of field.

   In either case the field's Properties dialog box will open.

3. If it is not already selected, click the **General** tab, as shown in Figure 8-9. Type the **Name** and **Tooltip** (the label that appears when the mouse hovers over a field), and click **Close**. In "Set Field Properties" next in this chapter, you'll consider the other field properties.

4. Continue adding additional fields. Repeat steps 2 and 3 for the same types of fields as originally selected. Then repeat steps 1 through 3 for the different fields you need.

Figure 8-9: Acrobat allows you to tailor a text field to your needs through the field's properties.

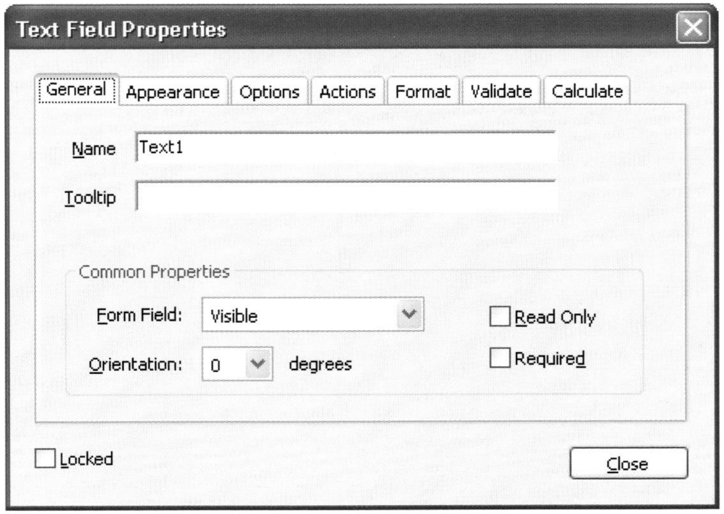

Text Field Properties

| General | Appearance | Options | Actions | Format | Validate | Calculate |

Name | Text1

Tooltip |

Common Properties

Form Field: Visible   ☐ Read Only

Orientation: 0 degrees   ☐ Required

☐ Locked   Close

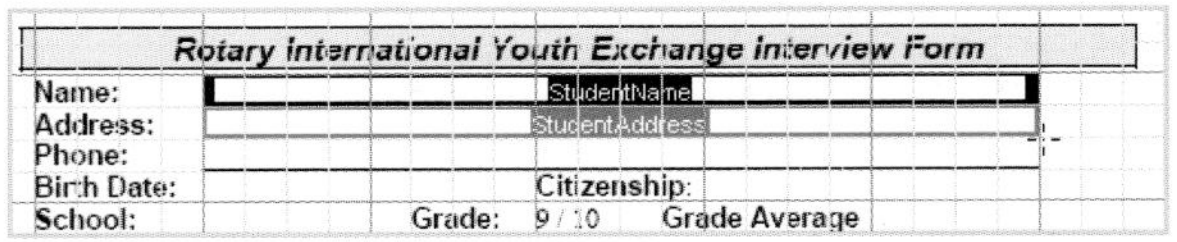

Rotary International Youth Exchange interview Form				
Name:	StudentName			
Address:	StudentAddress			
Phone:				
Birth Date:		Citizenship:		
School:	Grade:	9 / 10	Grade Average	

SET FIELD PROPERTIES

The properties that you can set for a field depend on the type of field you are working with, although many of the settings are common for two or more fields.

- The settings common to all fields in their respective tabs are:

  The **General** tab, shown in Figure 8-9, allows you to name the field; type a tooltip that appears when the mouse pointer passes over the field; determine the visibility of the field; and set the orientation of the data in the field, whether it is read only and if it is required.

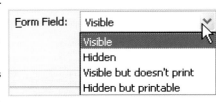

  The Appearance tab, shown in Figure 8-10, lets you determine the border and fill color; the thickness and style of the border; and the font size, color, and typeface.

Figure 8-10: Form fields can look many different ways depending on the settings in the Appearance tab.

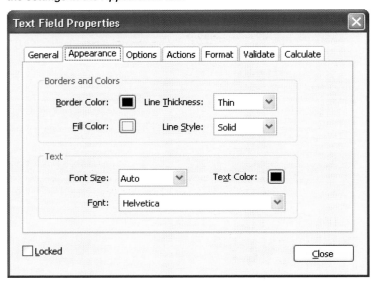

  The **Actions** tab lets you determine the action that will be taken on a selected mouse event, as discussed in "Determine the Actions on Mouse Events" later in this chapter.

- The **Button** unique settings in its tabs are:

  The **Options** tab allows you to specify if the layout for the button includes a label, an icon, or both; whether the button, when it is clicked, inverts its color, changes the color of its outline, or changes the label and/or icon when it is pressed or when the mouse passes over it; and to select the label and icon that will appear in various states of the button field. The button states are "Up" when the mouse button is released, "Down" when the mouse button is pressed, and "Rollover" when the mouse pointer passes over the field.

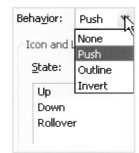

NOTE

Radio buttons with the same name are mutually exclusive; only one of them can be selected, unless you choose to override this default behavior.

- The **Check Box** and **Radio Button** unique settings in their tabs are:

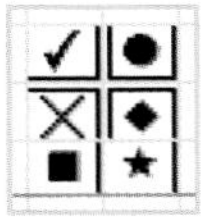

  The **Options** tab lets you determine how the check box or radio button will look when it is selected: a check mark, a circle, a cross, a diamond, a square, or a star; set the value that is returned when the box is selected; determine whether the box or button is selected by default; and specify whether radio buttons with the same name are selected in unison.

- The **Combo Box** and **List Box** unique settings in their tabs are:

  The **Options** tab allows you to enter the items that are displayed on the list, determine what their export values are, and set several options for them, as shown in Figure 8-11.

  The **Selection Change** tab lets you execute a script when a list box selection changes.

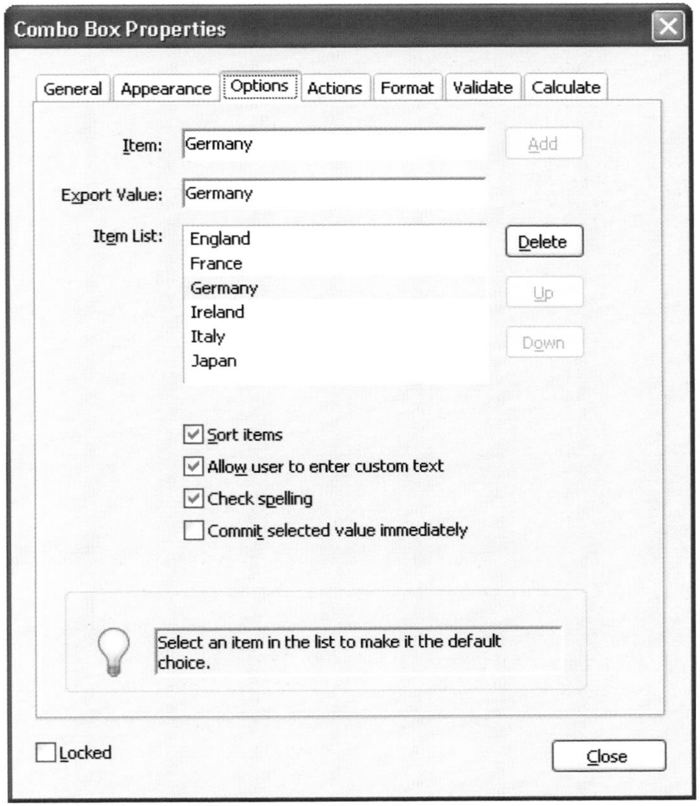

Combo Box Properties

General | Appearance | Options | Actions | Format | Validate | Calculate

Item: Germany   Add

Export Value: Germany

Item List:
England
France
Germany
Ireland
Italy
Japan

Delete   Up   Down

☑ Sort items
☑ Allow user to enter custom text
☑ Check spelling
☐ Commit selected value immediately

Select an item in the list to make it the default choice.

☐ Locked   Close

Figure 8-11: Items in a combo or list box can be sorted or ordered using the Up and Down buttons.

SELECTING FIELDS TO BE CHANGED

After a set of fields have been created, you can select them and make any desired change.

1. Open the form in Acrobat Professional, and open the **Forms** toolbar (see "Access a Form Tool in Acrobat" earlier in this chapter).

2. In the Forms toolbar click the type of field you want to change. Those types of fields will be highlighted with a black border around them and a name in the middle.

3. Click the individual field you want to select. The border and name will turn red.

4. Press **CTRL** while clicking second or additional fields you want simultaneously selected; press **CTRL** and click an already selected field to deselect just it.

   –Or–

   Press **CTRL** while dragging a selection rectangle around the set of fields you want simultaneously selected.

   –Or–

   Press **SHIFT** while clicking a second field to simultaneously select all fields between the previous field you selected and the present one.

5. Make all changes needed, and then click the **Hand** tool, or grabber hand, on the Basic toolbar to deselect all fields.

If you have multiple fields of a given type, you can change the properties of one, right-click that field, and click **Use Current Properties As New Defaults** to copy those properties to the other fields and any new fields of that type.

- The **Text Field** and **Combo Box** unique settings in their tabs are:

  The **Options** tab (Text Field only) allows you to determine the alignment of text that is entered, specify a default value in the field, and set several characteristics of the text.

  The **Format** tab lets you specify the type of information the field will hold and how to format it, as shown in Figure 8-12.

  The **Validate** tab allows you to determine if the field will be validated either by falling within a given range, or by running a custom script (the writing of scripts is not within the scope of this book).

  The **Calculate** tab lets you specify a calculated value in the field, as described in "Create Calculated Fields" later in this chapter.

- The **Digital Signature** unique settings in its tab are:

  The **Signed** tab allows you to determine what happens to the form, principally to set some or all of the fields as read-only—meaning that once signed, the fields cannot be changed.

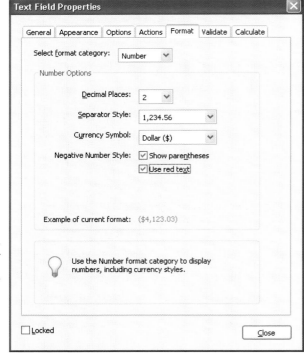

Figure 8-12: The Format tab is principally used to format numeric information, such as percentages, telephone numbers, and dates.

MOVE AND SIZE FIELDS ON A FORM

With a field selected (see the "Selecting Fields to Be Changed" QuickSteps), drag from the middle of the field to move it anywhere on the form, or drag one of its corners or sides to change its size.

DELETE FIELDS

With a field selected (see the "Selecting Fields to Be Changed" QuickSteps), press **DELETE** to remove the selected field from the form, and press **CTRL+Z** to undo the deletion and restore the deleted field to the form.

CHANGE FIELD PROPERTIES

A field's properties can be changed in the field Properties dialog box which is originally opened when a field is created (see "Add Fields to a Form" and "Set Field Properties" earlier in this chapter); a field's properties can also be changed in the Properties toolbar, shown in Figure 8-13. To open the Properties toolbar:

Click the **View** menu, click **Toolbars**, and click **Properties Bar**.

–Or–

Press **CTRL+E**.

To open the Properties dialog box:

Click **More** on the Properties toolbar.

–Or–

With a field selected (see the "Selecting Fields to Be Changed" QuickSteps), right-click either a highlighted or a selected field, and click **Properties** to open the Properties dialog box for that field. Make any desired changes, and click **Close**.

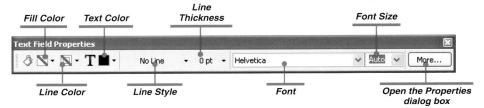

Figure 8-13: The form field Properties bar changes slightly for different types of fields.

TIP

A field's Properties dialog box can be opened by double-clicking the field.

CAUTION

When you copy a field, the new field has the same name as the original field. Two or more fields with the same name share the same property settings as well as the same information. So borders, colors, and other properties set for one field will automatically be set for another with the same name. Also, information entered by a form user into one field will automatically appear in another field with the same name. You can prevent this by simply changing the name of a copied field.

Figure 8-14: Groups of similar fields can be created and manipulated in the Create Multiple Copies Of Fields dialog box.

CUT, COPY, AND PASTE FIELDS

1. With a field selected (see "Selecting Fields to Be Changed"), right-click the selected field, click **Edit**, and click **Cut** to remove the field from its current location and temporarily hold it on the Windows Clipboard; or, you can click **Copy** to leave the field where it is and temporarily make a copy of it on the Windows Clipboard.

2. Right-click a highlighted, or selected, field, click **Edit**, and click **Paste** to have a copy of the field currently on the Windows Clipboard placed approximately in the middle of the current Acrobat window.

   –Or–

   Click the **Edit** menu and click **Paste** to have a copy of the field currently on the Windows Clipboard placed approximately in the middle of the current Acrobat window.

3. Drag the cut or copied field to the location you want on the current page.

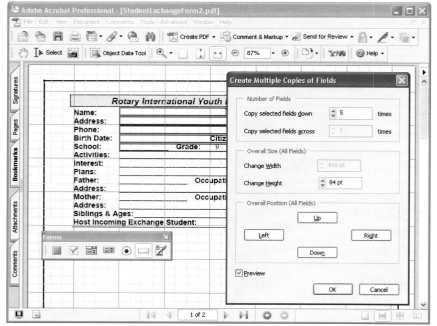

CREATE MULTIPLE COPIES OF FIELDS

Once you create one field in a set of similar fields, you can easily create the rest.

1. With the field selected that you want copied (see the "Selecting Fields to Be Changed" QuickSteps), right-click the field and click **Create Multiple Copies**. The Create Multiple Copies Of Fields dialog box will open.

2. Click the **Copy Selected Fields Down** spinner to select the number of copies of the selected field that you want. If Preview in the lower left of the dialog box is checked, the new fields will appear as blue outlines, as shown in Figure 8-14.

3. Click the **Change Height** spinner to adjust the overall height of the group of fields. Click the appropriate position buttons that move the group of fields in the direction selected.

4. When the new fields are the size and position you want, click **OK**. If desired, you can drag one or more fields to where you want them.

DUPLICATE FIELDS ACROSS PAGES

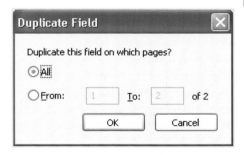

If you have a multipage form with one or more of the same fields on two pages, you can duplicate the original fields on the second page.

1. With the field or fields selected that you want duplicated (see the "Selecting Fields to Be Changed" QuickSteps), right-click the field and click **Duplicate**. The Duplicate dialog box will open.

2. Click **All** to duplicate the field or fields on all pages, or click **From** and enter the starting and ending pages on which to duplicate the fields, and then click **OK**.

   The fields will be duplicated into the same position on the new pages as they occupied on the original page.

SPECIFY THE TAB ORDER OF FIELDS

By default, the order in which fields are selected by the form user when TAB is repeatedly pressed is the order in which the fields were created. This can be changed in two ways: using Page Properties to select from several predefined tab orders for a particular page, and using Set Tab Order to individually set the tab order for each field.

- Use **Page Properties**:
  1. With the form whose tab order you want to set open in Acrobat, click **Pages** in the left navigation pane.
  2. Click the page thumbnail containing the form, click **Options**, and click **Page Properties**. The Page Properties dialog box will open.
  3. If needed, click the **Tab Order** tab.
     - Select **Use Row Order** to tab across each row from left to right and then down the rows from top to bottom.
     - Select **Use Column Order** to tab down a column from top to bottom and then across columns from left to right.
     - Select **Use Document Structure** to use the original hierarchical structure of headings or an outline created in the original document application.
     - Select **Unspecified** to not specify a tab order, and use Set Tab Order for that purpose.
  4. Click **Close** to close the Page Properties dialog box, and close the navigation pane.

- Use **Set Tab Order**:
  1. With the form whose tab order you want to set open in Acrobat, click the **Tools** menu, click **Advanced Editing**, and click **Select Object Tool**. All the fields on your form will be highlighted with a black border around them and a name in the center of the field.
  2. Right-click a field and click **Set Tab Order**. A number representing its tab order appears in each field.
  3. Click the first field on the form where you want the form user to start. Then click each field in the order that you want the form user to tab through them.
  4. Click the **Hand** tool to deselect all fields.

NOTE

Set Tab Order can be used only if Unspecified is selected in the Tab Order tab of Page Properties, opened from Options in the navigation pane.

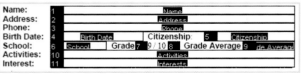

DETERMINE THE ACTIONS ON MOUSE EVENTS

You can use any field in a form to perform numerous actions at the time a form is being filled out. This is the purpose of the Action tab in the Properties dialog box for all fields. In the Action tab, you can specify the action that will take place on a selected trigger, or mouse event, such as pressing down the mouse button or moving the mouse pointer over an icon.

1. With the form you want to work on open in Acrobat, click the appropriate type of field in the Forms toolbar, and right-click the particular field in the form to which you want to attach an action (see the "Selecting Fields to Be Changed" QuickSteps earlier in this chapter).

2. Click **Properties** to open the field's Properties dialog box, and click the **Actions** tab. An Action tab with several actions enabled is shown in Figure 8-15.

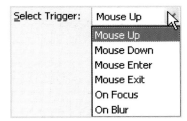

3. Click the **Select Trigger** down arrow, and click the trigger you want to use. The triggers, or mouse events, and their meanings are:

- **Mouse Up** occurs when the mouse button is released.

- **Mouse Down** occurs when the mouse button is pressed.

- **Mouse Enter** occurs when the mouse pointer enters the field.

- **Mouse Exit** occurs when the mouse pointer leaves the field.

- **On Focus** occurs when the field is selected by either the mouse or the keyboard.

- **On Blur** occurs when the field is deselected by either the mouse or the keyboard.

4. Click the **Select Action** down arrow, click an action, and click **Add**.

Figure 8-15: The primary means of automating a form is through the Actions tab of a field's Properties dialog box.

The dialog box for that action will open. Handle the options as needed, and click **OK**. The available actions and their usage are:

- **Execute A Menu Item** allows the selection of an Acrobat menu and submenu option.
- **Go To A 3D View** allows the selection of a 3-D annotation.
- **Go To A Page View** allows the selection of a page, magnification, and particular field.
- **Import Form Data** allows the selection of an FDF (Form Data Format) file to be imported.
- **Open A File** allows the selection of a file to be opened.
- **Open A Web Link** allows the entry of a URL of the site to be opened.
- **Play A Sound** allows the selection of a sound file to be played.
- **Play Media** (both Acrobat 5 compatible and Acrobat 6 and later) allows the selection of media already linked to the document to be played.
- **Read An Article** allows the selection of an article already linked to the document to be read using the sound system.
- **Reset A Form** allows the selection of fields to be reset or cleared.
- **Run A JavaScript** allows the entry of a JavaScript program to be run.
- **Set Layer Visibility** allows the selection of the layers of the form to be visible.
- **Show/Hide A Field** allows the selection of fields to be hidden.
- **Submit A Form** allows the entry of a URL or Internet address and the selection of a format and fields to be transmitted.

5. When you have the actions that you want for a particular field, you can change the action's position within the list by clicking the action and clicking **Up** or **Down**. With an action selected, you can also click **Edit** to reopen the dialog box you originally saw, and then click **Add** or click **Delete** to add new actions or delete existing ones.

6. When you have completed all the actions for a field, click **Close**.

Create Calculated Fields

Acrobat provides a capable calculation ability that you can use with forms. For example, the form in Figure 8-16 allows the user to enter a quantity for each of the three products, and select a tax rate. Using these amounts, the total for each product is generated and subtotaled, the tax is calculated, and a grand total is produced. To perform calculations such as these:

1. In a program such as Microsoft Word, create a form on which you want to add calculated fields, and leave spaces for the fields that you will add in Acrobat; save this form as a PDF file.

2. Open the form in Acrobat, and open both the Forms and the Properties toolbars. Turn on Rulers, place any guides as desired, and enter any noncalculated fields needed.

Quantity:		@		for a total of:	
Quantity:		@		for a total of:	
Quantity:		@		for a total of:	

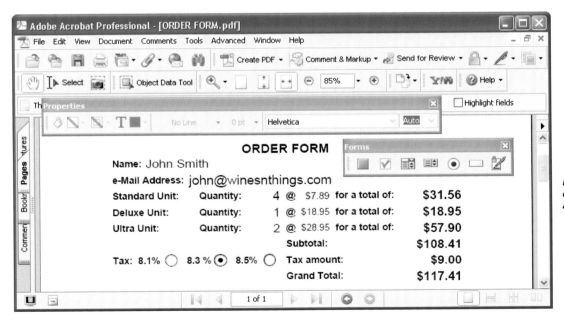

Figure 8-16: Reasonably complex calculations can be added to Acrobat forms.

3. In the Forms toolbar, click the **Text Field** tool, and draw a text box for the quantity to be purchased. In the Properties dialog box, make the following changes:

- In the **General tab**, type the name and tooltip.

- In the **Appearance tab**, make any desired changes.

- In the **Options tab**, click the **Alignment** down arrow, click **Right**, click to deselect **Scroll Long Text** and **Check Spelling**, and click **Limit Of** and enter a number of characters.

- In the **Format tab**, click the **Select Format Category** down arrow, and click **Number**; click the **Decimal Places** down arrow, and click **0**; and leave the rest.

- In the **Validate tab**, click **Field Is In Range,** and enter a range appropriate for your quantity field, probably beginning with 0 (given the user cannot make an entry).

4. Click **Close**, but leave the first Quantity field selected. Right-click the field and click **CreateMultiple Copies**. Reduce the **Copy Selected Fields Across** spinner to 1 and increase the **Copy Selected Fields Down** spinner to the number of quantity fields you want. Change the Height so the fields fit your form (see Figure 8-17), and click **OK**.

5. Open the Properties dialog boxes for each of the new copied fields, and change their name and tooltip accordingly.

6. With the Text Field tool, draw a text box for the price of the first item. In the Properties dialog box, make the following changes for a price entry:

- **General tab**: type the name (a tooltip isn't needed), and click **Read Only**.

- **Appearance tab**: make any desired changes.

- **Options tab**: click the **Alignment** down arrow, click **Right**, in the **Default Value** enter the price amount, and click to deselect **Scroll Long Text** and **Check Spelling**.

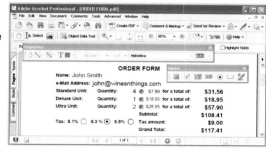

- **Format tab**: click the **Select Format Category** down arrow, and click **Number**; click the **Decimal Places** down arrow, and click **2**; click the **Currency Symbol**, and click **Dollar ($)**.

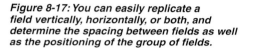

Figure 8-17: You can easily replicate a field vertically, horizontally, or both, and determine the spacing between fields as well as the positioning of the group of fields.

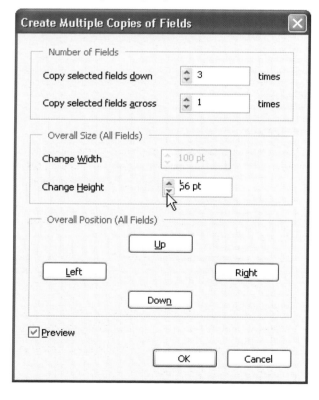

7. Click **Close**, but leave the first Price field selected. Right-click the field and click **Create Multiple Copies**. Follow the same procedure as in step 4, click **OK**, repeat the procedure in step 5, and enter the price for each item in the Options tab.

8. With the Text Field tool, draw a text box for the extended total of the first item. In the Properties dialog box, make the following changes for an extended total entry:

   ● **General tab**: type the name (a tooltip isn't needed), and click **Read Only**.

   ● **Appearance tab**: make any desired changes, and possibly make the font bold.

   ● **Options tab**: click the **Alignment** down arrow, click **Right**, and click to deselect **Scroll Long Text** and **Check Spelling**.

   ● **Format tab**: click the **Select Format Category** down arrow, and click **Number**; click the **Decimal Places** down arrow, and click **2**; leave the default for the separator style, click the **Currency Symbol**, and click **Dollar ($)**.

   ● **Calculate tab**: click **Value Is The**, click the **Of The Following Fields** down arrow, and click **Product (x)**. Click **Pick**, click both the first quantity and the first price, and click **OK**.

9. Click **Close**, but leave the first extended total field selected. Right-click the field and click **Create Multiple Copies**. Follow the same procedure as in step 4, and click **OK**; repeat the procedure in step 5, but enter the fields for quantity and price for each item in the Calculate tab.

10. Right-click the bottom extended total field, and click **Create Multiple Copies**. Follow the same procedure as in step 4, and click **OK**.

11. Double-click the **Subtotal** field to open the Properties dialog box. Change the name in the General tab; in the Calculate tab, select **Sum (+)**, click Pick, click all the extended total fields, and click **Close**.

12. In the Forms toolbar, click the **Radio Button** tool, and draw a radio button for the first tax choice. In the Properties dialog box, make the following changes for a tax entry:

   ● **General tab**: type the name and a tooltip, which will be the same for all tax amounts.

   ● **Options tab**: enter the tax amount in the Export Value.

TIP

Constant values—those not entered by the form user—such as prices and tax rates, can be entered as either read-only fields or values associated with check boxes and radio buttons.

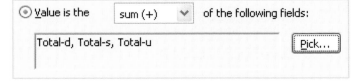

13. Click **Close**, but leave the first tax amount field selected. Right-click the field and click **Create Multiple Copies**. Decrease **Copy Selected Fields Down** to 1, increase **Copy Selected Fields Across** to the number of tax fields, increase **Change Width** until the fields fit in your form, and click **OK**.

14. Open the Properties dialog box for each tax field, change the name so that it is the same for all tax fields, change the Export Value so that it is correct for each of the tax fields, and click **Close**.

15. In the Forms toolbar, reselect the **Text Field** tool, double-click the **Tax Amount** field, and change the name as appropriate; in the Calculate tab, select **Product (x)**, click **Pick**, click the **Subtotal** and **Tax Amount** fields (since they are named the same there should only be one), and click **OK**.

16. Double-click the **Grand Total field**, and change the name in the General tab; in the Calculate tab, select **Sum (+)**, click **Pick**, click the **Subtotal** and **Tax Amount** fields, click **OK**, and click **Close**.

17. Click the **File** menu and click **Save**, assuming you have already named the file (if not, click **Save As**, give the file a name, and then click **Save**). Click the **Hand** tool to deselect the fields, and then move the mouse pointer over the **Quantity** and **Tax** fields to see the tooltips (there shouldn't be any tooltips for the other fields); observe that all the totals are zero.

18. If you see a problem, click the appropriate tool on the Forms toolbar, right-click the field that has a problem, click **Properties**, correct the error, click **Close**, and click the **Hand** tool.

19. Fill in the form and check the arithmetic. If you find a problem, repeat step 18. You probably do not want to save the form once it is filled out.

CHECKING THE SPELLING OF FIELDS

For those of us who make typos or can't spell, Acrobat has the ability to check the spelling of form fields.

1. With the form whose spelling you want to check open in Acrobat, click the **Edit** menu, click **Check Spelling**, and click **In Comments And Form Fields**. The Check Spelling dialog box will open.

2. Click **Start**. When a misspelled word is identified, it will be displayed under Words Not Found, and a suggested replacement will be displayed under Suggestions.

3. Click **Ignore** to leave the identified word as is, click **Change** to replace this instance of the identified word with the suggested word, click **Change All** to replace all instances of the identified word with the suggested word, or click **Add** to not change the identified word, and add it to the spelling dictionary for future reference. The spell checker will go on and check the next word.

4. When you finish checking the spelling of a form, click **Done**.

NOTE

Acrobat's spell checker checks the words that are entered in Acrobat and not the words that appear in Acrobat from another application.

Add Command Buttons

A form that is to be completed online needs a set of command buttons. At a minimum there needs to be a Submit button to send the form, a Cancel button to not submit the form, and a Reset button so the user can clear all the fields and start over; you can see these command buttons in Figure 8-18. To add these buttons:

1. With the form on which you want command buttons open in Acrobat, click the View menu and click Rulers. From the vertical ruler, drag a guide on which to align the left edge of the first button. From the horizontal ruler, drag a guide on which to align the bottom edge of all buttons.

2. Click the Button tool on the Forms toolbar, and drag a rectangle whose left and bottom edge are aligned on the two guides you just placed. As in all other field types, the button's Properties dialog box will open when you release the mouse button.

Figure 8-18: Command buttons allow the user to work with the form after they have filled it out.

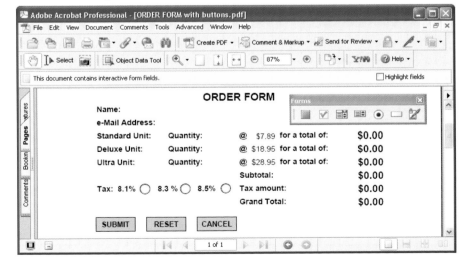

3. Click the General tab in the Properties dialog box. Type a name and a tooltip, such as Submit and Submit This Form for the first button.

4. Click the Appearance tab and make any desired changes. Adding a black border sets off the button, and the default 12-points font size is often too big—11 or 10 points is generally better.

5. Click the Options tab, type a label for the button, such as SUBMIT, and change the behavior if desired.

6. Click the Actions tab, click the Select Action down arrow, scroll to the bottom of the list, click Submit A Form, and click Add. The Submit Form Selections dialog box will open.

7. If you want to send the form using e-mail, then in Enter A URL For This Link, type an e-mail address preceded by mailto: without spaces (see Figure 8-19). For example:

    `mailto:jillsmith@excitingtravel.com`

Figure 8-19: You can choose whether to send form data by e-mail or to a web server that has a program to receive it.

8. If you want to send the form to a web server, then in Enter A URL For This Link, type the complete URL for the web server, and include in the URL the program to receive the form information (you will need to be given the complete URL by a server administrator).

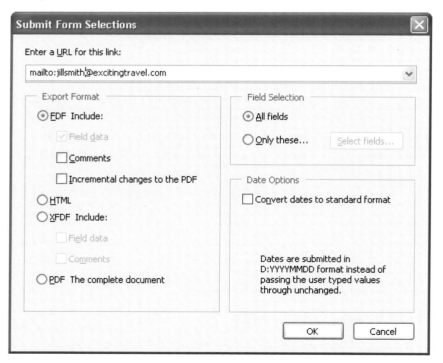

9. Choose what to send:

- An **FDF** file is just the form field data, any comments entered on the form, and any incremental changes made to the form (use the latter for digital signatures). An FDF file is the smallest file and is the easiest to handle at the receiving end.

- An **HTML** file of the entire form may be useful when sending the information to a web server.

- An **XFDF** file is just the field data and any comments entered in XML format.

- A **PDF** file is the complete form.

10. Choose whether to send all fields or only selected fields and whether to convert dates from the default, machine-readable format of YYYYMMDD to a more standard date of MM/DD/YYYY; when you are finished, click **OK** and click **Close**.

11. Right-click the new button, and click **Create Multiple Copies**; decrease the **Copy Selected Fields Down** spinner to 1, and increase the **Copy Selected Fields Across** spinner to 3. Increase the Change Width spinner to give you the separation you want.

12. Double-click the second button to open its Properties dialog box. In the General tab, change the name and tooltip to something like <u>Reset</u> and <u>Clear all the form's fields</u>, respectively; in the Options tab, change the label to <u>RESET</u>.

13. In the Actions tab, click the **Select Actions** down arrow, click **Reset A Form**, click **Add**, and click **OK** to accept all the fields. Click **Submit A Form** in the list of Actions, click **Delete**, and click **Close**.

14. Double-click the third button to open its Properties dialog box. In the General tab, change the name and tooltip to something like <u>Cancel</u> and <u>Close the form and do not submit it</u>; in the Options tab, change the label to <u>CANCEL</u>.

15. In the Actions tab, click the **Select Actions** down arrow, click **Execute A Menu Item**, and click **Add**; in the Menu Item Selection dialog box, click **File**, click **Exit**, and click **OK**. Click Submit A Form in the list of Actions, click Delete, and click Close.

16. Return to the first button, and correct the name, which has ".0" added to it. When the buttons are the way you want them, click the **Hand** tool to deselect all fields, and click **Save** on the File toolbar. You might also make a backup copy of this file with another name, in case it gets corrupted with data during testing.

17. To test this form, jump to the section "Use a PDF Form" later in this chapter. To make changes, click the tool in the Forms toolbar, and then double-click the tool with which you are having problems. Remember to clear the fields before resaving the form.

NOTE

You can use Designer to edit fields that you created in Acrobat Professional, but Acrobat can't edit Designer fields.

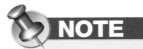

Create an Interactive PDF Form with Adobe Designer

To create an interactive PDF form from scratch, you should use Adobe Designer, which is a separate program that comes with Acrobat Professional. Adobe Designer is a full-featured page layout program that can be used for creating a number of different types of forms, from simple fill-in-the-blanks forms to forms in which sets of questions change depending on answers to earlier questions.

Adobe Designer is a sophisticated program almost on the level of Acrobat itself, and an entire book could be devoted to it. In this section we will skim some of its more important features and capabilities.

Advanced
Window
Help
Accessibility
Acrobat Distiller
Batch Processing...
Catalog...
Digital Editions
Export All Images...
Forms
JavaScript
Links
Migrate Comments...
Number Pages...
PDF Optimizer...
Security Settings...
Trusted Identities...
Web Capture
Use Local Fonts Shift+Ctrl+Y
Overprint Preview Shift+Ctrl+7
Output Preview...
Preflight... Shift+Ctrl+X
Make Form Fillable in Adobe Designer...
Edit Fillable Form...
Create New Form...
Open Form in Adobe Designer...
Initiate Data File Collection Workflow...
Create Spreadsheet From Data Files...
Import Data to Form...
Export Data from Form...
Fields
Page Templates...
Set Field Calculation Order...
Always Hide Document Message Bar

Figure 8-20: You can easily open an existing PDF form in Designer from Acrobat.

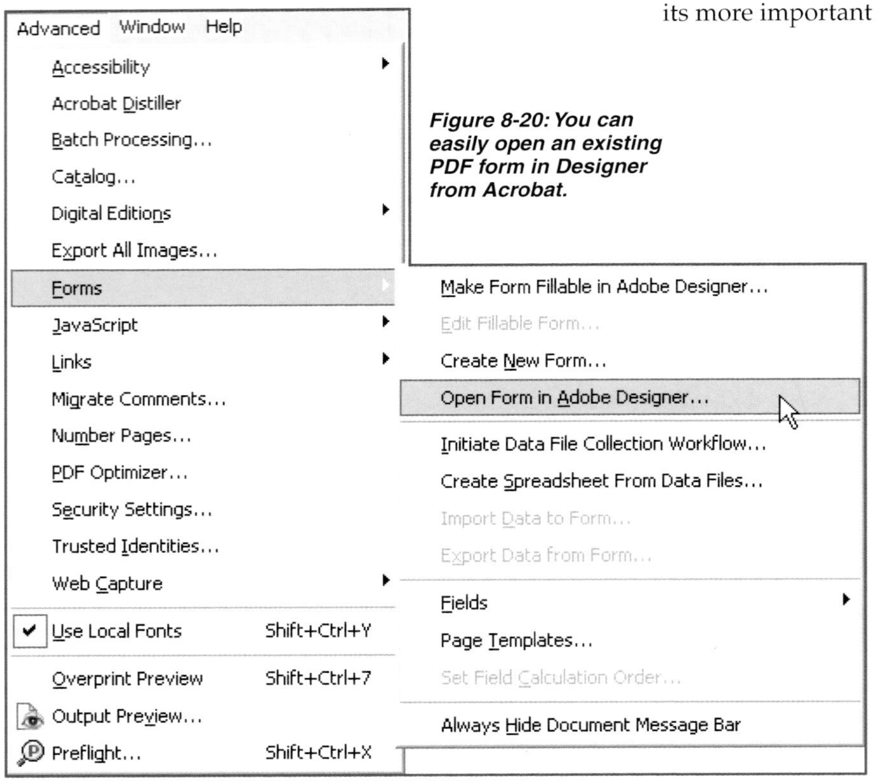

Start Adobe Designer

Adobe Designer can be started either from Acrobat or directly from the Start Menu.

- **Start Designer from Acrobat**

  With Acrobat running and, potentially with a form you want to make interactive open, click the **Advanced** menu, click **Forms**, and then choose one of the following options: Click **Create New Form** and click **OK** to start Adobe Designer with a new blank form. Acrobat will remain open.

  –Or–

  Click **Open Form In Adobe Designer** (see Figure 8-20), and click **OK** to start Adobe Designer and open a new copy of your form. Acrobat will remain open with the original copy of your form.

–Or–

- **Start Designer from the Start Menu**

  Click **Start**, click **All Programs**, and click **Adobe Designer 7.0**.

Designer will start and, depending on whether you started it with an existing form, will display different dialog boxes:

- When you have an existing form, the New Form Assistant dialog box opens and displays the path and file name of the form that is being imported.

  1. Correct the path and file name, if necessary, and click **Next**.

  2. Click either **Maintain Editability** or **Preserve Appearance**, and click **Next**.

  3. Click the form return method that is correct for you, and click **Next**.

  4. Type a return e-mail address, and click **Finish**. A Conversion Summary message box will open and describe how the existing form was converted to Designer. Click **OK**.

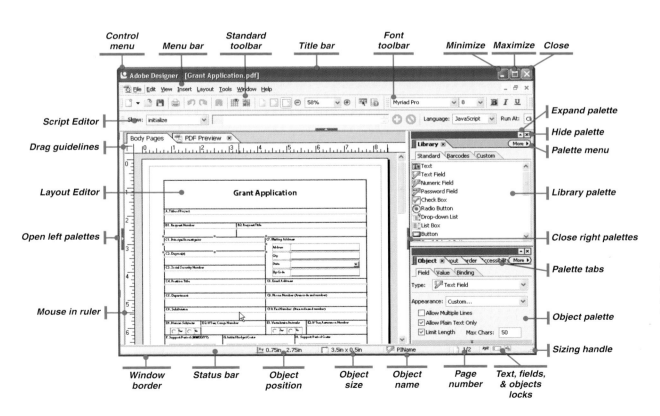

Figure 8-21: The default Designer window provides a large layout area on the left and a series of palettes on the right.

5. If the existing form used fonts that Designer can't readily find, the Missing Fonts dialog box will open and display those fonts and the proposed substitute fonts. If you want to change the substitutes, click **Change Substitute Font**, select the substitution, and click **OK**.

● When you want to create a new form, the Welcome Screen opens and displays several options.

1. Click **New Form** to open the New Form Assistant, and click **Next**.

2. Select a paper size and orientation, enter the number of pages, and click **Next**.

3. Click the form return method that is correct for you, and click **Next**.

4. Type a return e-mail address, and click **Finish**.

In either case the Designer window will open, as shown in Figure 8-21, with a form. Much of what you see in Figure 8-21 can be customized to suit your needs and tastes, but Designer customization is beyond the scope of this book.

Use PDF Form Fields

Interactive forms are produced either by adding fields to an existing form or by creating a new form and adding fields to it. In the following sections, you'll see how to work with fields in an existing form and when creating a new one. In both cases you can add several categories of fields to the form: standard form data collection fields (see Table 8-1), form creation elements (see Table 8-2), and custom form fields (see Table 8-3 for selected custom fields). You can also add many different types of barcode fields, but those are beyond the scope of this book.

To add a field to a form you simply drag it from the Library palette to the form.

TABLE 8-1: STANDARD FORM DATA COLLECTION FIELDS

LIBRARY ICON	DESCRIPTION	EXAMPLE
Text Field	**Text Field** allows the form user to enter text.	Text Field
Numeric Field	**Numeric Field** allows the form user to enter numbers.	Numeric Field
Password Field	**Password Field** allows the form user to enter a password.	Password Field
Check Box	**Check Box** allows the form user to indicate a nonexclusive choice, in which several items can be chosen.	Check Box
Radio Button	**Radio Button** allows the form user to indicate an exclusive choice, in which only one item can be chosen.	Radio Button
Drop-down List	**Drop-down List** allows the form user to open and choose an entry from a drop-down list of items.	Drop-down List
List Box	**List Box** allows the form user to choose from a displayed list of items.	List Box Choice 1 Choice 2 Choice 3
Button	**Button** allows the form user to perform some action by clicking the button.	Button
Email Submit Button	**Email Submit Button** allows the form user to send the form via e-mail by clicking the button.	Submit by Email
HTTP Submit Button	**HTTP Submit Button** allows the form user to send the form over the Internet by clicking the button.	Submit
Print Button	**Print Button** allows the form user to print the form by clicking the button.	Print Form
Reset Button	**Reset Button** allows the form user to clear all fields in the form by clicking the button.	Reset Form
Date/Time Field	**Date/Time Field** allows the form user to enter a date and/or time and have it validated.	Date/Time Field
Image Field	**Image Field** allows the form user to add an image to the data being submitted with the form.	Image Field
Signature Field	**Signature Field** allows the form user to add a digital signature to a form and lock the data that they have added.	Signature Field

TABLE 8-2: FORM CREATION ELEMENTS

LIBRARY ICON	DESCRIPTION	EXAMPLE
Text	**Text** adds a block of text on the form for titles, headings, and instructions.	ORDER FORM
Image	**Image** adds an image to a form.	
Line	**Line** adds a straight line to a form.	
Rectangle	**Rectangle** adds a square or rectangle to a form.	
Circle	**Circle** adds a circle or oval to a form.	
Subform	**Subform** groups fields, text, and other objects within a bordered and referencable area; it can be dynamically switched for another subform based on a form entry.	
Content Area	**Content Area** defines an area on a form that can contain fields and other objects. The default outer blue rectangle on a new form defines the initial content area.	

TABLE 8-3: SELECTED CUSTOM FORM FIELDS

LIBRARY ICON	DESCRIPTION
Address Block	**Address Block** adds a group of fields to a form, including name, address, city, state, ZIP, and country.
Countries	**Countries** adds a drop-down list of countries.
Current Date	**Current Date** adds a field and a script to display the current date.
Email Address	**Email Address** adds a field that will validate an e-mail address entered into it.
Name	**Name** adds a group of three fields for the first name, last name, and middle initial.
Page n of m	**Page N Of M** adds a field that displays, for example, "Page 3 of 8," in which the numbers are filled in by Acrobat.
Page Navigation	**Page Navigation** adds four buttons in order to go to the first page, the next page, the previous page, and the last page.
Phone Number - North Amer.	**Phone Number – North America** adds a field that formats numbers as a North American telephone number.
Signature - Print and Sign	**Signature – Print And Sign** adds a box to a printed form for the user's signature.
Signature - Print and Sign	**U.S. Social Security Number** adds a field that formats numbers as a Social Security Number.
U.S. States	**U.S. States** adds a drop-down list of states.

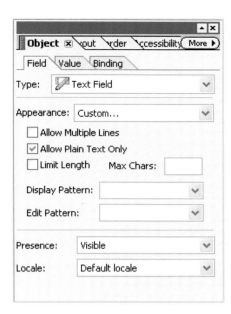

Change Field Properties

Each field that you add to a form has a set of properties attached to it; for example, its size, position, border color, and default value. A field's properties are set and changed in the Object palette, generally in the mid-right of the Designer Window. When a field is selected, because you just dragged it as a new field to a form, or because you clicked in a field on the form, the Object palette will reflect the properties for that field. The Object palette, of course, must be enabled or opened, and can have a number of different tabs, depending on the field being described.

OPEN AND USE PALETTES

The Library, Object, and How To palettes are opened by default when you first start Designer, after installing Acrobat Professional. These palettes can be turned off by clicking their **Close** button in the upper-right of the palette. To open one of these (or other) palettes:

Click the **Window** menu and click the palette, such as **Library** or **Object**, that you want to open.

The Library, Object, and How To palettes are on the right by default. Other palettes, such as Hierarchy and Report, if they are open, are on the left by default. You can move palettes anywhere you want them. For example, Figure 8-22 shows the Object palette on the left, achieved by opening the Hierarchy palette from the Window menu and then dragging the Object palette from the right to the left pane.

UNDERSTAND THE OBJECT PALETTE

The Object palette, used to set the properties of every field, is heavily used with a number of detail settings. As you are adding fields to a form, it is important that you look at all options available for that type of field until you become familiar with all of them. For all new fields, click each tab in the Object palette to determine if the settings are relevant to what you want to do.

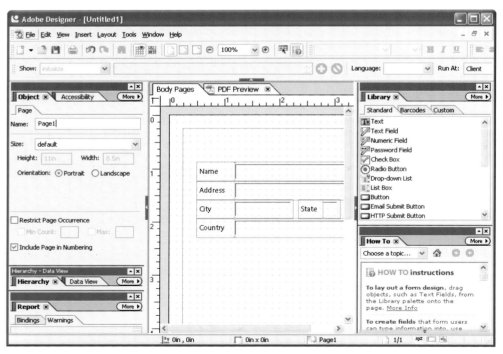

Figure 8-22: Any of the numerous palettes in Designer can be in panes on the left, the top, the right, or the bottom of the Designer window.

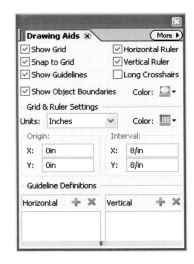

Prepare a New Form In Designer

The forms that can be created in Designer can be reasonably sophisticated with complex fields, static text, borders, and shading. Designer also provides a number of tools to place and align the many objects on a form.

ADD GUIDELINES AND USE THE GRID

As you build a form, you will want to align fields and other elements to give the form a professional look. To help you do that, Designer has provided:

- Horizontal and vertical rulers to measure distances
- A grid set on an interval you specify to align objects
- A property called "Snap To Grid" to attract objects to the grid
- Guidelines you set to provide major alignment guides
- Drawing Aids palette to control all of these features

To set up a form:

1. Click the **Windows** menu and click **Drawing Aids** to open that palette. Drag across first the **X Interval** and then the **Y Interval** and set them to what is appropriate for you. Often 4 per Inch is too coarse, and 8 or 16 is better.

2. In the upper-left corner of the Layout Editor, point on the intersection to drag a pair of guidelines to where you want them, or drag within the horizontal or vertical ruler to get the opposite line. For example, if you want just a horizontal line at 2 inches, point on the intersection in the upper-left corner, and drag it down the vertical ruler (stay in the ruler) to 2 inches.

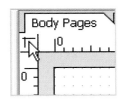

3. Remove a guideline by dragging the small triangle in the ruler just above or to the left of a line off the form.

4. If Show Grid is selected, you can use the tiny dots that represent the grid to visually align objects; or if Snap To Grid is selected, objects that are dragged to the form will "snap to" those points like a magnetic property.

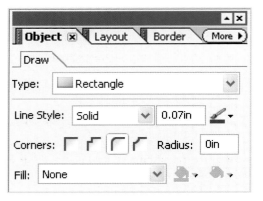

ADD BORDERS, LINES, AND SHADING

Borders, lines, and shading are added to a form by placing an object, such as a line, rectangle, or circle, on a form, and then defining the border and background color and the border size in the Object palette.

1. From the Library palette, drag a rectangle to what will be an outer border of your form. In the Object palette, set the line style, size, color, corner type, and fill (the shading), as desired.

2. From the Library palette, drag a line to be used as a divider. In the Object palette, set the line style, size, and color, as desired.

PLACE STATIC TEXT

Static text on a form, such as titles, labels, and instructions, is just another object that you drag from the Library palette; however, the principal properties of text, font, font size, style, and paragraph alignment, are set in the Font and Paragraph toolbars or palettes, not in the Object palettes.

1. From the Library palette, drag the **Text** element to the form. Do not drag the full rectangular area you want to use for text. As you type the text, the area will automatically expand to provide room for the text.

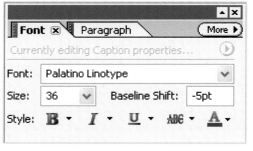

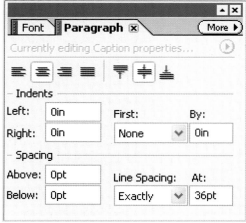

2. Drag over the word **Text** to select it. In either the Font toolbar or the Font palette, select the font, font size, style (bold, italic, or underlined), font color (palette only), and paragraph alignment. You can make additional paragraph settings in the Paragraph palette.

3. Type the text you want, and then drag and size the text box as needed.

Add Fields to a Form in Designer

Adding fields to a form in Designer includes dragging the fields that are needed, setting the properties appropriately, duplicating where necessary, and then aligning the fields to create an attractive form.

DRAG FIELDS TO A FORM

1. From the Library palette, drag the first field you want. Place it roughly where you want it, and make it the size you want.

2. In the Object palette, choose the appearance you want in the Field, Value, and Binding tabs, enter a default value if appropriate, and type a field name.

3. In the Font palette, choose the font, font size, and style to be used.

4. Repeat the first three steps, as needed, for all the fields you want.

SELECT, COPY, AND DUPLICATE FIELDS

To create multiple copies of one or more fields, you must first select the field(s):

- Click an object to select it. A border with eight sizing handles (little squares on the corners and midpoints) will appear around the object.
- Press and hold **CTRL** while clicking as many objects as you want to select.
- Press and hold **SHIFT** while clicking the first and last objects in a stack to select all the objects in the stack.
- Press **CTRL+A** to select all the objects on the form.
- Click the object or objects in the Hierarchy palette.

Once you have the object(s) selected, Designer has three ways to copy and duplicate them:

- Click the **Edit** menu and click either **Cut** (removes the original object) or **Copy** (leaves the original object), and then click the **Edit** menu, and click **Paste** to place the object in the upper-left of the form, or press **CTRL+V** to have the new object appear immediately under the mouse pointer, if the mouse pointer is on the form.
- Click the **Edit** menu and click **Duplicate** to have the new object appear immediately below and slightly offset from the original object.
- Click the **Edit** menu and click **Copy Multiple** to open the Copy Multiple dialog box. Click the vertical and horizontal placement and spacing that is correct for you, and click **OK**.

TIP

If you need fields that are similar in many respects, you can copy or duplicate fields and have all the properties carry over.

TIP

If you are using Duplicate several times, complete the steps the first time, move the field to where you want it in relation to the original field, and then perform the duplicate again. The next new field will be in the same relative position to the second field as the second was to the first.

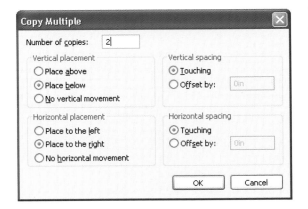

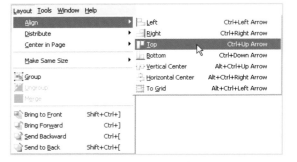

TIP

Be sure to click *last* the field to which you want the other fields to align.

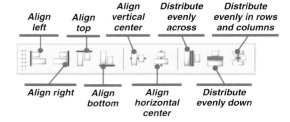

Align left
Align top
Align vertical center
Distribute evenly across
Distribute evenly in rows and columns

Align right
Align bottom
Align horizontal center
Distribute evenly down

ALIGN, DISTRIBUTE, AND CENTER FIELDS

Designer has a number of tools to align, distribute, and center multiple fields, and that's why we said not to worry about the exact placement of fields when you first place them. You can do this manipulation through the Layout menu or with the Layout toolbar.

1. Select the fields you want to align (see "Select, Copy, and Duplicate Fields" earlier in this chapter), click the **Layout** menu, click **Align**, and click the way you want the alignment.

2. Select the fields you want to distribute, click the **Layout** menu, click **Distribute**, and click the way you want the distribution.

3. Select the fields you want to center, click the **Layout** menu, click **Center In Page**, and click the way you want the centering.

Use a PDF Form

You might use many kinds of PDF forms, from ones you print out and manually fill in, to ones you fill in online and print out, to ones you fill in online and send out over the Internet. This section will concentrate on the last type and in the process discuss how forms are filled in online. Printing a blank form is just printing a PDF document, as discussed in Chapter 2. This section will also discuss how to handle and use the data collected with a PDF form collected over the Internet.

Fill In and Send a PDF Form

An interactive PDF form can reach you via e-mail, on a CD, or downloaded from an Internet site. In any case you need to be able to get around the form, enter information on it, and send it out over the Internet.

GET AROUND A FORM

You can use a PDF form that is on your computer, regardless of how it got there.

1. Locate and double-click the form, either directly on your desktop or through Windows Explorer. Acrobat will open and display the form.

2. Click the **Hand** tool in the Basic toolbar if it isn't already selected. Move the mouse over the form. As you pass over a field, the field border will appear and, if the form creator added it, you'll see a tooltip appear describing the field. The mouse pointer changes depending on the type of field:

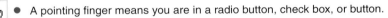
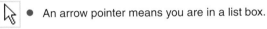
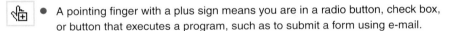

- An I-beam pointer means you are either in a text field or a combo box.

- An arrow pointer means you are in a list box.

- A pointing finger means you are in a radio button, check box, or button.

- A pointing finger with a plus sign means you are in a radio button, check box, or button that executes a program, such as to submit a form using e-mail.

Figure 8-23: Acrobat allows you to quickly see the fields on a form, and it designates required fields as well.

3. Click in the first field you want to use. The field is said to be "selected."

4. Press **TAB** to go to and select the next field, and press **SHIFT+TAB** to go to and select the previous field.

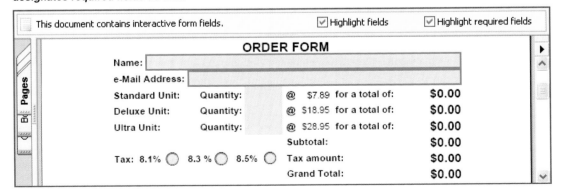

USING AUTO-COMPLETE

If you have previously used a form, the information that you entered for each field is stored and is available the next time you use the form; this feature is called *Auto-Complete*.

COMPLETING AN ENTRY

1. Begin to type into a text field. The system looks to see if the first few letters you type match anything that has been in that or similar fields in the past. If so, a drop-down list will open and display the similar items.

J
John Staley

2. Click one of the options in the drop-down list.

   –Or–

   Keep typing and the remainder of the name will automatically be filled in (or automatically completed).

3. Press **TAB** to go on to the next field.

EDIT AUTO-COMPLETE PREFERENCES AND LISTS

To change the Auto-Complete Preferences and list contents:

1. Click the **Edit** menu, click **Preferences**, and click the **Forms** category. The lower part of the dialog box includes a section for Auto-Complete.

2. Click the drop-down list and choose:

   - **Basic** to implement the Auto-Complete capability
     –Or–
   - **Advanced** to implement the Auto-Complete capability and have the field automatically filled in when you **TAB** to it if there is only one choice
     –Or–
   - **Off** to turn off Auto-Complete

3. Click **Remember Numerical Data** if you want numbers included in Auto-Complete.

4. Click **Edit Entry List** to open the Auto-Complete Entry List dialog box. Click an entry and click **Remove** to delete a single entry, or click **Remove All** to do that—in both cases click **Yes**, you are sure. Click **Close** when you are done deleting entries.

5. Click **OK** to close the Preferences dialog box.

How information is entered into a field depends on the type of field. In all cases, though, the field must first be selected, as described in "Get Around a Form" immediately above.

- **Text Field** –Type the information you want directly in the field. Use:

  DOWN arrow to open a list of previous values in that field if you have used the form in the past (see the "Using Auto-Complete" QuickSteps)

  LEFT and **RIGHT** arrow keys and **END** and **HOME** keys to move within the text box

  ENTER to accept the contents of the text field and move to the next field

  ESC to reject the contents of the text field and move to the next field

- **Check Box** – Click to select. Use:

  ENTER or **SPACE** to select, and press a second time to deselect a box

- **Radio Button** – Click to select. Use:

  LEFT or **UP** and **RIGHT** or **DOWN** arrow keys to select the previous and next radio buttons

- **List Box** – Click to open the spinner (if the list box is small), click the spinner to display an option, and click the option to select. Use:

  LEFT or **UP** and **RIGHT** or **DOWN** arrow keys to select the previous and next option

  ENTER to open or close the spinner if the list box is smaller than the number of options

- **Combo Box** – Click the down arrow to open the drop-down list, and click the option to select. Use:

  LEFT or **UP** and **RIGHT** or **DOWN** arrow keys to select the previous and next option

- **Button** – Click to select. Use:

  ENTER to select

  ESC to deselect

If the PDF form you are filling out has a Submit button, then it is meant to be transmitted electronically either over a local area network (LAN) or the Internet. In either case the transmittal can be accomplished using e-mail or using an Internet protocol to a web server. In the latter case, you simply click the **Submit** button, and you are done. In the e-mail case it is a little more complex:

1. Move the mouse pointer over an e-mail-enabled **Submit** button, and the default tooltip will tell you to whom the data will be sent.

2. Click an e-mail-enabled **Submit** button, and the Select Email Client dialog box will open (see Figure 8-24). Click:

- **Desktop E-mail Application** if you use Eudora, Outlook, or Outlook Express

- **Internet E-mail** if you use Hotmail, Gmail, or Yahoo

- **Other** if you want to delay choosing a mail client and simply store the results

3. Click **OK**. What happens next depends on what you chose.

Select Email Client

Please indicate the option which best describes how you send mail.

⦿ **Desktop Email Application**

Choose this option if you currently use an email application such as Microsoft Outlook Express, Microsoft Outlook, Eudora, or Mail.

○ **Internet Email**

Choose this option if you currently use an Internet email service such as Yahoo or Microsoft Hotmail.

○ **Other**

Choose this option if your preferred desktop email application is not available or you do not know which option to choose.

| Help | | OK | Cancel |

Figure 8-24: An e-mail-enabled form submittal gives you a choice of the e-mail client.

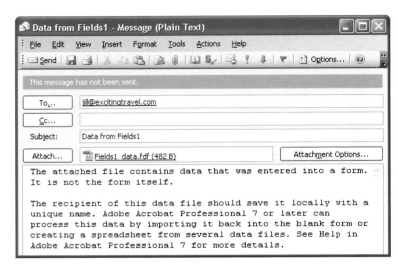

Figure 8-25: Acrobat can e-mail form data using a standard e-mail message.

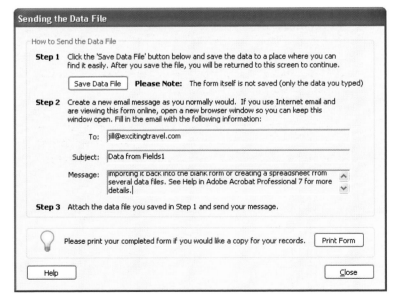

Figure 8-26: If you use Internet e-mail, you must save the form data to a file, create an e-mail message, and attach the data.

If you clicked **Desktop e-mail Application**, the Send Data File dialog box will open.

1. Click **Print Form** if you wish, and then click **Send Data File**. A normal message window from your e-mail application will open with an attachment containing the form data and some text generated by Acrobat, as shown in Figure 8-25.

2. Click **Send**, or whatever is the equivalent button in your e-mail client. You will get a message that the e-mail message has been handed off to your e-mail program. Depending on how your e-mail program is set up, you may need to open it, and click Send/Receive or the equivalent in your program.

USE INTERNET E-MAIL OR OTHER

If you clicked **Internet e-mail** or **Other**, the Sending The Data File dialog box will open (see Figure 8-26).

1. Click **Print Form** if you wish, and then click **Save Data File**. The Export Form Data As dialog box will open. Navigate to a file location in which to store the form data, and click **Save**.

2. If you want to use Internet e-mail, open your browser, go to your mail server, and start an outgoing message. Copy and paste from the To, the Subject, and the Message in the Sending The Data File dialog box to your mail message.

3. Click **Attach A File**, or the equivalent in your mail program, and locate and attach the file you just saved.

4. Click **Send** or the equivalent button in your program. When you are done, click Close to close the Sending The Data File dialog box.

5. If you want to use some other method to transmit the form data, such as dragging it across a local area network (LAN), do so now.

In Outlook and Outlook Express (and possibly other programs), you can sort your e-mail messages by subject. All form data messages will have a subject that begins "Data from" and the name of your form. If you sort by the subject, all of your form data messages will be grouped together.

Use PDF Form Data

Once you have created a form, you can do three things to put it to use:

● Distribute it to the people you want to fill it out.

● Collect the data entered on the form.

● Analyze the data using a spreadsheet.

Acrobat has created an automated process (a "wizard") called Form Data Collection Workflow to help you start this. To begin:

Click the **File** menu, click **Form Data**, and click **Initiate Data File Collection Workflow**.

The **Initiate Form Data Collection Workflow** dialog box will open, as shown in Figure 8-27, and lead you through the process of using a form.

DISTRIBUTE PDF FORMS

To distribute a PDF form:

1. With the Form Data Collection Workflow wizard open, click **Next**.

2. Type the e-mail addresses for the people you want to fill out the form. Click **Next**.

3. Review and change, as needed, the proposed subject and the message of the invitation e-mail.

4. Click **Send Invitation**. An e-mail message window will open with the subject and message you just worked on and the form you want to send attached. Click **Send**. If needed, go to your e-mail program, and make sure that the invitations were sent.

Figure 8-27: The Form Data Collection Workflow wizard lets you distribute, collect, and analyze form data.

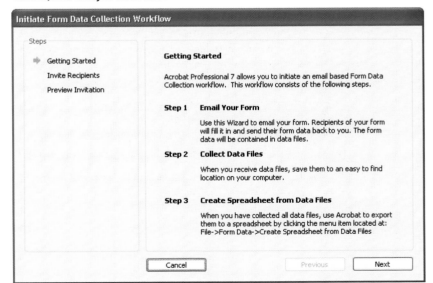

Initiate Form Data Collection Workflow

Steps

➡ Getting Started
　Invite Recipients
　Preview Invitation

Getting Started

Acrobat Professional 7 allows you to initiate an email based Form Data Collection workflow. This workflow consists of the following steps.

Step 1　Email Your Form

Use this Wizard to email your form. Recipients of your form will fill it in and send their form data back to you. The form data will be contained in data files.

Step 2　Collect Data Files

When you receive data files, save them to an easy to find location on your computer.

Step 3　Create Spreadsheet from Data Files

When you have collected all data files, use Acrobat to export them to a spreadsheet by clicking the menu item located at: File->Form Data->Create Spreadsheet from Data Files

Cancel　　　Previous　　　Next

TIP

The Export Data From Multiple Forms dialog box converts the data in .fdf, .pdf, .xfdf, and .xml files to comma separated values in a .csv file. A .csv file can be read by a number of different programs.

HANDLE FORM DATA FROM E-MAIL

To handle the e-mailed data that you receive from your PDF form:

1. Open Windows Explorer and create a new folder to store the data.

2. Open your e-mail program and locate the e-mail messages that contain form data.

3. Using the facilities of your e-mail program, transfer the form data attachments to the new folder you created, giving each a unique name. For example, in Outlook Express, double-click the message, right-click the attachment, click **Save As**, locate the new folder, change the file name to make it unique, and click **Save**. Close the message.

PUT FORM DATA INTO A SPREADSHEET

After collecting responses from a PDF form, you can analyze the data in a spreadsheet. This requires that you export the data in a form that a spreadsheet program, such as Excel, can read. This is the function of the Export Data From Multiple Forms dialog box.

1. In Acrobat open the Export Data From Multiple Forms dialog box by clicking **Form Tasks** in the Tasks toolbar, and clicking **Create Spreadsheet From Data Files**.

The Export Data From Multiple Forms dialog box will open.

Figure 8-28: By putting form data in a spreadsheet, you can summarize it, compute averages, and look at distributions.

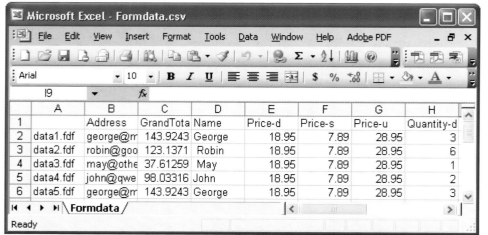

2. Click **Add Files**, locate the folder in which you stored the data files, select one or more files by holding **CTRL** while clicking several files separated by other files, or by holding **SHIFT** while clicking on the first and last file in a contiguous group, and click **Select**.

3. Click **Export**. Select the folder in which to save the converted form data, and click **Save**. The Export Progress dialog box will open and display the conversion.

4. When the conversion is complete, click **View File Now**. Excel, or your spreadsheet program, will open and display the data, as you can see in Figure 8-28.

5. When you are finished, close Excel or your spreadsheet program.

Chapter 9
Adding Navigation and Multimedia

When you display a PDF file in Acrobat, you have a number of ways of getting around, or *navigating*, within the document, and can even jump out of the current PDF and Acrobat and open other documents and web sites. The two major tools that Acrobat provides for this are bookmarks and interactive links. Another kind of link that Acrobat provides allows the PDF reader to start a multimedia presentation. In this chapter you'll see how to add both bookmarks and links, including multimedia links, and how to modify and use them once they are in a PDF.

Add Bookmarks

A *bookmark* is a link in the Bookmark tab of the navigation pane. When a user clicks a bookmark, it is displayed in the document pane. Bookmarks can be created automatically when a PDF is created, or manually after the PDF is created. Once created, bookmarks can be modified and rearranged and used in several ways. Special-purpose bookmarks can be created and used to perform functions other than just opening a page, such as executing a menu command.

Figure 9-1: The PDFMaker installed in Microsoft Word allows you to select the headings and styles that will become bookmarks.

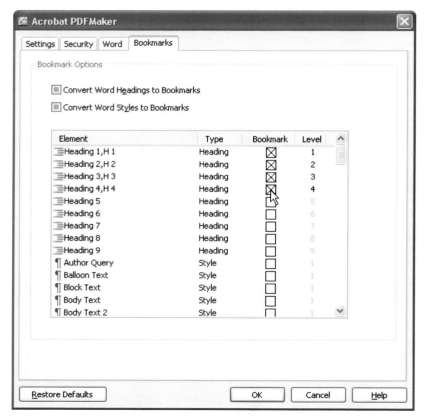

Create Bookmarks Automatically

You can automatically create bookmarks when a PDF is made from a document with a document structure, like a table of contents, or with styles that lead to a hierarchical structure. For example, a Microsoft Word file contains settings in the PDFMaker that provide for the conversion of headings and other Word styles to bookmarks in the resulting PDF.

1. Start Word and open the document you want to convert to a PDF with bookmarks.

2. Click the **Adobe PDF** menu, and click **Change Conversion Settings**. The Acrobat PDFMaker dialog box appears with the Settings tab displayed.

3. If it is not already selected, click **Add Bookmarks To Adobe PDF**, and then click the **Bookmarks** tab.

4. Click the **Bookmark** box for each of the headings and styles that you want to be bookmarks (if they are not already selected); if a heading or style is selected and you want to deselect it, click its corresponding box (see Figure 9-1).

5. To change the hierarchical level of a bookmark, click the level number opposite the heading or style to display a drop-down list box. Click the **Level** down arrow, and click the new level number.

Element	Type	Bookmark	Level
Heading 1,H 1	Heading	☒	1
Heading 2,H 2	Heading	☒	2

6. When finished, click **OK**. To create the PDF, click **Convert To Adobe PDF** in the PDFMaker toolbar, enter the location to store the new PDF, and click **Save**. The PDF opens in Acrobat. Click **Bookmarks** in the navigation pane. You should see the bookmarks that parallel your headings and styles, as shown in Figure 9-2.

Figure 9-2: Bookmarks provide an easy way to locate and jump to part of a document.

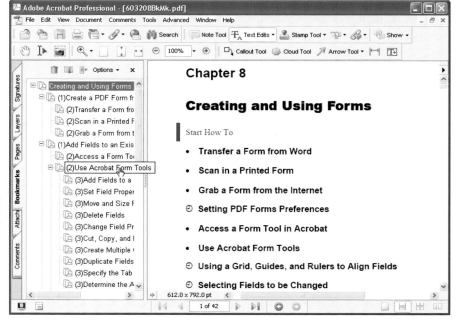

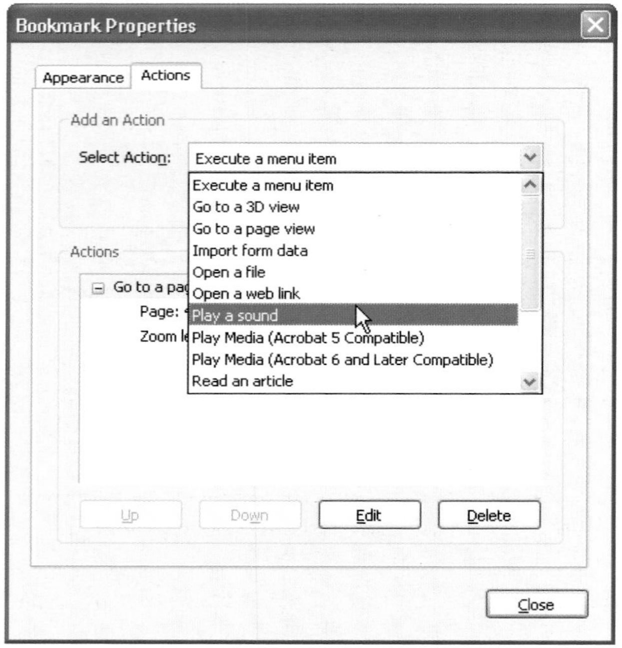

Create Bookmarks Manually

You can manually set bookmarks on anything in a document.

1. Start Acrobat and open the PDF and the page on which you want to add bookmarks. Click the **Select** tool.

2. Select the text or object you want to bookmark:

   - Drag across text to select it.

   - Click an image to select the entire image.

   - Press **CTRL** and drag a rectangle around any object to select it.

3. Click the **Bookmarks** tab in the navigation pane.

   If there are existing bookmarks and you want the new bookmark to go under a particular bookmark other than at the very end, click the bookmark the new one is to go under.

4. Click the **New Bookmark** icon in the navigation pane toolbar. The new bookmark appears in the navigation pane.

5. If the new bookmark is from selected text, the text will appear as the name of the bookmark and will be selected so you can easily replace the name or change it. If the new bookmark is from an image or other object, you will need to type a name for the bookmark and press **ENTER**.

6. If you want the bookmark to be something other than black text on a white background, click the bookmark, click the **View** menu, click **Toolbars**, and click **Properties Bar**. Click the **Color** down arrow, and click a color. Click the **Style** drop-down list, and click a style.

7. If you want to use the appearance of a bookmark for future bookmarks, right-click the bookmark and click **Use Current Appearance As New Default**.

8. If you want a bookmark to perform an action when it is clicked, other than going to the page it references, right-click the bookmark, click **Properties**, click the **Actions** tab, click the **Select Action** down arrow, click an action (as shown in Figure 9-3), and click **Add**. One or more dialog boxes associated with the action may require you to do something. When you are finished, click **Close** in the Bookmark Properties dialog box. This procedure is covered in more detail in "Change Bookmarks" later in this chapter.

Figure 9-3: Clicking a bookmark can perform a number of actions in addition to opening a page in the PDF.

SELECTING BOOKMARKS

Many operations on bookmarks can be performed on one or several bookmarks. Also, in some cases, a bookmark may be hidden and need to be exposed before it can be selected.

SELECT ONE OR MORE BOOKMARKS

If you simply click a bookmark, it will take you to its related page. If you want to work on a bookmark itself, however, you don't want to open the related page:

- To select a single bookmark and not open its related page, move the mouse cursor to the bookmark, press and briefly hold the mouse button down, and then release it (known as a *slow-click*).

  –Or–

  Press and hold **CTRL** while clicking the bookmark, called ***CTRL-click***.

- To select several noncontiguous bookmarks, press and hold **CTRL** while clicking the bookmarks.

- To select several contiguous bookmarks, slow-click the first bookmark in a list, press and hold **SHIFT**, and click the last bookmark.

HIDE OR EXPOSE BOOKMARKS

In a hierarchical list of bookmarks, as you would have with a table of contents, you can hide or expose (collapse or expand) each level of bookmarks:

- To hide or collapse all bookmarks under a given bookmark, click the minus sign (–) located to the left of the bookmark.

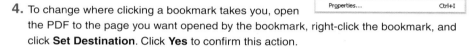

- To expose or expand all bookmarks under a given bookmark, click the plus sign (+) located to the left of the bookmark.

- To hide or expose the top-level bookmarks, click the **Options** down arrow in the Bookmarks toolbar, and click **Collapse Top-Level Bookmarks** or **Expand Top-Level Bookmarks**.

Change Bookmarks

Once a set of bookmarks has been created, you can change the name, its appearance, where it takes you, and any other action it performs.

1. With the PDF whose bookmarks you want to change open in Acrobat, click the **Book-marks** tab to display the bookmarks in the navigation pane.

2. To rename a bookmark, right-click it and click **Rename**. Retype or edit the existing name, and press **ENTER**.

3. To change a bookmark's appearance, slow-click the bookmark (see the "Selecting Bookmarkes" Quick-Steps), click the **View** menu, click **Toolbars**, and click **Properties Bar**. Click the **Color** down arrow, and click a color. Click the **Style** drop-down list, and click a style.

Go to Bookmark	
Cut	Ctrl+X
Delete	
Set Destination	
Rename	
Use Current Appearance as New Default	
Wrap Long Bookmarks	
Properties...	Ctrl+I

4. To change where clicking a bookmark takes you, open the PDF to the page you want opened by the bookmark, right-click the bookmark, and click **Set Destination**. Click **Yes** to confirm this action.

5. To add an action performed when a bookmark is clicked, right-click the bookmark, click **Properties**, click the **Actions** tab, click the **Select Action** down arrow, click an action, and click **Add**. Make the needed entries or selections in the dialog boxes that appear, and click **Close**.

6. To edit an action performed when a bookmark is clicked, right-click the bookmark, click **Properties**, click the **Actions** tab, click the action in the Actions list, and click **Edit**. Make the needed entries or selections in the dialog boxes that appear, and click **Close**.

7. To delete an action performed when a bookmark is clicked, right-click the bookmark, click **Properties**, click the **Action** tab, click the action in the Actions list, and click **Delete**. Click **Close** to close the Properties dialog box.

8. To delete a bookmark and all its subordinate bookmarks, right-click the bookmark and click **Delete**.

   –Or–

   Select the bookmark and click the **trash can** icon in the Bookmarks toolbar.

9. To wrap long bookmarks, click the **Options** down arrow in the Bookmarks toolbar, and click **Wrap Long Bookmarks**.

NOTE

Changing the order of bookmarks does not change the order of the pages represented by the bookmarks.

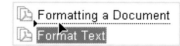

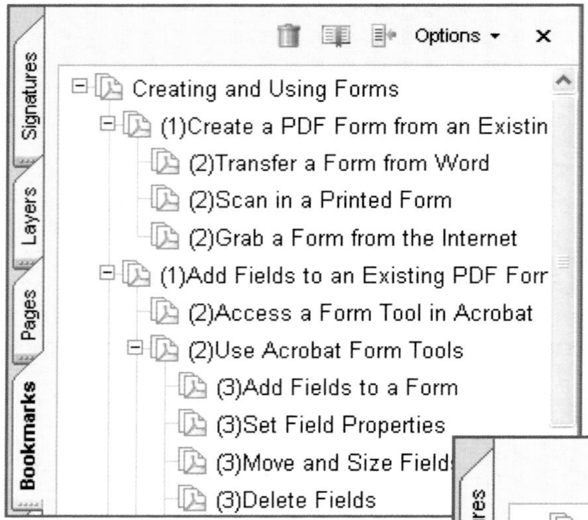
Options
Signatures
Layers
Pages
Bookmarks
Creating and Using Forms
(1)Create a PDF Form from an Existin
(2)Transfer a Form from Word
(2)Scan in a Printed Form
(2)Grab a Form from the Internet
(1)Add Fields to an Existing PDF Forr
(2)Access a Form Tool in Acrobat
(2)Use Acrobat Form Tools
(3)Add Fields to a Form
(3)Set Field Properties
(3)Move and Size Field
(3)Delete Fields

Figure 9-4a: Bookmarks created with the PDF bring with them the document structure.

Rearrange Bookmarks

When you create a set of bookmarks based on a document structure, as discussed in "Create Bookmarks Automatically" earlier in this chapter, the hierarchical structure of headings (heading 3s within headings 2s within heading 1s) are automatically duplicated in the bookmarks and are linked so you can collapse each level, as shown in Figure 9-4a. When you create bookmarks manually, they are initially all independent without hierarchy or linking, as shown in Figure 9-4b, but you can manually arrange the hierarchy and order of the bookmarks, as well as link them.

1. With a PDF with bookmarks you want to reorder open in Acrobat, click the **Bookmarks** tab to open the navigation pane.
2. Select one or more bookmarks (see the QuickSteps "Selecting Bookmarks" earlier in this chapter).
3. Drag the selected bookmark(s) up or down until it is under the bookmark you want to be its parent. A line is displayed under the parent.

Formatting a Document
Format Text

4. To move a selected group (one or more) of bookmarks, select the bookmarks and drag them to the new parent.

   –Or–

   Select the bookmarks, click the **Options** down arrow, click **Cut**, right-click the new parent, and click **Paste**.

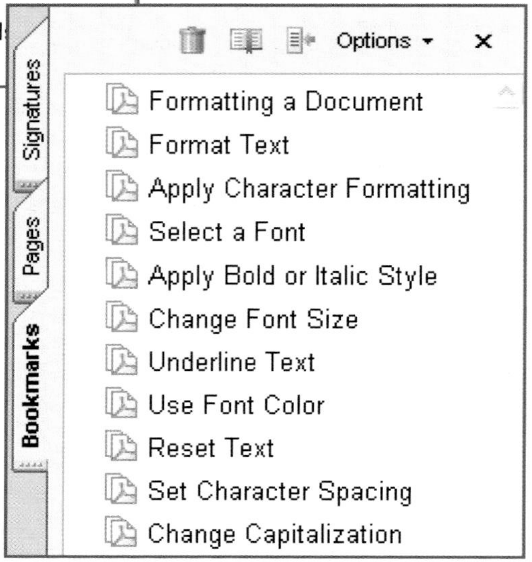
Options
Signatures
Pages
Bookmarks
Formatting a Document
Format Text
Apply Character Formatting
Select a Font
Apply Bold or Italic Style
Change Font Size
Underline Text
Use Font Color
Reset Text
Set Character Spacing
Change Capitalization

Figure 9-4b: Manually created bookmarks do not have a structure.

Add Interactive Links

Interactive links are objects, text, graphics, or just a spot on a page within a PDF that, when clicked, open a different page in the current document, open a different electronic document, open a web page, or perform some action, such as playing multimedia (see "Add Multimedia" later in this chapter). Links in PDFs are the same as links, or hyperlinks, in web pages and can serve as a primary means of navigation and automation.

Create Interactive Links

Links can be created in another program and carried over to the PDF in the conversion process, or you can add links to an existing PDF. In both cases, the links look and work the same.

BRING LINKS FROM ANOTHER PROGRAM

Links can be brought into a PDF from many different programs and from web pages. To create links in Microsoft Word and convert them to a PDF (the links in this case will be internal to other locations in the same document):

1. Start Word and open the document in which you want to create links prior to converting the document to a PDF.

2. In the Word document, locate and select the text that will be the destination of the link.

3. Click the **Insert** menu and click **Bookmark**. The Bookmark dialog box appears.

4. Type a one-word name and click **Add**. Repeat steps 2 through 4 to create all the bookmarks you need.

5. In the Word document, locate and select the text that will be the actual link.

6. Right-click the selected text and click **Hyperlink**. The Insert Hyperlink dialog box appears.

7. Click **Place In This Document** on the left side of the dialog box. The list of bookmarks that you created should appear in the center.

8. Double-click the bookmark that you want to be the destination of the link. The link is created. If you **CTRL-**click it (see Figure 9-5), the destination page will open.

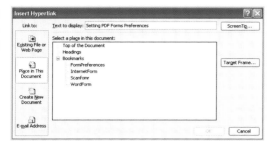

9. Save the Word document, click **Convert To Adobe PDF**, and create the PDF in the normal way. When the PDF opens in Acrobat, clicking the link will open the page with the Word bookmark.

Figure 9-5: Links in Microsoft Word will directly convert to links in a PDF.

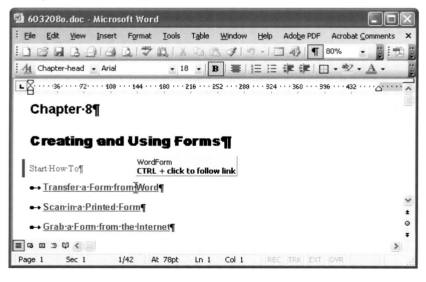

ADD LINKS TO A PDF

In a PDF, a link can open a page in the current document, open another document, open a web page, or perform an action. In Acrobat, you can select text, an image, or an area to act as a link in two different ways.

1. Click the **Select** tool in the Basic toolbar. Drag across text, click an image, or drag a rectangle around an object to select it. Right-click the selected text or object, and click **Create Link**.

–Or–

Click the **Tools** menu, click **Advanced Editing**, and click **Link Tool**. Drag a rectangle around text, an object or image, or blank space.

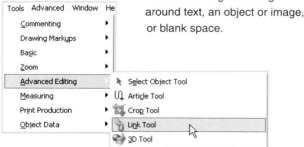

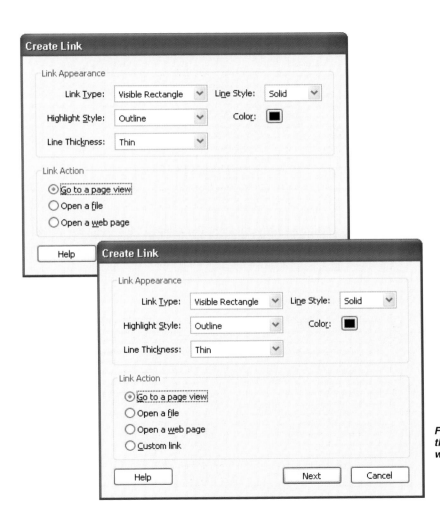

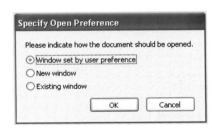

In both cases, the Create Link dialog box appears, as shown in Figure 9-6. The dialog box on the bottom comes from the Select tool, while the dialog box on the top is from the Link tool. You can see the Link tool has the ability to create custom links.

2. Click the drop-down arrows opposite each of the four Link Appearance drop-down lists, and select the appearance attributes you want to use. Finally, select the color you want.

3. To go to a page in the current document, click **Go To A Page**, and click **Next**. Use the scroll bars, mouse, and zoom tools to open the page the link will open. When ready, click **Set Link**.

4. To open a file, click **Open A File** and click **Next**. Locate the folder and file to open, and click **Select**. If a PDF file is selected, choose how the document should be opened.

5. To open a web page, click **Open A Web Page**, and click **Next**. Enter the URL for the page to be opened. If the page is one that has been selected in the past, click the drop-down arrow and click the URL. When finished, click **OK**.

6. To perform an action, use the **Link** tool, click **Custom Link**, and click **Next**. If needed, click the **Actions** tab. Click the **Select Action** drop-down list, click an action (such as **Play A Sound**), and click **Add**. Locate the folder and file containing the music file, and click **Select**. Repeat this step for additional actions. When finished, click **Close**.

Figure 9-6: Only the Link tool has the ability to create custom links with an action attached to them.

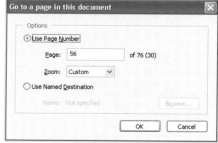

TIP

Any links created with an "invisible rectangle" display a link rectangle when the Link tool is selected.

TIP

Clicking the **Edit** menu and clicking **Undo**, or pressing **CTRL+Z**, repeatedly can undo a lot of changes made to links.

Modify Links

You can modify one or more links by selecting them, changing their selection rectangles, changing their appearance, changing what they open or do, or changing their other properties.

1. With the PDF whose links you want to modify open in Acrobat, click the **Tools** menu, click **Advanced Editing**, and click **Link Tool**.

2. Move the mouse pointer over the link rectangle. The link is identified by eight *sizing handles*:

   - Drag any of the four corner handles to diagonally change the size of the link rectangle.

   - Drag any of the four side handles to move a side in or out.

   - Move the mouse pointer inside the rectangle, and drag the entire rectangle to a different location.

3. Right-click in a link rectangle to open the link's context menu:

   - Click **Edit** and click **Delete** to delete the link, or click **Cut** or **Copy** to do either of those operations.

   - With a number of links selected, click **Edit** and click **Align**, **Center**, **Distribute**, or **Size** to make all the selected link rectangles similarly aligned.

   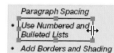

4. With one or more links selected, right-click the selection and click **Properties** (to select multiple links on a page, press **CTRL** and click each link; to select all links in a stack, click the first link, press **SHIFT**, and click the last link):

   - Click the **Appearance** tab if it isn't already displayed. Use the drop-down lists to change any of the appearance attributes.

   - Click the **Actions** tab. If the action is Go To A Page In This Document and you want to change it, click the action (Go To A Page...), and click **Edit** to open the Go To A Page In This Document dialog box. Change the page number and click **OK**.

   - When finished modifying link properties, click **Close**.

NOTE

To play media files, you must have speakers and a sound card, as well as player software, such as Windows Media Player, Apple QuickTime, or RealOne.

CAUTION

Sound and video files can be quite large, and when embedded in the PDF file, the PDF can become huge.

Figure 9-7: When you add music to a PDF, you can also add an image of the album cover.

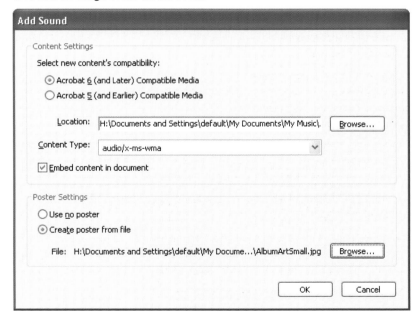

5. Click the **Advanced** menu and click **Links**:

- To create links from text that looks like a URL, for example: http://www.osborne.com, click **Create From URLs In Document**.

- To remove all links in the document, click **Remove All Links From Document**.

Add Multimedia

Adding multimedia to a PDF adds sound and/or video clips that the user of the PDF can play using custom links, as you saw in "Create Interactive Links" earlier in this chapter. Acrobat has two tools, the Sound tool and the Movie tool, that are used to add clips.

Add Sound

To add sound to a PDF:

1. With the PDF open in Acrobat, click the **Tools** menu, click **Advanced Editing**, and click **Sound Tool**.

2. Drag a rectangle to identify the area within which the sound clip will be activated. The Add Sound dialog box appears.

3. Select the type of compatibility you want: **Acrobat 6 And Later** or **Acrobat 5 And Earlier**. Under most circumstances, you want Acrobat 6 And Later because it adds a number of features for multimedia.

4. Click **Browse** to locate and select the sound file you want to use. The content type is filled in automatically based on this selection. With Acrobat 6 compatibility, **Embed Content In Document** is selected by default.

5. Choose whether you want an image of the album cover displayed (called a "poster") and, if so, browse for its file (usually stored in the same folder with the music) (see Figure 9-7).

6. When finished, click **OK**.

Add Video

To add video to a PDF:

1. With the PDF open in Acrobat, click the **Tools** menu, click **Advanced Editing**, and click **Movie Tool**.

2. Drag a rectangle to identify the area within which the movie clip will be activated. The Add Movie dialog box appears.

3. Select the type of compatibility you want: **Acrobat 6 And Later** or **Acrobat 5 And Earlier**. Under most circumstances, you want Acrobat 6 And Later because it adds a number of features for multimedia.

4. Click **Browse** to locate and select the movie file you want to use. The content type is filled in automatically based on this selection. With Acrobat 6 compatibility and known file types, **Snap To Content Proportions** and **Embed Content In Document** are selected by default.

5. Choose whether you want a "poster" from the first frame of the movie, or browse to locate the file you want to use (see Figure 9-8).

6. When finished, click **OK**.

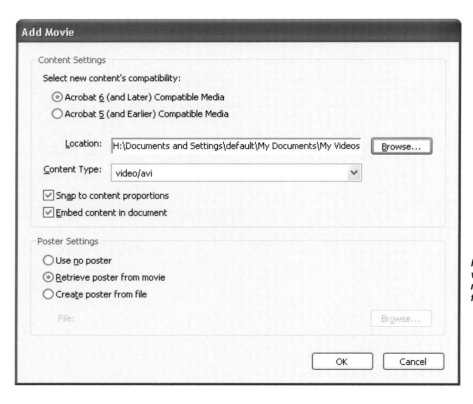

Figure 9-8: When you add video to a PDF, you can also make a "poster" from the first frame of the movie.

Modify Sound and Video in a PDF

If a multimedia file has been added to a PDF, you can modify the file by moving and/or resizing the activation area, changing its properties, or deleting it.

1. Open the PDF with the media clip you want to modify, and click **Tools**, click **Advanced Editing**, and click either **Movie Tool** or **Sound Tool**.

2. Move the media tool (Movie or Sound) over the activation area, and eight sizing handles appear. Drag any one of these handles to modify the size of the area.

3. With the media tool inside the activation area, drag the area to a new location.

4. Right-click in the activation area to open its context menu:

   • Click **Edit** and click **Delete** to delete the media clip, or click **Cut** or **Copy** to do either of those operations.

   • Click **Center** to center the activation area horizontally, vertically, or both.

5. Right-click the activation area and click **Properties**:

   • Click the **Settings** tab if it isn't already displayed. Modify the **Annotation Title** and **Alternate Text** fields as needed. Select the event that will play the media. If you want to add or edit a rendition, or version, of a media, click either of those buttons and change the settings as needed (see Figure 9-9).

   • Click the **Appearance** tab and use the drop-down lists to change any of the appearance attributes.

   • Click the **Actions** tab. If you want to add additional actions, select the trigger and the action, click **Add**, and click **OK**.

   • When you are finished modifying multimedia properties, click **Close**.

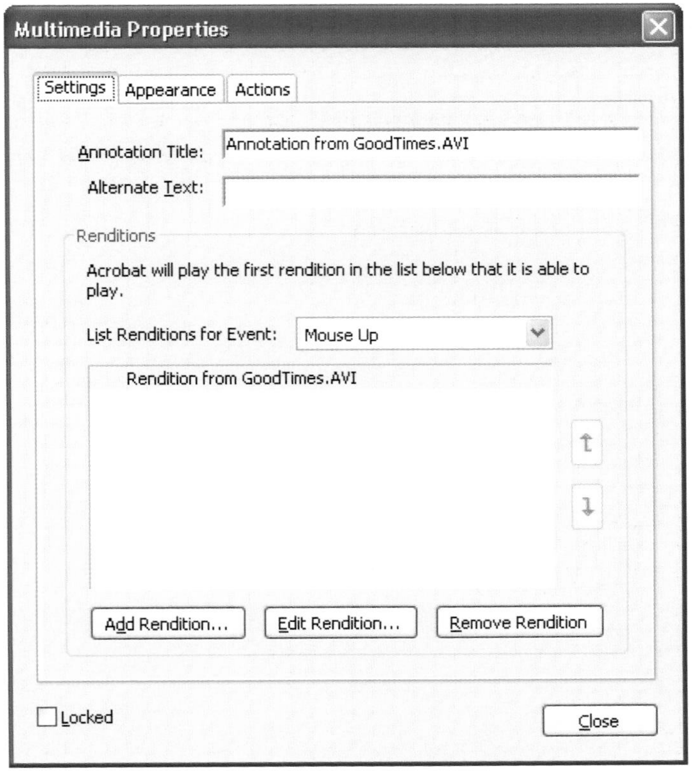

Figure 9-9: Use different renditions if you believe users of your PDF will be using different players.

Chapter 10
Establishing Security

If the PDF you are creating needs to be secure from the many computer threats out there, Acrobat gives you a number of ways to accomplish that. You can use passwords to restrict who can open a PDF, set up security levels to limit changes, encrypt a PDF, use certificates to implement digital signatures and file verification, and create a policy to manage security. In effect, you have four major degrees of security:

- Limiting access with passwords
- Restricting document usage
- Using certificates
- Implementing a security policy

QUICKSTEPS

LOOKING AT PDF SECURITY SETTINGS

If you can open a PDF file, you can look at the security settings pertaining to that particular document. If you can't open a file, your only recourse is to go to the originator of the file and get the appropriate permission.

CHECK DOCUMENT SECURITY

1. Open the document in Acrobat or Adobe Reader.

2. Click the **Document** menu, click **Security**, and click **Show Security Settings For This Document**. The Document Properties dialog box appears with the Security tab displayed, as shown in Figure 10-1.

3. Click **Show Details**. The Document Security dialog box appears.

4. When you are done looking at the security details, click **OK** and then click **OK** again to close the dialog box.

NOTE

The discussion on security in this chapter relates to Acrobat 7 and Windows XP. Older versions of Acrobat and Windows have different types of and ways to implement security. From a security standpoint, it is strongly recommended that you use these products, especially Windows XP SP2, which, at this writing, is the latest version of Windows and has a number of security enhancements.

This chapter will discuss these degrees of security. It is important to understand that looking at security is much like peeling back the layers of an onion—it seems endless and hurts your eyes after a bit. Our discussion here will be brief and focused on how to implement security without providing much background on the different types of security.

Figure 10-1: Security settings are a part of a PDF document's properties.

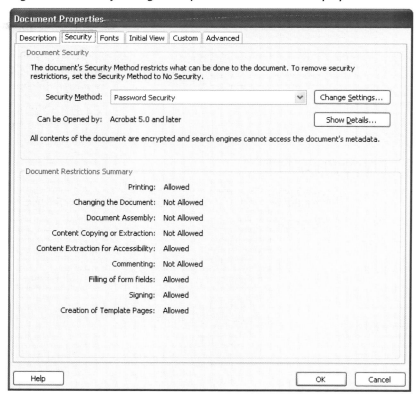

10

You cannot recover a password that is lost or forgotten. Your best course of action is to keep a copy of a PDF without password protection on a CD or DVD and store it in a safe place.

Set Up Password Access

The simplest form of security is to require a password in order to open a PDF file. With the password, the document is protected by encryption and would be exceptionally hard for someone to open.

Add Access-Password Protection

To add a password to a PDF:

1. In Windows Explorer, make a copy of the PDF you are about to password protect, renaming it, and possibly putting it on a CD that you can place in safekeeping. This protects you should you forget and/or lose the password.

2. Open the PDF in Acrobat, click **Secure** in the Tasks toolbar, and click **Show Security Settings For This Document**. The Security tab of the Document Properties dialog box appears, as shown in Figure 10-1.

3. Click the **Security Method** down arrow, and click **Password Security**. The Password Security – Settings dialog box appears, which contains the Document Open Password field, as shown in Figure 10-2.

Figure 10-2: Implementing a password automatically encrypts the PDF.

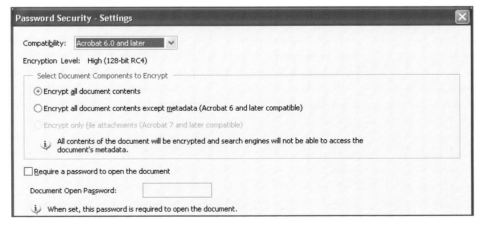

USING PASSWORDS

The type of password you use and the way in which you use it has a lot to do with how good your password security is. To create and maintain strong passwords:

- Use passwords of at least seven characters.
- Use passwords with a mixture of letters, numbers, and special characters, except the following: ! @ # $ % ^ & * , | \ ; " " < > _
- Do not use your birth date, wedding anniversary, pet's name, street address, or any recognizable words or number groupings.
- Change your password often, although you may not want to do this when protecting documents you give to others.
- If you write down your password, store it in a safe place.
- Do not transfer your password over the Internet.

NOTE

If you click Save instead of Save As and save the file to the same location as the original file, you will be asked if you want to replace the current, unprotected file with a protected one.

4. Click the **Compatibility** down arrow, and choose the version of Acrobat with which you want to be compatible. The key is to determine which Acrobat version is used by the majority of users of the PDF that you are encrypting. See the "Understanding Encryption" QuickFacts for a description of the encryption types available with various Acrobat versions.

5. Depending on the Acrobat version that you have chosen, select the document components you want encrypted.

6. Click **Require A Password To Open The Document**, and type a password in the Document Open Password field.

7. Note the password and click **OK**. Confirm the password by retyping it, and again click **OK**. You are reminded that the password will only take effect after you save and close the document. Click **OK** again.

8. In the Document Properties dialog box, the Security Method field now shows "Password Security." Click **OK**, click the **File** menu, click **Save As**, choose the location and type the file name you want to use, and click **Save**. Close the document.

9. In Acrobat, reopen the PDF you just closed. The Password dialog box appears. Type the password you created earlier, and click **OK**. The PDF should open.

Change or Remove Password Protection

To change or remove password protection, you must know the existing password and have the ability to open the PDF.

CHANGE A PASSWORD

To change a password:

1. Open the PDF in Acrobat using the correct password. Click **Secure** in the Tasks toolbar, and click **Show Security Settings For This Document**.

2. In the Document Properties dialog box, click **Change Settings**. The Password Security – Settings dialog box appears.

3. In the **Document Open Password** text box, type the new password you want to use. Make any other changes in the dialog box, and click **OK**.

UNDERSTANDING ENCRYPTION

Encrypting a PDF file scrambles the information using a mathematical algorithm with a numeric key. No matter how someone tries to look at what is stored on a disk, all he or she will see is gibberish. When the correct password is provided, the key is presented to the algorithm, allowing it to unscramble the information. For basic password security, the same key is used both for encryption and decryption and is called a *private key*. (Later in this chapter we'll talk about a public key; see the "Understanding Public Keys" QuickFacts.)

Depending on the version of Acrobat you chose for compatibility in the Password Security – Settings dialog box, the encryption will use different types of numeric keys and algorithms, and you will be able to encrypt different parts of the document:

- **Acrobat 3.0** compatibility uses a low level of encryption with a 40-bit key and the RC4 (Rivest Cipher 4) algorithm. The only choice is to encrypt the entire document.

- **Acrobat 5.0** compatibility uses a high level of encryption with a 128-bit key and the RC4 algorithm. Only the entire document may be encrypted.

- **Acrobat 6.0** compatibility uses a high level of encryption with a 128-bit key and the RC4 algorithm. The entire document may be encrypted; or you may exclude metadata, such as title, author, description, creation date, and so on, to allow a search to read this information.

- **Acrobat 7.0** compatibility uses a high level of encryption with a 128-bit key and the AES (Advanced Encryption Standard) algorithm. The entire document may be encrypted; or you may exclude metadata, such as author, creation date, and so on; or you may encrypt only the attachments.

4. Confirm your new password, click **OK**, and click **OK** again to acknowledge that the settings will not be changed until you save and close the document.

5. Click **OK** to close the Document Properties dialog box, save your PDF, and close it.

6. Reopen the PDF you just closed. The Password dialog box appears. Type the password you created earlier, and click **OK**. The PDF should open.

REMOVE A PASSWORD

To remove a password:

1. Open the PDF in Acrobat using the correct password. Click **Secure** in the Tasks toolbar, and click **Remove Security Settings For This Document**.

2. Click **OK** to remove the security settings. Save and close the PDF.

3. Reopen the PDF you just closed. The PDF should open without prompting you for a password.

Limit PDF Use and Changes

Acrobat allows you to use passwords in two ways: to limit the opening of PDF files, as described in "Set Up Password Access" earlier in this chapter; and to limit the use and changes to the PDF file once it is opened. The latter is called a "permissions password," and with it you can control:

- The type of printing allowed

- The changes allowed in terms of inserting and deleting pages, filling in forms, and commenting

- The copying of content

- The use of screen readers to read text

NOTE

If you use a password to open a file and a permissions password to control the use and changing of a file, the permissions password can also be used to open the file. To change the permissions password, however, a person must have the password required to open the file.

TIP

When a PDF document has limited permissions, a padlock icon is displayed in the lower-left corner of the Acrobat window . If you move the mouse pointer over the icon, you will see a message telling you about the security features that have been implemented. Also, with limited permissions, the menu items and toolbar buttons are disabled for any unavailable features.

This document has been encrypted and may use security features that prevent you from modifying certain aspects of it.
Use the Security panel in the Document Properties dialog to view these settings.

Set the Permissions Password

To set and change the permissions password and the features it protects:

1. Open the PDF in Acrobat, click **Secure** in the Tasks toolbar, and click **Show Security Settings For This Document**. The Document Properties dialog box appears with the Security tab displayed, as shown in Figure 10-1.

2. Click the **Security Method** down arrow, and click **Password Security**. The Password Security – Settings dialog box appears, the Permissions part of which is shown in Figure 10-3.

3. Click the **Compatibility** down arrow, and choose the version of Acrobat with which you want to be compatible. See the "Understanding Encryption" QuickFacts earlier in this chapter for a description of the types of encryption available with different versions of Acrobat.

4. Click **Use A Password To Restrict Printing And Editing**, and type a password (see the "Using Passwords" QuickFacts earlier in this chapter).

5. Click the **Printing Allowed** down arrow, and click the type of printing that can be used.

6. Click the **Changes Allowed** down arrow, and click the types of changes you will allow.

7. If desired, click **Enable Copying Of Text, Images, And Other Content** (this option is not selected by default).

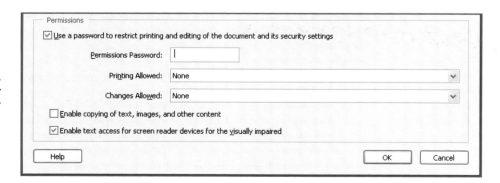

Figure 10-3: You can limit what people do in a PDF without limiting their access to it.

NOTE

In this section, we don't create an unprotected copy at the beginning as we did earlier; but by using the Save As command, we're creating an unprotected copy (the original file).

CAUTION

The permissions password provides a restriction on usage in Adobe products, but it may not in non-Adobe products, which can allow unrestricted changes, printing, and copying. The best protection is to make sure that a password is required to open the file, which also encrypts it.

8. If not desired, click **Enable Text Access For Screen Reader Devices For The Visually Impaired** (this option is selected by default).

9. Note the password and click **OK**. You are reminded that permissions passwords may not prevent changes by non-Adobe products. Click **OK**.

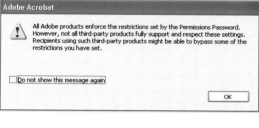

10. Confirm the permissions password by retyping it, and again click **OK**. You are reminded that the password will only take effect after you save and close the document. Click **OK** again.

11. In the Document Properties dialog box, click **OK**, click the **File** menu, click **Save As**, choose the location and type the file name you want to use, and click **Save**. Close the document.

Use Permission Restrictions

If you set up a permissions password and limit what the user can do but don't use a password to limit the opening of a PDF, the user will not know the file has permission restrictions until he or she tries to perform a restricted action. If he opens the Edit menu, he might notice that many of the options are unavailable. If she goes to print using the icon in the File toolbar, she might notice that the Print icon is unavailable. The only way to use these disabled features is to remove the restrictions using the permissions password.

1. In Acrobat, reopen the PDF that has a permissions password. If there is no password required to open the file, then it will simply open.

2. Look at several pages and observe that you can view them normally. Open several menus and observe the unavailable options. Note the potentially unavailable Print icon on the File toolbar.

3. Click **Secure** in the Tasks toolbar, and click **Show Security Settings For This Document**. The Document Properties dialog box appears with the Security tab displayed. Note the Document Restrictions area in the lower part of the dialog box.

4. Click **Change Settings**. The Password dialog box appears, as shown in Figure 10-4. Type the permissions password and click **OK**.

5. Change the permission restrictions, if desired; or simply use the restricted-features settings, such as printing, as they are by default, and click **OK**. Click **OK** again for the third-party software notice, and click **OK** once more in response to the message that changes will not be applied until you save and close the file. Close the Document Properties dialog box.

You now have full use of all of Acrobat's printing and editing capabilities. Given that you did not change the use of permissions restrictions, when you save, close, and reopen the PDF, it will once more have restrictions on the features you originally chose to restrict.

Document Properties

Description | **Security** | Fonts | Initial View | Custom | Advanced

Document Security

The document's Security Method restricts what can be done to the document. To remove security restrictions, set the Security Method to No Security.

Security Method: Password Security   [Change Settings...]

Can be Opened by: Acrobat 5.0 and later   [Show Details...]

All contents of the document are encrypted and search engines cannot access the document's metadata.

Password   [X]

⚠ '860803.pdf' is protected. Please enter a Permissions Password.

Enter Password: [   ]

[OK]   [Cancel]

Content Extraction for Accessibility: Allowed
Commenting: Not Allowed
Filling of form fields: Allowed
Signing: Allowed
Creation of Template Pages: Allowed

[Help]   [OK]   [Cancel]

Figure 10-4: To use permission-restricted features, you must open the Document Properties dialog box and proceed as if you are going to change the password.

Use Digital Signatures

Digital signatures identify either the author of a document or a reader who is agreeing to the contents of the document. Acrobat allows you to digitally add both of these types of signatures. These signatures not only identify the person, but the author signature also assures the authenticity of the document, because the presence of the signature proves that the document has not been changed.

To use a digital signature with a PDF, you need to create a digital ID with a user profile and a password. This is placed in a certificate with two keys. One is a *private key* that is used only by you to sign, certify, and encrypt a document. The second key is a public key that can be given to others to verify your signature and read the document without giving them the ability to change it. See the "Understanding Public Keys" QuickFacts in this chapter.

Create a Digital ID

You can create a digital ID and have it authenticated within Acrobat, by Windows XP or Windows 2003 Server, or by third-party authentication services. This section will discuss how a digital ID is created and authenticated in Acrobat. When you have created a digital ID, it is important that you copy it and store it in a safe place, because once you use it to sign and encrypt a file, you must have the ID to open it again.

Figure 10-5: You may already have digital IDs that were created in Windows.

1. In Acrobat, click the **Advanced** menu and click **Security Settings**. The Security Settings window opens, as shown in Figure 10-5. (In Acrobat Reader, click the **Document** menu and click **Security Settings**.)

2. Click **Digital IDs** in the left pane, and click **Add ID** in the toolbar at the top. The Add Digital ID dialog box appears. This gives you the choice of using an existing digital ID, such as one you created in Windows, a self-signed digital ID created in Acrobat (discussed here), or a third-party digital ID.

3. Click **Create A Self-Signed Digital ID**, and click **Next** twice. Accept the default **New PKCS#12 Digital ID File**, and click **Next**. The Identity Information dialog box appears.

4. Type the requested information through the Country field. Leave the default values for the Key and Usage fields, and click **Next**.

5. Leave the default value for the file location, type and confirm a password of at least six characters, and click **Finish**. Write down this password and store it in a safe place.

6. Click **Digital ID Files** in the Security Settings window's left pane, and place the mouse cursor over the Folder column to see the full path, as shown:

C:\Documents and Settings\Marty Matthews\Application Data\Adobe\Acrobat\7.0\Security\

7. Open Windows Explorer, find the folder you just identified in step 6, and locate your digital ID file, which will have a .pfx extension. Copy this file to another drive and to a CD or DVD, which you store in a safe place.

Add a Digital Signature to a PDF

When you have a document exactly the way you want it, you are ready to sign it. If you make a change after signing it, a warning is placed in the signature field so the reader will have less assurance that the document is as you wrote it. You can simply sign a document, or you can sign and certify the contents of the document. If a change is made to the document after it is certified, the signature is invalidated. Finally, you can choose if the signature is visible on the actual document or if it is displayed on the Signature tab of the navigation pane.

1. With the finished document you want to sign open in Acrobat, click the **Document** menu, click **Digital Signatures**, and click **Sign This Document**.

   –Or–

   Click **Sign** in the Tasks toolbar, and click **Sign This Document**.

   In either case, if the document is not certified, you will receive a message to that effect.

2. If needed, click **Certify Document**. You are told about the need for a digital ID in order to create a certified document. Click **OK**. The Save As Certified Document dialog box appears.

3. Click the **Allowed Actions** drop-down arrow, make the relevant choice, and click **Next**.

Allowed Actions:	Disallow any changes to the document
☑ Lock the Certif	Disallow any changes to the document
	Only allow form fill-in actions on this document
	Only allow commenting and form fill-in actions on this document

4. Choose whether you want to show the certification on the document, and click **Next**. Read about drawing a rectangle for the area with the certification, and click **OK**.

5. Drag a rectangular area. When you release the mouse button, if you have more than one digital ID, the Apply Digital Signature dialog box appears. Double-click the digital ID you want to use, and the Save As Certified Document – Sign dialog box appears.

6. Type your password, select the reason for signing the document, click **Show Options**, select the appearance, and fill in the city and contact information, as shown in Figure 10-6.

7. Click **Sign And Save As** to save the certified and signed file with a new name, or click **Sign And Save** to sign the file with the existing name. If needed, select the folder, type a file name, and click **Save**.

8. Click **OK** to acknowledge the message that the document was successfully signed. A digital signature is displayed in the area you identified, as shown:

   Digitally signed by Marty
   cn=Marty, c=US, o=Matthews Technology, ou=Matthews, email=marty@mtech.com
   Reason: I attest to the accuracy and integrity of this document
   Location: Seattle, WA
   Date: 2005.02.24 21:36:10 -08'00'

Figure 10-6: To certify and sign a file, you must enter the password that is part of your digital ID.

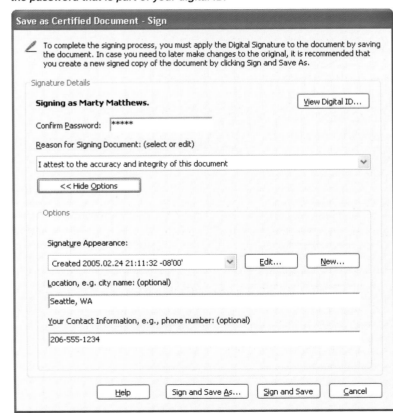

Save as Certified Document - Sign

To complete the signing process, you must apply the Digital Signature to the document by saving the document. In case you need to later make changes to the original, it is recommended that you create a new signed copy of the document by clicking Sign and Save As.

Signature Details

Signing as Marty Matthews.   [View Digital ID...]

Confirm Password: [*****]

Reason for Signing Document: (select or edit)

[I attest to the accuracy and integrity of this document   ⌄]

[<< Hide Options]

Options

Signature Appearance:

[Created 2005.02.24 21:11:32 -08'00'   ⌄] [Edit...] [New...]

Location, e.g. city name: (optional)

[Seattle, WA]

Your Contact Information, e.g., phone number: (optional)

[206-555-1234]

[Help]   [Sign and Save As...]   [Sign and Save]   [Cancel]

Export Your Digital ID

In order for others to view your signed PDFs, they must have a copy of your digital ID with the public key. They can then open and read the document, and possibly sign it, but they can't change it in any other way. This is called "exporting your certificate" or "sending a public key."

1. In Acrobat, click the **Advanced** menu and click **Security Settings**. (In Adobe Reader, click the **Document** menu and click **Security Settings**.) The Security Settings window opens.

2. Click **Digital IDs** in the left pane, in the right pane, click the digital ID file you want to export, and click **Export Certificate** in the toolbar. The Data Exchange File – Export Options dialog box appears and gives you the choice of creating a file you can distribute any way you want or directly e-mailing the file to someone.

3. If you choose **Email The Data To Someone** and click **Next**, the Compose Email dialog box appears. Type the e-mail address of the person to whom you want to send the file. Make any other changes to the subject line or body of the message, and click **Email**.

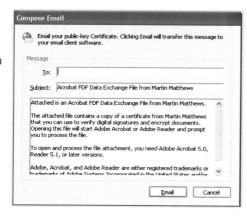

4. If you choose **Save The Data To A File** and click **Next**, the Export Data As dialog box appears. Identify the folder where you want the file stored (leave the file name as is), and click **Save**. Click **OK** to acknowledge the completion of the save operation.

5. Close the Security Settings window.

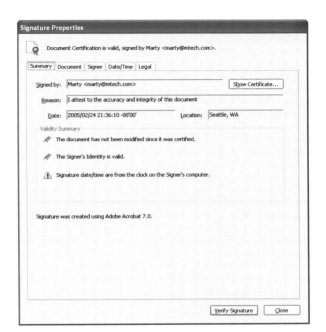

Figure 10-7: You can learn a lot of information about a document and the signer from the Signature Properties dialog box.

Verify a Digital Signature

If someone sends you a document with a digital signature, you can open the document and see the signature. If the signature uses third-party authentication and you are connected to the Internet, you may be able to authenticate the signature over the Internet. Otherwise, you will get a questionable signature message along with a dialog box explaining that a questionable signature may certify the document but that your computer had no way to verify the signature. To verify it, you need to use the same means the author of the document used to validate his or her signature—either an Internet-based third-party service, or through a certificate, which the author created and will need to send you.

To verify a signature using a certficate that was sent to you:

1. Open in your e-mail program the message containing the certificate as an attachment. Save the attachment on your hard drive, noting the folder it is in.

2. In Windows Explorer, locate the certificate and double-click it to open it in Acrobat or in Reader. This file has an .fdf extension and a name like CertExchangeMartinMatthews.fdf. The Data Exchange File – Import Contact dialog box appears.

3. Click **Set Contact Trust** to open the Import Contact Settings dialog box.

4. Click **Signatures And As A Trusted Root** and/or **Certified Documents (And Then For Dynamic Content And/Or Embedded JavaScript)**, click **OK**, and click **OK** again to acknowledge that one issuer certificate has been imported.

5. Close the Data Exchange File – Import Contact dialog box.

If you now reopen the file with the signature, the Document Status dialog appears telling you the signature is valid. If you close the dialog box, right-click the signature, and click **Properties**, the Signature Properties dialog box appears, as shown in Figure 10-7, providing a significant amount of information.

UNDERSTANDING PUBLIC KEYS

In the "Understanding Encryption" QuickFacts earlier in this chapter, it was explained that a private key is used to encrypt files on your computer. Private keys are useful when the key never leaves your computer, but if you send it over the Internet, or even by private courier, it is possible that someone else might get it, and then the key is not so private.

A *public key* is actually a pair of keys that only work together: a public key that you don't care who has, and a private key that you want to keep private. The combination of public and private keys work in one of two ways:

- As has been discussed in this chapter, you can use a private key to lock the document to prevent changes, and encrypt, certify, and sign it. Then a public key can be used to only decrypt the document so it can be read. With this method, the original locking and certification are the important features and the encryption is not that important. You do not care who reads the document; you just don't want anyone to change it or represent they wrote it.

- You can also reverse the process. You can create a digital ID and export it to the author of a document, keeping the private key and sending the author the public key. The author uses the public key to lock, certify, sign, and encrypt the document and then sends it to you. You, and you alone, can use the private key to decrypt and read the document. With this method, the encryption and prevention of others from reading the document are the important features; anybody can send you the document, but only you can read it.

Implement a Security Policy

If you want to apply the same security settings to more than a couple of documents, then you need to establish a security policy that can be used over and over for encryption; permission settings; and to certify the author, signer, and authenticity of a document. Individuals can create security policies and repeatedly use them, and an organization can set up a policy server to store and control security policies. The use and function of a policy server is beyond the scope of this book.

Create a Security Policy

You can create two kinds of security policies that are stored on your computer: password policies and certificate policies.

1. In Acrobat, click **Secure** in the Tasks toolbar, and click **Manage Security Policies**. The Managing Security Policies dialog box appears.

2. Click **New** to open the New Security Policy dialog box.

3. Click **Use Passwords** or **Use Public Key Certificates**, and click **Next**.

4. Type a policy name and description, and, for passwords, click **Save Passwords With The Policy**. For certificates, select the document components to encrypt, and determine if you want to enter the recipients each time you apply the policy. In either case, click **Next**.

5. For passwords, fill out the section(s) pertaining to the type of password (open document or permissions) and their use, and then enter and confirm the passwords as described in "Set Up Password Access" earlier in this chapter. Click **Next** and click **OK** to move through the dialog boxes. At the end, you are given a summary of the policy. Click **Finish**.

Policy Details	
Name:	Marty's passwords
Description:	General password policy
Encrypted Components:	All document content
Type:	User
Modification Date:	2005.02.25 22:25:28 -08'00'
Document Open Password:	Required
Permissions password:	Required
Changes:	None
Printing:	None
Copying:	Not Allowed
Accessible:	Allowed

NOTE

Sample password and certificate policies are added when Acrobat is installed. You can edit and use these in place of creating your own if you wish.

TIP

You can also click the policy you want to apply from the list on the Secure button drop-down menu.

6. For certificates, if you don't select the recipients each time you apply the policy, select the permanent recipients and their permissions. Click **Next**. At the end, you are given a summary of the policy. Click **Finish**.

When you return to the Managing Security Policies dialog box, your policy will be displayed, as shown in Figure 10-8.

Apply a Security Policy

To apply a security policy to a PDF:

1. With the PDF open in Acrobat, click **Secure** in the Tasks toolbar, and click **Secure This Document**. The Select A Policy To Apply dialog box appears.

2. Click a policy in the list, and click **Apply**.

Once you create the policy, handling security the way you want is quite simple.

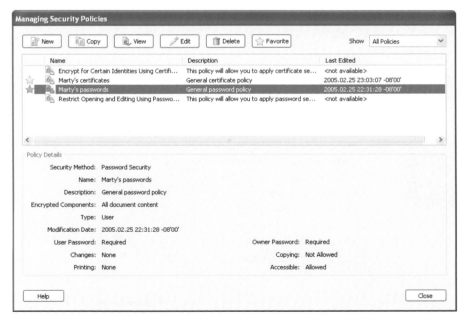

Figure 10-8: You can set up several security policies to be applied under different circumstances.

Note: Italicized page numbers denote definitions of terms.

NUMBER

4-up printing layout, example of, 42

SYMBOLS

— (em dash), adding to text, 87
! (NOT Boolean operator), performing searches with, 118
& (AND Boolean operator), performing searches with, 117
(()) parentheses, using with Boolean searches, 118
^ (Exclusive OR Boolean operator), performing searches with, 117
| (OR Boolean operator), performing searches with, 117
" (quotation marks), using with Boolean searches, 118

A

Access, conversion options for, 54
Acrobat
  customizing, 16–18
  leaving, 3
  obtaining in-depth information about, 14
  versus Reader, 19–20
  starting, 2–3
  updating, 18
Acrobat settings, location of, 101
Acrobat shortcuts, dragging files to, 50
Acrobat window, features of, 3–5
Add Adobe PDF Settings dialog box, displaying, 105
Add Headers & Footers dialog box, displaying, 78
Add Movie dialog box, displaying, 208
Add Sound dialog box, displaying, 207
Add Watermark & Background dialog box, displaying, 82
Address Block icon in Designer, description of, 184
Adobe Acrobat. *See* Acrobat
Adobe Designer. *See* Designer
Adobe Distiller print driver, description of, 46. *See also* Distiller
Adobe Expert Support, accessing, 15

Adobe PDF Explorer bar, using, 58–59
Adobe PDF printer driver
  changing options for, 69
  creating PDFs with, 56
Adobe PDF Settings dialog box, displaying, 69–70
Adobe programs, creating PDFs from, 56
Adobe Reader. *See* Reader
advanced searches, performing, 115–117
All Programs option, starting Acrobat with, 2
ampersand (AND Boolean operator), performing searches with, 117
AND Boolean operator (&), performing searches with, 117
annotation tools, definition of, *131*
Arrow Drawing tool, function of, 149
articles, 9
  creating, 89–90
  editing, 91–92
  reading, 90
attachments
  adding, 91–92
  sending documents as, 132
audio
  adding to PDF files, 207
  modifying in PDF files, 209
audio comments, adding, 147
Auto-Complete feature, using with forms, 192

B

backgrounds, adding to PDF content, 82–83
Baseline Offset text attribute, description of, 88
binders, creating, 48–49
Bookmark Properties dialog box, displaying, 200
bookmarks, 8
  changing, 201
  creating automatically, 198–199
  creating manually, 200
  definition of, *198*
  displaying in PDFs, 33
  rearranging, 202
  selecting, 201
  using, 32–33
Boolean search operators, using, 117–118

borders, adding to Designer forms, 188
bounding boxes, including text in, 86–87
boxes created in layout programs, displaying, 78
browsers, setting up reviews in, 138
browsing with Hand tool, 9
Button icon in Designer, description of, 183
buttons, applying 3-D look to, 163

C

calculated fields, creating for forms, 173–176. *See also* fields in forms
Callout Drawing tool, function of, 149
cascading documents, example of, 31
Catalog dialog box, displaying, 126
certificates, verifying digital signatures with, 223
Character Spacing text attribute, description of, 88
Check Box icon in Designer, description of, 183
Circle icon in Designer, description of, 184
clicking mouse, effect of, 7
Clipboard content, using as stamps, 148
Close button
  in Acrobat window, 4–5
  in Designer window, 181
Close Right Palettes button in Designer window, location of, 181
Cloud Drawing tool, function of, 149
collections, using with Organizer, 23
Combo Box Properties dialog box, displaying, 165
command buttons, adding to forms, 177–179
comment options, changing, 141
comment text, viewing, 141
comment windows, examples of, 140
commenting tools
  accessing, 144
  availability of, 140
comments, 151. *See also* Note tool; recorded comments
  attaching files as, 147
  versus comment windows, 143
  exporting, 152
  identifying and selecting, 151
  importing, 153
  integrating, 137
  managing, 151

  merging, 136
  moving, sizing, and removing, 143
  preventing changes to, 142
  reviewing and returning, 135–136
  showing and hiding, 143
  summarizing, 153–154
  using Properties bar with, 141
  viewing, 138
Connect to Printer dialog box, displaying, 39
Content Area icon in Designer, description of, 184
context menus, creating PDF files from, 51
Control menu
  in Acrobat window, 4–5
  in Designer window, 181
conversion settings, 46
  changing, 70–72
  customizing, 71
  location of, 70
conversion settings, modifying, 67–69
converted files, saving, 51–52. *See also* documents; files; PDF files; reviewed PDFs
Copy Multiple dialog box in Designer, displaying, 189
copying text, 84–85
Countries icon in Designer, description of, 184
Create Custom Stamp dialog box, displaying, 148
Create Link dialog box, displaying, 205
Create Multiple Copies of Fields dialog box, displaying, 174
Create PDF from Scanner dialog box, displaying, 64
Create PDF From Web Page dialog box, options in, 61
Crop Pages dialog box, displaying, 76–77
cropped pages, printing, 77
Current Date icon in Designer, description of, 184
customizing Acrobat, 16–18

D

date, inserting in headers and footers, 79
Date/Time Field icon in Designer, description of, 183
Delete Pages dialog box, displaying, 75
Designer, 181

parentheses (()), using with Boolean searches, 118
Password Field icon in Designer, description of, 183
passwords. *See also* permissions passwords
  adding to PDF files, 213–214
  changing, 214–215
  removing, 215
PDF concept, explanation of, 8
PDF content, adding backgrounds and watermarks to, 82–83
PDF conversion settings, 46
  changing, 70–72
  customizing, 71
  location of, 70
PDF documents. *See* documents
PDF files. *See also* converted files; documents; files; reviewed PDFs
  adding digital signatures to, 220–221
  adding headers and footers to, 78–80
  adding interactive links to, 204–205
  adding navigation pane and navigation bar page numbers to, 80
  adding page numbers to, 80–81
  adding sound to, 207
  adding video to, 208
  adding web pages to, 58–59, 62
  browsing and viewing with Organizer, 21–23
  converting, 48
  converting from PostScript to, 97–98
  converting Microsoft Office content to, 47
  converting screen captures to, 66
  converting to other file types, 52
  creating from Adobe programs, 56
  creating from scans, 63–65
  creating in Acrobat, 46–51
  creating in Office programs, 53–55
  creating with PDF printer driver, 56
  displaying bookmarks in, 33
  indexing, 121–124
  inserting, 74
  listening to, 36
  modifying audio and video in, 209
  opening, 21
  saving after modification, 52
  saving source files as, 51
  scanning printed forms into, 157–158

scrolling through automatically, 35
searching on Internet, 119–120
searching with Find toolbar, 112
searching with Search PDF pane, 113–114
sorting in Organizer, 23
testing with Preflight, 108–110
using for presentations, 76–77
PDF forms. *See* forms
PDF Optimizer, using, 110
PDF pages
  selecting for printing, 41
  viewing in Organizer, 22
PDF printer driver
  changing options for, 69
  description of, 46
PDF settings files, adding and removing, 104–105
PDFMaker macro
  description of, 46–47
  Security tab in, 67
PDFMaker-supported programs, changing conversion options in, 67–68
Pencil and Pencil Eraser Drawing tools, functions of, 149
permission restrictions, using, 217–218
permissions passwords, setting, 216–217. *See also* passwords
Phone Number icon in Designer, description of, 184
photo-printing options, availability of, 44
Pictures Tasks button, appearance of, 44
PKCS#12 ID, explanation of, 220
pointing with mouse, effect of, 7
Polygon Drawing tool, function of, 149
PostScript format
  converting files from, 97–98
  handling fonts in, 105–106
  opening in Distiller, 98
  overview of, 95–96
PowerPoint, conversion options for, 54
Preferences dialog box
  displaying, 17
  options in, 16
Preflight, testing PDF files with, 108–110
presentations, using PDFs for, 76–77
print areas, selecting, 41
Print Button icon in Designer, description of, 183
Print dialog box, displaying, 40, 42
Print Setup dialog box, displaying, 38

printed forms, scanning, 157–158.
  See also forms
printer driver, creating PDFs with, 56
printer options, selecting, 38
printers, connecting to, 39
printing
  cropped pages, 77
  documents, 40–44
  options for, 40, 43
  PDF documents, 37–44
  previewing, 41
  through Distiller, 99
profiles, selecting and executing with Preflight, 109
program-specific conversion options, changing, 67–69
Properties bar
  using with comments, 141
  using with form fields, 167
public keys, explanation of, 224
Publisher, conversion options for, 54

Comparing PDF Documents, 152
Creating PDFs from Pages, 49
Editing Articles, 91
Listening to a PDF, 36
Looking at PDF Security Settings, 212
Opening a PDF File, 21
"Printing" through the Distiller, 99
Refining a Multidocument Search, 115
Selecting an Area to Print, 41
Selecting Bookmarks, 201
Selecting Fields to Be Changed, 166
Selecting Text with the Select Tool, 86
Setting PDF Forms Preferences, 160
Setting Search Preferences, 120
Setting Up a Browser-Based Review, 138–139
Starting Acrobat in Different Ways, 2
Understanding Public Keys, 224
Using a Grid, Guides, and Rulers to Align Fields, 162
Using Acrobat Toolbars, 5–6
Using Auto-Complete, 192
Using Menus, 7
Using PDF Optimizer, 110
Using PDFs for Presentations, 76–77
Using the How To Window, 11–12
Using Zoom Tools, 28–29
Viewing Multiple Documents, 31
Working with Collections, 23
Working with Headers and Footers, 80
Working with Images, 89
quotation marks ("), using with Boolean searches, 118

R

Radio Button icon in Designer, description of, 183
Read Out Loud feature, using, 36
Reader
  versus Acrobat, 19–20
  installing, 20
recorded comments, attaching, 147. *See also* comments; Note tool
Rectangle Drawing tool, function of, 149
Rectangle icon in Designer, description of, 184
Replace Pages dialog box, displaying, 75
reply threads, establishing for comments, 141

Reset Button icon in Designer, description of, 183
resolution, choosing, 103
review status, displaying for comments, 141
reviewed PDFs. *See also* converted files; documents; files; PDF files
organizing and managing, 139
viewing, 138–139
reviews
definition of, *132*
setting up, 132–137
setting up in browsers, 138
tracking, 138–139
right-clicking mouse, effect of, 7
rotating layouts, 29
rulers, aligning fields with, 162

S

Save As DOC Settings dialog box, displaying, 53
scanning printed forms, 157–158
scans, creating PDFs from, 63–65
screen captures, converting to PDFs, 66
Script Editor in Designer window, location of, 181
scroll arrow and button in Acrobat window, locations of, 4–5
scroll bar in Acrobat window
location of, 4–5
properties of, 9
scrolling behavior, controlling with buttons, 25
Search PDF pane
closing, 114
searching PDF files with, 113–114
Search PDF pane, features of, 112
searches
performing advanced searches, 115
performing with indexes, 128–129
refining, 115
setting file properties for, 123–124
setting preferences for, 120
using Boolean operators with, 117–118
security policies
applying, 225
creating, 224–225
security settings, checking, 212
Select Email Client dialog box, displaying, 193

Select Page Links to Download window, displaying, 63
Select tool
copying text with, 84–85
selecting text with, 86
Set Transitions dialog box, displaying, 77
Settings button, unavailability to file types, 52
settings files, adding and removing, 104–105
shading, adding to Designer forms, 188
Signature - Print and Sign icon in Designer, description of, 184
Signature Field icon in Designer, description of, 183
Signature Properties dialog box, displaying, 223
sizing handle in Designer window, location of, 181
Snap to Grid feature, accessing, 162
sound, adding to PDF files, 207
sound, modifying in PDF files, 209
source files, saving as PDFs, 51
space usage, analyzing with PDF Optimizer, 110
spelling, checking for fields in forms, 177
Split view, using, 29–30
spreadsheets, putting form data in, 196
Spreadsheets Split view, using, 30–31
stamps
creating and using, 147–148
displaying, 144
Standard toolbar in Designer window, location of, 181
Start menu, launching Acrobat from, 2
status bar
in Acrobat window, 4–5
in Designer window, 181
Stroke and Stroke Width text attributes, descriptions of, 88
Subform icon in Designer, description of, 184
Submit Form Selections dialog box, displaying, 178

T

tab order, specifying for fields in forms, 169–170
Taskbar, locking, 3

Tasks toolbar in Acrobat window, location of, 4–5
text
copying with Select tool, 84–85
modifying in Acrobat, 85–87
placing with Designer, 188
repositioning, 87
selecting with Select tool, 86
text, fields & objects locks in Designer window, location of, 181
text attributes, descriptions of, 88
Text Box Drawing tool, function of, 149
Text Box Properties dialog box, displaying, 142
Text Edit tools, using, 145–146
text elements, adding, 86
Text Field icon in Designer, description of, 183
Text Field Properties dialog box, displaying, 163, 166, 171
Text icon in Designer, description of, 184
text properties, changing, 88
thumbnails, using, 34
Thumbnails tab in navigation pane, description of, 9
tiled documents, example of, 31
title bar
in Acrobat window, 4–5
in Designer window, 181
toolbars, using, 5–6
TouchUp Properties dialog box, displaying, 88
TouchUp toolbar, modifying text with, 85
Tracker feature, using with reviews, 138–139

U

UDF (Universal Disk Format), significance of, 123
units of measurement, changing, 83
U.S. States icon in Designer, description of, 184

V

vertical panes, displaying information in, 32
video
adding to PDF files, 208
modifying in PDF files, 209

views
fitting documents into, 26–27
splitting documents into, 28–29
Views buttons
using Hand tool with, 9
viewing single or facing pages with, 24
Visio, conversion options for, 54

W

watched folders, using, 107–108. *See also* folders
watermarks, adding to PDF content, 82–83
web links. *See* links on web pages
web pages
adding in IE (Internet Explorer), 58
adding to active PDFs, 62
adding to PDF files, 58–59
capturing in Acrobat, 60–61
capturing in IE, 57–59
changing conversion settings for, 72
converting, 60–61
web tree structure, example of, 60
Windows, converting files from, 49–51
Word
conversion options for, 54
transferring forms from, 158–159
Word Spacing text attribute, description of, 88
words
looking up meanings and pronunciations of, 84
removing highlights from, 113

X

XFDF file, explanation of, 179

Z

Zoom tools, using, 28–29
zooming capabilities, explanations of, 25

International Contact Information

AUSTRALIA
McGraw-Hill Book Company Australia Pty. Ltd.
    TEL +61-2-9900-1800
    FAX +61-2-9878-8881
    http://www.mcgraw-hill.com.au
    books-it_sydney@mcgraw-hill.com

CANADA
McGraw-Hill Ryerson Ltd.
    TEL +905-430-5000
    FAX +905-430-5020
    http://www.mcgraw-hill.ca

GREECE, MIDDLE EAST, & AFRICA
    (Excluding South Africa)
McGraw-Hill Hellas
    TEL +30-210-6560-990
    TEL +30-210-6560-993
    TEL +30-210-6560-994
    FAX +30-210-6545-525

MEXICO (Also serving Latin America)
McGraw-Hill Interamericana Editores S.A. de C.V.
    TEL +525-1500-5108
    FAX +525-117-1589
    http://www.mcgraw-hill.com.mx
    carlos_ruiz@mcgraw-hill.com

SINGAPORE (Serving Asia)
McGraw-Hill Book Company
    TEL +65-6863-1580
    FAX +65-6862-3354
    http://www.mcgraw-hill.com.sg
    mghasia@mcgraw-hill.com

SOUTH AFRICA
McGraw-Hill South Africa
    TEL +27-11-622-7512
    FAX +27-11-622-9045
    robyn_swanepoel@mcgraw-hill.com

SPAIN
McGraw-Hill/Interamericana de España, S.A.U.
    TEL +34-91-180-3000
    FAX +34-91-372-8513
    http://www.mcgraw-hill.es
    professional@mcgraw-hill.es

**UNITED KINGDOM, NORTHERN,
EASTERN, & CENTRAL EUROPE**
McGraw-Hill Education Europe
    TEL +44-1-628-502500
    FAX +44-1-628-770224
    http://www.mcgraw-hill.co.uk
    emea_queries@mcgraw-hill.com

ALL OTHER INQUIRIES Contact:
McGraw-Hill/Osborne
    TEL +1-510-420-7700
    FAX +1-510-420-7703
    http://www.osborne.com
    omg_international@mcgraw-hill.com